stories from the middle seat

the four-million-mile journey to building a billion dollar international business

Best regards,

Bob Hemphill

R. F. Hemphill

Published in the USA by

Strelitzia
Ventures

dedication

This book is dedicated to Paul Hanrahan and Barry Sharp, who helped save AES in the dark days of 2002 and 2003; and to Dave Freeman, who taught me everything about energy that I know.

Contents

foreword

Robert Hemphill was an author with a small following of close friends long before he knew he could write. I was lucky enough to be on his mailing list for the "Christmas letter" every year .The letters were not only entertaining but had a unique sense of humor. After reading them I always felt I had been along on the journey.

Robert Hemphill's new book will enable a much larger audience to enjoy the same experience. Bob doesn't just tell you about his adventures, he takes you along with him. You are not just reading about Pakistan or Peru; you are there as you read.

What is unique about this book is that you can learn a lot about the electric power business worldwide as you travel with Bob. And you can stay in the best hotels for the price of a book.

I have known Robert Hemphill as a close and dear friend for forty years. For all those years I considered him professionally as the most effective manager I ever worked with. I did not realize that he was also a gifted author. Now I do. And if you read this book, so will you.

S. David Freeman
Former chairman, Tennessee Valley Authority;
Former CEO of Los Angeles Department of Water and Power
Former chairman and CEO of the Sacramento Municipal Utility District

introduction

I am a storyteller. This is a book of stories.

I worked in a time of radical change in the world. In the period of my energy career, the Arabs shut the tap on the world's oil and taught everyone that energy mattered, the Berlin wall came down, the old Soviet Union was broken up, and mobsters were running much of eastern Europe. China had only just let Westerners in at all and then Tiananmen Square happened. Africa was urbanizing at the same time that large parts of the continent were engaged in extensive and debilitating and continuing warfare. And I worked in an industry that was changing overnight. The demand for electricity was growing at a double-digit rate. In order to bring electricity quickly and efficiently to masses of people, many countries privatized their systems. These were billion dollar projects and many billion dollar deals. Fortunes were made and lost quickly, often in exotic parts of the world. It was a wonderful, wild time to be in the electricity business and it produced great stories.

My colleagues and I had a fascinating time working in this milieu. Of course, the company was always short of funds and looking for more, the countries we worked in were often challenging and deals failed more often than they succeeded, but despite all that we were delightfully successful overall and it was fun. Yes, fun. Working in different cultures was weird and often downright funny. I found great humor—not in laughing at people—but in laughing with them or at ourselves. I have made a point of recounting these funny stories as they happened. Some of them were hard to believe even at the time. Snakes where? Eat the eyeballs of what?

One of the best aspects of international business is the opportunity to visit exotic places. Often these are not places where you would want to take a vacation—I have traveled and done business in Kazakhstan; Cameroon; Northern Ireland, when it wasn't so peaceful; and western China, back when there were zero other Westerners, whom the Chinese politely referred to as "big noses." I think the setting of these exotic places—especially at the time that they were just opening to American business developers—makes these stories particularly interesting.

I learned a huge amount about business while I was doing this work, a particularly nerve-wracking form of disorganized on-the-job training. Often I learned it more slowly than I would have liked, but still there was progress. After all, you don't forget your first run-in with a Russian oligarch who looks exactly like a thug and who has determined that you are his "partner" and never mind what you think. Or your official driver of the company car who refuses to drive you around the capital of his African country unless he is carrying his AK-47 with him in the front seat. Or your first interaction with a local government official who is determined to be paid off or he won't let your project, now complete and ready to go, interconnect with the electric system, never mind the Foreign Corrupt Practices Act. As these interactions developed into learnings, we did our best to share them with new employees in the company. My theory was that I would pass along what I knew to save the new guys from making the same dumb mistakes, knowing full well that they would find new mistakes to make. I hate duplication. As you read these stories I'm sure you will learn more about business in general and the energy business in particular, but the stories are just stories and it's probably best if you come to your own conclusions about how they apply to your own business situation.

Finally, people have asked me about the format of this book. Why letters to my dad? These are stories embodied in letters that I really wrote to my dad as they were happening. He was a successful career air force officer, a WWII P-47 pilot who flew combat missions in the Pacific theater and stayed in after the war ended. He was a pretty straight guy from Nebraska, and he was a storyteller also. He told us kids wonderful bedtime stories that he made up out of his head. But he knew nothing about business except what he read in the papers. Nothing about how it worked, what success meant or what it took, the intricacies of raising money and structuring financings. He would have strongly preferred for me to have ended up in the air force as well. But I couldn't fly, so I went down my own headstrong path. Nonetheless, I wanted him to know about it, and maybe I wanted him to realize that, as is said in Asia and about a thousand self-help websites, there are many paths to enlightenment.

So that is where this book of stories came from. From business, from travel, some from both, and all as truthful and as honest as I can make them. I would not have written them if I didn't think they would be entertaining; I hope that they are.

R. F. Hemphill
June 2015

nobody's perfect

There are plenty of "business" books around where a successful entrepreneur explains how brilliant he or she is, and if you only follow their simple formula for success, you too can have a billion dollar company and date scrawny fashion models and go to fancy places wearing a hoodie. The only infallible formula to achieve this level of success is actually being born with a billion dollars, and then not screwing it up, drinking it away, or sending it to a deposed prince in Nigeria who promises to send it back pretty soon, just as soon as he sells all the gold he has inherited from his father the chief. This is somewhat difficult to achieve if you have already been born, however. Absent that, you'll have to try it the hard way.

Our company, AES, was established in 1981 by Roger Sant and Dennis Bakke, two of the finest executives I have ever worked with. We had capital of a million dollars, six people, and offices in Rosslyn, Virginia, in a building that had been seized by the IRS from its original owners. Our business plan was to build power plants costing many millions of dollars, and sell electricity to established utility companies in the US. The companies, institutions like Duke Power and Texas Utilities (now TXU Energy) and Pacific Gas and Electric, would then further distribute the power to their own retail customers. None of us had ever built or run a power plant. Despite this somewhat inauspicious beginning, some people listened to our pitch and signed contracts with us. We prospered and grew. At the end of ten years we had six plants and six hundred people, all in the US, and a tiny office in the UK.

Then the industry began to open up internationally, and we went where the deals were. By the time the first chapter of this book was written, we had grown dramatically to a company with 123 business units, most of them power plants, in 33 companies, employing 30,000 people. My first book, *Dust Tea, Dingoes and Dragons*, is full of stories from that fascinating ten-year period in our history.

Lots of power assets had changed hands from government to private ownership, some at very low prices and with little or no competing bidders. But sometimes there are reasons why things are on sale.

The least successful business venture in our history was the purchase of the electric utility in Tbilisi, the capital of Georgia—the country, not the state—as we frequently reminded ourselves. The company was in the retail business—it owned a power plant, and then distributed that electricity in the capital area.

We bought this woebegone utility in the heyday of privatization, where governments all over the world were embracing the idea that maybe they weren't so good at running industrial activities and perhaps they should sell them to people who thought there were good at it, and would give the government owners some nice hard currency to take over the assets. In January of 1999, we ponied up about $50 million to the Georgian government to buy Telassi, the distribution business for the capital of Tbilisi and a bit of the surrounding countryside. Georgia at that time was a bit of a darling in the West, as it was being run by Eduard Shevardnadze, the former foreign minister of the USSR during the glasnost period. He was out of a job when the Soviet Union splintered and Putin took over, so since he was a native Georgian, he went home and got into politics. Not everyone liked him; in February of 1998 he was attacked in Tbilisi by ten or fifteen unpleasant people armed with rifles and RPGs. The latter, an anti-tank rocket, is not a weapon one usually associates with disgruntled loner citizens trying to shoot the president. He survived, and shortly there-after we bought the utility. Given the unpleasantness, we thought we had gotten a great deal. There were no other bidders, which might have told us something had we paid attention. This was the largest privatization ever done in Georgia, also a clue. To something. But we were in the liberal glorious expansion phase of AES, buying things left and right and just borrowing more money.

We sent an accountant to run the place, a very good accountant who had never run an organization of any size, let alone a big electric distribu-tion company in a country where he didn't speak the language and almost no one in the business spoke English. Even with these obvious handicaps, we immediately began to find problems.

There was a staff of 1,300 and a total of one computer. All the records were kept by hand. And there weren't many records since the meters were mostly shoddy and easy to wire around so that your electricity never went through the meter and it looked like your monthly consumption was zero. But wouldn't a smart meter reader catch this? Well . . . the meter readers also collected the bills. Then they brought back the money and the meter reading to the office, where it was all entered. In many or even most cases the meter reader read the meter low, then split the difference with the customer. Or maybe he read the meter right, took all the money, then entered a false lower reading in his log and kept the remainder. The records of the utility indicated that of all the electricity sent out, only 18% was actually paid for. Hard to run a good system this way, so suppliers were routinely stiffed. But most suppliers had bribed Telassi to select them in the first place, so maybe it was what they expected. But invoices were on average six months overdue.

This system was so corrupt that the supervisors routinely sold the meter reading jobs to the highest bidder. It should also be noted that once a customer figures out how to bribe the meter reader or to avoid the meter, a culture of nonpayment grows up and breaking this is difficult. And it is especially difficult when the economy is in free fall and unemployment hovers around 30%. And Russian-inspired bad guys keep trying to assas-sinate the president.

To make matters worse, our deal with the government was that we could spend whatever was needed to upgrade the system, starting with all new meters as well as serious upgrades to transformers and substations, and then just raise the rates enough to recover all the capital in three years. I analyzed what this meant, and the result was to have been rates that were two and a half times higher within a year or two. There was no chance that this was politically doable, and in fact when we tried to raise the rates, the increases were never approved, despite what our carefully negotiated agreements said.

The only smart thing we did was to get the World Bank to give us a nonrecourse loan for about 80% of the purchase price. Why they thought that Telassi, the borrower, could ever pay this back cannot be determined.

So we have a completely broken system that will cost millions to fix, and these funds realistically will never be recovered, never earn a "return on investment" for AES. We have an entirely unprofessional staff with almost no English language capability and no computer or computer systems. We have an entirely corrupt revenue collection system. We have an earnest but completely inexperienced general manager. He has no support staff that he can understand. We slowly supplemented this, but it was difficult to attract expats to the country. I wonder why.

The final straw came when our CFO, a good guy and a qualified expat, was found dead in his office, shot in the back of the head with a .22 caliber weapon. There was no evidence of a struggle, and naturally we had no security guards and no security system in the building. We tried an audit to see if something was awry, and much was, but audits only work when you have reasonable records. We did not. The murder was investigated by the local police, under a lot of pressure from the US Embassy, but no one was ever apprehended.

Finally, we gave up. We told the World Bank we weren't going to pay back the loan, ever, and we then sold the business to a group of Russians for twenty cents on the dollar. The Russians charitably told us at the closing, "We know how to deal with Georgians." Personally, I believe that they overpaid.

But not everything we did was quite this feckless. We bought a 4,000

Mw coal-fired power plant in Kazakhstan for $1.7 million dollars, at the request of the Kazakh government. It was located on the northern border of the country, and was really in the middle of nowhere. It certainly didn't look like a bargain the first time I saw it. And none of the workers had been paid in six months.

The plant was physically enormous. The turbine hall was two football fields long—you literally couldn't see the end of it. This was at least partly because the roof had collapsed at the far end.

It was in awful shape; of the sixteen turbines, each identical and sized at 250 Mw, only one actually worked. We didn't have a contract to sell to anyone, but we were the only electricity provider around. At least in this case we could simply stop making power if we didn't get paid. So we got to work on rationalizing the three thousand-person work force (we needed maybe three hundred) and fixing the many, many things that didn't work.

Eventually the government and the country got back on its feet and the president for life, an unattractive man in many ways named Nazarbayev, began to hint that it would be good if we sold the plant to some local organization. And since we had fixed up the plant a bit and it had become a principle power supplier for northern Kazakhstan, there were several legitimately interested parties. We ended up getting a billion dollars for the plant from Kazakhmys, the Kazakh national copper company. That made up for a lot of other places where we weren't as smart or as lucky.

chapter
one

i hope we get to
see castles ...

Author's Note: It had been literally years since I had taken a real "vacation." The timing never seemed to be right, something at work always intervened—a financing that needed to close, a dispute with a vendor that needed to be resolved, a new territory to open up. These all seemed more important than getting away. I counted up and at one point I had cancelled seven straight vacations, including some with deposits that were not refundable. All the literature says that you're supposed to take breaks from work, but somehow . . .

Finally I resolved to commit to a cruise to places where I had not gone before, and then stick with it. Just as long as it wasn't a long cruise.

It could also be said that taking a vacation just before the largest terrorist attack in history on American soil was a bit thoughtless. But think back—who knew?

September 2001

Dear Dad,

I was planning on sending you postcards from our recent trip in various parts of the Mediterranean, and I had even collected some of this soon-to-be outmoded style of communication. But it was hard to find the correct postage from each country, and hard to find a post office and a mailbox and so forth. So instead I have tried to describe what the postcard might have been, which means I get to select any image I want, not just the images in the cards in the little columnar wire rack in front of the ubiquitous souvenir stands selling hats and mugs and T-shirts. This also means you have to use your imagination on the picture part until I get digital enough to both take pictures and then incorporate the images. Don't hold your breath.

We start with the image of a large white boat sitting in the Venice harbor beside other equally large (and even larger) white boats, a small plume of blackish diesel smoke coming out of its stack, the name *Sea Goddess I* on the side. I tell Linda that this shall be her new name, at least for the week. Except without the "I." This shall be our home for the next seven days, until we get to Athens.

Once we board the big white boat we find that the theme is caviar and champagne. Not a bad start. I have convinced a somewhat reluctant Linda to sign up for a cruise (high end, of course) around the Greek islands except it includes Italy and Croatia (one stop each) and only the Greek islands on the west, not Mykonos and Santorini and all those other cute ones. Everyone wears white on this boat and also is white—crew and passengers. Well, the passengers don't wear white; the Americans wear T-shirts and baseball caps and the Europeans wear exotic stuff with matching shoes. There are two inside lounges, one with a dance floor, and a dining room and an outside bar and a pool the size of a pool table (is this where the name came from?). Also a library with lots of videos but not, strangely, *Zorba the Greek, Never on Sunday* or *Chariots of Fire*, although it does have *The Poseidon Adventure*, but not *Titanic*. I am somewhat incensed that they want to charge $5.00/kb for e-mail, which you send from the one computer in the library. Also, they promise to bring any incoming e-mail to your cabin. I try to think how this could be—a small pile of ones and zeroes? There is much to learn here of the ways of the sea. All the drinks seem to be free, however, so perhaps we will be able to learn less than might have otherwise been the case.

OK, we're on the boat, then off the boat. Please envision the lovely old Italian hill town of Urbino, complete with big castle, sitting sure enough on a hill—couple of towers, turrets, walls, the whole castle thing. Just imagine a generic hill town with a castle, then save the image on the back of your eyelids. You'll see why later.

"What exactly kind of damn fool vacation is this anyway?" asks the Sea Goddess, quite reasonably, as the alarm rings at 0715. Good question. Unfortunately, her not-very-foresighted husband has arranged this early annoyance so we can get up and get on the 0800 tour bus to drive quickly through the sort of interesting looking port town of Ancona, and then one and a half hours through the only routinely interesting countryside to Urbino, referred to in our materials as "Jewel of the Marches." I am confused about the translation for this region of Italy—I don't think they mean "marshes," since there aren't any, but we have along no Italian, only four Greek dictionaries, which seem to be written in the Greek alphabet and thus are only useful for looking up sororities and fraternities—we should have checked that prior to purchase. They are unlikely to mean "marches," as in music or brownshirts. Haven't seen any hikers. It is also, everyone notes repeatedly, the birthplace of Raphael, although he only lived there until he was eleven and then went off to Florence like any sensible artist. Follow the money.

The Duke of Montefeltro built the town and the palace and had a very crooked nose and a wife who looked like a ghost, if their portraits are to be believed. His palace was pretty good, but it's now a museum of medieval religious art, never my favorite, and the tour guide wants to tell us about each painting, fresco, icon, and what have you. Then we get to go to Raphael's house, which is house-like. They give us a "tourist lunch," which since this is Italy is fine, then more bus time and then back to the boat. We are pooped since we had flown overnight to get here and natu-rally hadn't slept all that much on the plane. But dinner is quite good and our stateroom is spacious, and now we have officially been to Urbino. On to Greece!

Now please envision a quaint little Mediterranean port town, with an old fortress perched on a hill overlooking the port. OK, kind of like your last vision, see why you saved it? But wait.

We have now proceeded, at a leisurely pace, to the town and island of Korcula in Croatia. The boat cleverly stays at nice locations during the day, then travels at night, docking in the early morning at the next stop while all passengers are asleep. Almost all. "I've been lying here since five thirty listening to the engines and the whistle," says my darling wife as we get ready for our next early morning tour. I, of course, sleeping the sleep of the pure at heart, have heard nothing. "Want to hear my ship engine imitation?" she asks jovially. "Huh?" I respond. She points out that she has been awake and full of energy and ready to get at this vacation stuff for some time, while some *other* parties in the room (I look suspiciously about to see if anyone has joined us) were having trouble opening their eyes. . . .

Korcula is on the Dalmatian Coast of Croatia. Well, it's on the way to Greece. We go on a walking tour of Old Town with some others from the ship and see nice old buildings, carved lions representing the hegemony of Venice (boy, those guys owned the whole Aegean for a while—pretty impressive—and they held off the Turks quite ably while they were at it!), the odd gargoyle, and then more museums with religious art, including my favorite, a silver replica of Jesus standing hip deep in a wine glass. We abandon the tour at the entrance to the third museum, and go back to the boat for breakfast.

Afterwards, we return and poke around the town some more—it really is clean and not very crowded and very Mediterranean/European. Funny that we've never heard of this part of the world much, other than for the last ten years in terms of blood and hatred, but the Dalmatian Coast is full of nifty islands. I ask where the spotted dogs are, and if there are by some coincidence one hundred and one islands, and then I remind everyone of the townspeople's invention of a unique bottle-opening device called, naturally, the Korcula screw. Several people consider returning to a museum and leaving me to my own devices.

OK, get ready for your next image: think of a quaint but slightly Bulgarian-looking Mediterranean port town, with an old Venetian castle/ fortress purchased on a rocky promontory overlooking the harbor. Yes, you can use the previous images if you like, the ones with ports and castles.

This morning we skipped the predawn tour of the town of Corfu, on the island of Corfu, and slept in, one of us with more success than the other, who in a saintly fashion, quietly read the NIH report on stem cells, patiently waiting for the first party finally to awake. Then we went on our own to explore Corfu, at least the town thereof. Results of exploration: weather frying hot, city crowded and jostle-y, architecture uninspiring, hard to get a drink served without ice. All 350 million residents of Europe and a certain portion of the US are here, walking around town in the blazing sun, looking at cheap replicas of Greek artifacts, T-shirts, pizza restaurants, and each other. No Japanese, however. No snow globes. Reminds me of when we went to Cannes in August and it was so crowded that you could hardly move, anywhere. Note to self: avoid popular vacation spots reachable cheaply by Europeans in August. Put Corfu next to Cannes on this list.

We return to the boat and spend the rest of day fruitlessly trying to connect to the Internet. We opine to each other, several times, that the cruise industry needs to get into the twenty-first century, there is no excuse for this, and we can't be the first people to ever ask this question, etc. We even call the two nicest hotels in Corfu to see if either has a business center we can use. No have. These may not be the geek islands.

Your next vision: think of a lovely old, small castle/fortress of Venetian origin on a rocky promontory overlooking a quaint Mediterranean port town. Jesus, more of these?

Yes, castle and small port fans, it's the town of Fiscardo on the island of Cephalonia, in Greece, finally.

Travel tip: it's not good to buy seventeen guidebooks to Greece and then forget to pack any of them, at least if you want to have access to the information therein. Last night we raided the ship's library and got their only Greece guidebook, determined to avoid the next Corfu. The guidebook says of the island of Cephalonia itself, "This is a place for the old-fashioned traveler. . . . Don't go looking for glamour or excitement or even significance. Cephalonia is what's permanent and real." Bad news for e-mail here. With regard to said quaint Greek fishing town, it was even less encouraging: "A picturesque village that's been so exploited, especially by tourists from the UK, that its original charms are all but overwhelmed. Do not go expecting to see a quaint Greek fishing port." There's also a standard line about "oppressive British rule," although Brits are always given credit for building roads, schools, and hospitals. I think someone is getting a bad deal in the imperial credit department. I bet the guidebooks written by Brits don't say that.

Faced with this gloomy assessment, we decided to go on the tour even though it meant getting up in the morning. The tour bus took us for an hour through the Cephalonia countryside, which is rugged and rocky, dry and hot, with steep, mountainous, and narrow winding roads with no guardrails and one thousand-foot sheer drops to one's death in the crashing surf; lots of pencil-thin cypress trees; terraced hillsides with the terraces falling into disrepair and no crops growing therein; abandoned olive trees; bougainvillea in full and gorgeous flower; and not much people. Note: *Captain Corelli's Mandolin* was filmed here, but nobody seems too exercised about it—no "Nicolas Cage or Penelope Cruz slept here" stuff. Maybe they do know what's real.

First stop was the underground lake of Melissani—sort of like a Mayan cenote, more a pond really, where they take you for a little rowboat ride of perhaps seven minutes and, according to the guidebook, the "rays of sunlight when hitting the surface of the lake shatter into myriad colorful shards." Or just shine into your eyes. They also had a snazzy digital camera setup where they took your picture while you were sitting in the rowboat and then immediately printed it on a digital printer. There are some geeks here after all. We forgot to ask them about e-mail.

Second stop was the small port town of Asos, which is not, despite the sound of it, a place harboring badly behaved and rude people. Actually picturesque and nice—water unbelievably clear, as it has been at each location. Beach is composed of pebbles, as has also been true at each stop. Final stop, Fiscardo, *not* crowded with British. Or other vacationing hordes.

Architecture pretty and well maintained. So much for guidebooks. But it's very, very hot and very sunny. No wonder everybody jumps into the ocean from every available beach, pier, pile of rocks, etc. Also they like to swim while wearing their hats. It's a European thing.

OK, ready for one with no castles? Picture a rocky, steeply wooded hillside with ruins of a medium size with marble/limestone buildings—most of the floor still there, all the columns out front, but none of the walls or ceiling—the Temple of Apollo at Delphi.

We have arrived at the Port of Itea which provides access to Delphi. The tender deposits us at the not especially attractive waterfront, in a town bounded on both sides by very serious and very dry, brown, scrub vegetation-covered hills, and more hills behind it. We get on the bus for Delphi, a thirty-minute ride uphill, and our guide says, accurately, "Most people when they come to Greece for the first time are surprised by the mountains." All of us in the bus nod in unison. Actually I'm surprised at how very hot and dry it is. It really does look like Northern California up past Sacramento, but after a long drought, and with olive trees.

Delphi itself, Second Most Important Ceremonial Site in Greece after Olympus, is slammed into the side of a very steep hill about two-thirds of the way up. It's all on layers and terraces and switchbacks. Not much of it is standing, and very many pieces of it are lying all over the ground. You can see the Temple of Apollo (with help from the guide in telling the front from the back) and the amphitheater (sort of small) and the stadium (slightly bigger) and you pretty much have to take their word for it as to the storehouses and sacred springs and stoas and gymnasiums and such, since mostly it's piles of big rectangular marble pieces lying around, sometimes stacked two to a pile, and at various locations arranged on the edges of a small marble plaza, also usually rectangular. It's a nice excursion, with terrific views out over the ruins down into the valley, but it isn't nearly as impressive as and doesn't have the feeling of power of many ceremonial centers in Mexico. Maybe you had to be there. Or maybe too many tourists and too many archaeologists have been here, and the power of the site has drained away.

The museum is excellent—only the good stuff is on display, not overwhelming amounts of it, and it is well labeled and dramatically presented. And no gloomy religious art; well, actually, all of it is probably religious, just none of it is Christian. For the record, the site is clean, well organized, and has no—repeat no—hawkers of souvenirs, slightly expired film, bottled water, Cokes, images of Zeus, images of Zeus with Europa, etc. All of this necessary material is in the town, down the road a bit, where we stop briefly. But even there it's all nicely done in stores, not by street peddlers. But no Temple of Apollo snow globe.

OK, I cannot help it. For your image collection we have yet another semi-broken-down Venetian fort on a rocky promontory overlooking a small quaint fishing village. . . .

We are at the island of Hydra, and the town of Hydra, still in Greece. And finally, finally, whitewash!!! Don't these people read their own tourist literature?? Don't they realize we're looking for whitewashed houses tumbling down to the water? With red-tiled roofs? And crooked streets navigated by donkeys? And black cassocked fathers with those funny #10 can black hats on and long beards, jovially greeting large-stomached shipping tycoons sitting smoking cigars in waterside cafés, fresh off their white yachts anchored nearby? And a stray artists' colony in residence? OK, Hydra, you got it!! Also, apparently, an island so steep and so unproductive agriculturally that everybody finally gave up and said, "Well, maybe it's the ocean then," so, while there are miscellaneous towns on the island (with names like Agios Mamas and Vlyhos) there are, as far as one can tell, no roads between these towns. We are almost due south of Piraeus, the port of Athens, but not that far south, so lots of large boats/ferries of people come here regularly, and we watch with fascination from the shore as these babies speed in, thinking (at least me) of the scene in *Airplane!* where the 747 bursts through the wall of the airport, and the scene in (an otherwise unremarkable early Sandra Bullock movie for those not in the trade) where the cruise ship smashes through the dock and goes up onto the port. But the boats stop, hunker up to the dock (pulled in by people, not machines), drop gangways, a couple hundred folks get off, they back out (the boats, not the people), and away they go! I think to myself about the Greece Facts that I know: there are only ten million people in this country.

It's pretty big in terms of square miles, about half the size of the UK. There are 1,500 islands in the country, and besides that the non-island part is cut in half by a big sea. Aha! Boats 'R' Us! "The Greeks have been a seafaring people since the time of Homer," intones the commentator.

From what I have seen with regard to real estate and natural resources, the Greeks weren't dealt four aces or even the chance to draw to an inside straight. No flat terrain; no rain in the summer; crumby, cold, rainy winters; no oil/gas; no coal; average to minimal amounts of other good stuff; and a country chopped up by the ocean. Good thing they had the gods early, and thank goodness they invented the phonetic alphabet and democracy and Socrates and the proscenium arch and the Olympics and olive oil and feta cheese. Things like stuffed grape leaves can be forgiven. Oh yes, Hydra is lovely. But get a room and stay a couple of days. Of course, the same advice could be given for each of the places that we liked. This cruise might be entitled "Whitman's Sampler of the Greek Islands and One Croatian Island and a Stray Italian Port That You Don't Get to See."

This is pretty good, and it is an image you have no doubt seen before: the Parthenon atop the Acropolis, in Athens.

This *is* an impressive site—it does sit in the middle of Athens, but it's on top of a really big hill and so it's visible from all parts of the city, almost. And it is lovely and in very good condition, considering how many times it was blown up by the Turks (twice, each time because the building was being used to store gunpowder and lightning set off the explosion). The Turkish ordnance corps needed additional training. And it was looted many times, by everybody, but especially Lord Elgin, as all the guides point out with clarity and force. And reconstructed—four times, I think, but I lost count. And now going on five.

The whole thing seems to have been restitched together with rebar one of the recent times that it was rebuilt, but now the iron connecting bars are being replaced with titanium, which won't suffer from Athens's poor air quality. It's also hot as blazes and crowded as the dickens. Midday on a weekend in August may not be the exactly correct time to visit. But we take lots of pictures. Eventually I decide that we must seek shade and air-conditioning, and I am even willing to go into the museum on site, where more large fragments of broken marble showing eroded muscular torsos and pieces of horses are fetchingly displayed.

And then, well, unless one wishes to linger at the statue of Harry Truman, or see more plazas with a few standing columns, that's about it. Rome it isn't. So we walk to a sidewalk taverna in the Plaka area, where we can get neither fish soup, a Greek specialty, nor tiramisu. However, the Mythos beer is quite cold and good, if not mythical; the outdoor tables are all bathed in the glow of green lights (a unique look); and, unlike Nicholas Cage in the movie, the guy playing the mandolin doesn't look like he's had a lobotomy. And the next morning home.

Love and kisses,
Bob

Afterword: And so we returned from probably the last "luxury travel" vacation we would take for a while, maybe ever. We returned to the US on September 2 of 2001. Everyone knows what happened nine days later. The world as we knew it changed dramatically.

On that morning, I was walking down our long driveway in Potomac to pick up the paper, when I saw a very large column of dark black smoke to the south, where it should not have been, and it was growing. I went inside and turned on the television, as had millions of Americans, and saw that the Pentagon was on fire from a plane crashing into it. Then I saw the World Trade towers in New York, the second plane crash, the smoke and fire and confusion and the horror of people jumping to their deaths. And the two buildings crumbling, one after the other.

Over the next weeks and months I watched as the price of AES stock, my only real asset, accelerated from a downward spiral to a crash. It was the end of the good times and the beginning of times much more troubled and challenging, for my country and my company, as the next chapter tries to recount.

chapter
two

AES Collapse and Recovery (Or Near-Death Experiences Are a Gyp, As You Don't Even Get to See Jesus)

May 2003

Dear Dad,

You may have noticed that I haven't written you in a while about the energy business. Perhaps this was a relief. You may have also noticed that AES has gone through some major perturbations in the last year and a half, at least if you're looking at the stock price or some of the public announcements. I think we're through the worst of it, but I thought I'd try and detail for you what's been going on. Note that the fact that we haven't shown up on your doorstep in Hawaii and asked to stay in the guest bedroom for a couple of months is a good sign.

The business has been way more fun on the going-up part than on the going-down part. I suppose that's not much of a surprise. Several years ago in our annual report, we quoted this line from a popular country song: "Sometimes you're the windshield, sometimes you're the bug." It has been mostly bug since September of 2001.

Ever since we went public in 1991, we have had to engage every quarter in a standard corporate ritual called the "earnings release," wherein you disclose to the world how well the business did. Or how poorly. This is measured in good old dollars and cents—revenues, costs, income, assets. All the serious business thinkers deplore the fact that the "market" is focused on short-term earnings, while most businesses, especially capital-intensive ones like ours, can do little to influence what happens over a three-month period. There are few ways we can encourage customers to buy more electricity, or actions we can take to drive down the price of the fuels we buy, or the rain to fall more generously in the areas where we have hydro plants, like Colombia. But no one has a lot of sympathy for these arguments, which will be made by most companies. While the business thinkers urge a long-term focus as ultimately good for the business and its owners, there is a whole nother group of people to whom we respond—the analysts.

Sounds harmless enough, but these are the Wall Street guys who focus on a company, get to know it as intimately as they can while not receiving any insider information, and then publish forecasts of what they think quarterly earnings for the next quarter and the next year are going to be. I never knew these people existed until we went public, and now we live in fear of them. We coddle them and we respond to them while playing by the rules. Their reports are read by the large institutional shareholders—the people who hold probably 90% of our stock, and buy or sell it in large chunks. The days of the mom-and-pop investor, buying a hundred shares from time to time, are long gone. Instead it is mutual funds and pension funds and insurance companies, with large amounts of money to invest, who drive our stock price. They all will say they do their own research, and I suppose that's true, but they also read the analyst reports carefully, so these things matter.

A great, positive analyst report can really move your stock price up a couple of dollars.

But it's a double-edged sword. A good company must have "analyst coverage," so when we get the Merrill Lynch power industry analyst to "cover" us, it's a reason for celebration. In general, more analysts and more coverage is better. The more you can stand out, positively of course, in the welter of public companies, then the more likely investors will buy your stock, your stock price will go up, and your board of directors will be happy. If you're a girl at the prom, getting more fine young men asking to have a dance on your dance card is better than fewer, and quite a lot better than none. You're popular; you don't have to dance with another girl or just hang around the punch bowl as if you had just come off a long hike in the Sahara desert. Do they even have dance cards anymore? I've never seen one except in the movies. Besides if you were that thirsty, wouldn't water be better than punch? OK, never mind.

The other side of the bargain is the quarterly earnings estimates that each of these analysts prepares. Someone else adds the various estimates together, averages them, and this becomes the Wall Street consensus forecast of how you're going to do on the fateful day every three months when you come clean. And on that day, not only do you send out a press release, you also get on a conference call with all the analysts and try to explain why you didn't quite get to their numbers. If you beat the estimates, then this is an easy phone call, but pure statistics would lead one to conclude that you are above half the time, and less successful the other half. You can try to "guide" the analysts, and release your own forecasts, but everyone realizes that doing better than a forecast makes you look like a great manager, and falling below makes you look like a doofus, so you inevitably lowball your own forecasts. The analysts just want to be right—they don't look clever if you beat their numbers, or fall below them. They look best when your company's numbers are exactly the same as theirs. This is difficult to pull off. We and most others have avoided giving out forecasts of quarterly numbers and only provide annual ones; but while this seems wise, it only magnifies the importance of analyst quarterly estimates.

OK, enough on that. I could have just said, "Analyst quarterly estimates of earnings are important, it's good to do better than expected," and you probably would have gotten it.

There is never a good time to miss analyst estimates, but the third quarter of 2001 was a particularly bad choice. Oh really, why?

One of our major competitors, Enron, had its stock price just go below $10.00 from a high of $90.00 a year ago, and they were looking for someone to bail them out. They subsequently declared bankruptcy on December 3.

And even more damaging was that they eventually were found guilty of a number of illegal and deceptive business practices, mostly about messing around with their own numbers and reporting fraudulent results to the public and their investors and regulators. The ultimate result, in addition to their bankruptcy, was the imprisonment of a number of senior officers of the company, including the CEO. We tried hard to distinguish ourselves from Enron, even though we were in pretty much the same business. I was even heard to remark to a group of our own disgruntled investors, "Hey, we lost the money fair and square."

A substantial number of our competitors also got caught in the downdraft and went bankrupt—Calpine, a PG&E affiliate called National Energy Group, Covanta, Mirant, and Dynegy—to name some of the biggest. These names won't necessarily mean anything to you, but they were all significant players. And the more companies who looked like us but collapsed, the harder it became to convince the banks and our investors that we were OK. It was a very bad time.

And really, we weren't looking that wonderful ourselves. Our stock price had peaked at around $68.00 in September of 2000, and then began to feel the impacts of the general Internet bubble crash. By a year later we were down to $13.00. Not reassuring.

Some guys flew some airplanes into some buildings. This catastrophic event affected the whole market, and probably us even more so as we were and are so "international." Suddenly it didn't look like such a clever strategy.

Ever since 1991, when we went public, we had NEVER missed our earnings estimates.

And so our stock price continued to slide. Down.

In February of 2002, we had our big annual meeting for our board in Florida, at the Turnberry resort. This was a four-day meeting, and for two of those days we invited the thirteen analysts who were then covering us to come and meet with senior management and sit in on some of our internal presentations. And of course there was time for golf and tennis and schmoozing the analysts. We had been doing this for five years, and it is common practice among large corporations. Some of us were worried that going to such a fancy place, given our already challenging situation, was sending the wrong signal, but we had already paid for the whole four days on a nonrefundable basis, so we went.

The evening of the second day Dennis, our CEO, got up and gave a presentation on the state of the company. He has always been an enthusiastic and upbeat guy, and that has been one of his strengths. But maybe not this time. In addition to the general carnage in the markets, we had specific problems. I won't bore you with the details, but they included:

— We had major assets in Brazil, which were operating under long-term contracts with protection against currency changes. This was pretty important as these generated a lot of revenue, paid in reals, the Brazilian currency. And we had financed them with debt in dollars. As long as the exchange rate stayed steady, we were fine. But Brazil had undergone a big drought, which was a problem, and then they had decided on a three-to-two devaluation in order to make their products cheaper and more competitive as exports. But we weren't exporting, and so we were suddenly getting one-third less dollars, and so we couldn't pay back the loans we had taken out. We were negotiating with BNDES, the Brazilian Development Bank, and lead lender. We were surprised to find that our currency protection wasn't working, and they were surprised to find that our loan from them was not a corporate loan but a project loan, which meant there was no recourse to AES, the parent of the Brazilian subsidiary. Apparently neither of us had read our documents very carefully when the loans were taken out. We ended up swapping our majority ownership for a much smaller ownership in the Brazilian plants, with BNDES taking the majority as payment for their debt. But this significantly reduced our cash flow from one of our major investments.

— In the late 1990s, most US states set up wholesale electric markets open to anyone with a power plant. No long-term contracts were available; these were essentially "spot" markets, and you bid your power into them every day. Plus gas was plentiful and cheap, and seemed the ideal fuel for this. All of us independent power producers said to ourselves, "Hey, this is interesting, we can go out and develop, permit, and construct merchant plants—plants with no long-term customers—and instead rely on these new markets as a place to sell the power. And this is so hard to do, that

NO ONE ELSE will be able to do it but us. Gangway!" And so we all did. Fortunately, we proved not quite as good as everyone else, but we had two plants like this, one in New Hampshire and one in Texas. They both were financed with a bit of project debt but mostly corporate equity. And they were both in trouble.

In 1999, the US electric industry had about 900,000 megawatts of installed power plants. It needed maybe 30,000 megawatts per year of new capacity to replace old coal plants that were being retired. Through our combined efforts the independent power industry brought on 130,000 megawatts in that year. Supply/demand balances shifted dramatically, and now instead of bidding in power at five cents a kWh, we had to bid one or two cents. Plants started defaulting on their debt right and left. Our two did as well, and we had to write off the equity. Ugh.

— September 11 had caused a crisis of confidence in the financial sector, and new debt financing became very, very hard to find. Our stock price was so low that we couldn't issue equity, so we in essence had no way to finance the remaining build-out of power plants under construction, nor to roll over and refinance existing debt whose term was up and whose repayment was due. And yet we still kept announcing new projects, including my personal favorite, purchasing a local telephone company in Bolivia. Huh? We had no assets in Bolivia, so we knew little about the poorest country in South America. Plus we owned no telephone companies, so we had no idea how to run one. Perhaps not our finest hour in terms of common sense or good business judgment. Unfortunately the list went on.

— Most of the leadership recognized that we were in a serious cash crunch, so there was a random effort to sell assets. We sold a power plant in construction in Tennessee called Greystone. I didn't even know we had one, and I have been an AES executive and then board member for twenty-two years.

Soooo—our cash position was not good, we couldn't raise debt or sell equity, we were running around trying to sell stuff, but also still making silly investments. We couldn't sell the best plants because we weren't getting very good offers. We couldn't sell the bad plants, although we were trying, because everyone else in the power business was in the same situation. It was quite unsettling, and a remarkable change from a few years before, when we could do no wrong and the banks fell all over themselves to fund our purchases of assets in Sri Lanka and Kazakhstan.

Looking back, I conclude that no matter how grounded and sensible you are, no matter how experienced or humble, if every time you do a transaction (buying a broadband company in Brazil, a wood-fired plant in Hungary) the market applauds and your stock price goes up $2.00, at some point you look at yourself and say, "Damn, I AM a business genius." But eventually gravity works, markets rationalize, and you're not. The Internet guys had found that out a year or so before we did. We didn't get the lesson.

Back to Turnberry, where Dennis gives the after-dinner speech. It is a PowerPoint presentation with reasonable graphics, made to a big audience in a large ballroom. The analysts were all there. The AES board members were all there. The one hundred-plus senior leaders of the company were there. We were all expecting the same thing—acknowledgement of the bad place in which we found ourselves, reassurance, and maybe even some contrition, and a sensible way forward. But the CEO's presentation seemed to ignore everything that kept the rest of us up at night. His message was, "We're doing fine and we're going to keep doing what we've always done." His final slide was one of pioneers in a wagon train, heading west. He might as well have shown a clip from the old John Ford movie *Wagon Master*. We at AES were the Mormons, run out of town for our religion, but forging ahead secure in the certainty of our beliefs, and glorying in the opportunities lying ahead for us in the new territories. I wanted to crawl under the table.

A board member was sitting with us. He turned to me at the end of this speech and said, "The stock price will be in single digits in a month." It was $5.00 by mid-February—two weeks later.

Things continued to deteriorate. By June the board had lost all confidence in Dennis, and after several troubled meetings removed him as CEO. Roger Sant, the chairman of the board and the company's senior founder, had also offered his resignation, but the board was not so inclined. Instead he was asked to return full time to the company, and Paul Hanrahan, my old friend and a man I had helped recruit from Harvard Business School, was voted in as the new CEO. Participating in firing a good friend and a colleague with whom I had worked for twenty-five years, in the government and in AES, was one of the least pleasant things I have ever had to do. It was the right thing to do, and even so we were far from out of the woods.

Paul and Barry Sharp, our CFO, had a big mess on their hands. The basic problem was that we had several large pieces of debt that were coming due and we didn't have the money to repay them. See how easy business is to understand? Plus we were held in remarkably low regard in the financial markets, and besides the markets in general were still only slowly coming out of the 9/11 shock. Liquidity was poor overall and especially poor for us. We couldn't sell our shares at the low price at which we were trading—$3.75 per share on June 3. It is remarkable how quickly you go from market darling to market pariah.

The origins of the problem stemmed from our rapid growth, generally by acquisitions, over the past five years. We had gotten so big so quickly that we had ignored some of the tenets that had served us well in the early days. We had started using corporate money, usually debt, to pay for the acquisitions of power plants in foreign countries. And so we no longer had the insurance that we could walk away from the plant if things became dicey. We began to refer to this as "handing the keys to the banks," although electric plants take a bit more than a key to turn on. But if it's corporate money, then the obligation is at the AES level and ultimately the financing parties had a claim on all the assets that we owned. Very bad indeed. We also had to use short-term financing, usually one to five years in term, because that was the best we could do. We frequently structured "balloon" payments with these borrowings, as we couldn't pay back much of the principal during the term of the loan. This meant we had a big nut to pay at the end. And we were financing in dollars, which was cheaper than borrowing in Chilean pesos. But if the peso devaluated, then you were screwed, as you got less dollars for the same pesos and your ability to make even the interest payments went away. Sorry for the finance lesson, but all of these things hit us more or less at once. It was a very gloomy period.

But neither Paul nor Barry were much given to gloom, so they went to work. We had two pieces of very troublesome debt; the first was a $300 million bond coming due December 9. This was insurance company provided debt. We also had a $1.3 billion line of credit, which had been given to us by a bunch of banks, fifty-three to be exact. This was a short-term loan, and we of course had borrowed all of it. It was due January 15. It was in theory a sort of a backstop to be used if we had a stumble. Well, we had not just a stumble; we had fallen flat on our face, fractured our jaw, and blown out a kneecap. And we did all this, to continue the analogy, while the medical system was shut down and the ambulance drivers all on strike.

We needed both sets of parties to refinance our obligations and to "roll" the debt. There were really no other lenders or investors willing to step in and provide us "new" money to pay off the old lenders. We forecast that we would have just about enough money in the AES treasury to repay the $300 million of bonds, but not to pay off any of the banks. Barry and Paul enlisted Citibank to help, which they were more than willing to do as they were the most exposed member of the bank group. Our proposal to the two groups of lenders was simple: everybody stays in and everybody refinances, or we declare bankruptcy and then all of you can fight about the scraps.

None of the lenders liked the solution. Everyone's first reaction was: "Give us all the cash and let the other guys refinance." No surprise there. We held fast to our position, strengthened by something called a claw-back in bankruptcy. What the law says is that creditors in bankruptcy can "look back" sixty days before the filing and undo any transactions that have occurred. This is so that you can't give your house to your brother, then declare bankruptcy the next day and claim that you have no assets. In our case, even if we had paid out the insurance companies with our remaining money, a month later when the bank debt came due, the banks would immediately force us into bankruptcy and then go after the insurance companies to claw back whatever we had paid them. Years of costly litigation were the most likely outcome for everyone. It was a variant to the classic "If you aren't nice I am going to shoot myself, and then you'll all be sorry you were so mean to me"—the thoughtful ultimatum that works so poorly in personal relations.

The board by this point was having weekly calls, providing Paul and Barry with another group to respond to, as if they weren't busy enough. It turns out that boards aren't really hugely useful in this sort of situation. Our weekly advice to the management was: "Hurry up and get something done. Don't go bankrupt, and don't do anything else stupid." This is not, you will be surprised to hear, useful advice. The only exception to this was the excellent support we got from John McArthur, the dean of the Harvard Business School, who had agreed (probably to his regret at this point) to be on the board and to be the chairman of the Audit Committee. His deep experience in dealing with banks and other financiers in other dicey situations was especially useful in reassuring us that perhaps the world was not ending.

Slowly and unhappily, all the creditors, insurance companies, and banks fell in line. Except two: the Bank of Hawaii, where we had our very productive Barbers Point Plant; and Riggs Bank of Washington, our "hometown bank." Each had a ten million piece of the $1.3 billion bank credit line. They each said, in essence, "We're small, we don't like AES anymore, so some of you big guys take our piece and we'll go home and have a cup of tea." The Citibank guys were clear—everyone stays. The minute you let one bank off the hook by increasing the exposure of other banks, the stampede starts. If this sounds to you like a huge game of chicken, except the chickens are fifty feet tall, you're correct. And it was a game with which none of us had any experience.

This negotiation went on all through the summer and fall, and the stock market didn't like it a bit, and was betting that we were done. Our stock hit a low of $0.91 on October 21. Yes, $0.91 versus its high of $68.00 per share on 2 October of 2000. In two years, almost to the day, us smart guys had managed to lose 99% of the value of the company.

On December 9, the last day before the insurance company bonds were due, Bank of Hawaii and Riggs were still holding out. Everyone was in New York, working on the documents for the new debt. Finally Citibank and Bank of America, the other big guy in the credit line, took the Riggs and Bank of Hawaii delegations aside, without us in the room. We speculate on what was said to these two recalcitrants—probably something akin to "We know where you live, we know where your wife plays tennis, and we know what school your kids go to," except in bank talk. Forty-five minutes later, everyone came out of the meeting and Riggs and Bank of Hawaii were in the new deal. They looked a little pale. Hence we were not going to go bankrupt, and I didn't have to sell the house in Potomac and get a real job.

We all were hugely relieved, although the stock market didn't really get the news for some time. We came back up to around $3.00 per share and stayed there. But it was better than ninety-one cents. Way better.

Here is the most interesting part of the story. We still needed to raise money on better terms, because the December deal had limitations and was a short-term one, ending in three years. In April of this year, we were sufficiently out of the hole, through a combination of very hard work, a lot of assets sales, and excellent efforts by Barry and Paul to rebuild our destroyed credibility with lenders, so we were able to go back to the debt markets and raise about $3 billion of "junk" bonds. The interest rate was high, but the tenor was much better—about five years. This allowed us to refinance some remaining pieces of unattractive debt and finally get our house in order.

Personally I thought that this was a miracle of sorts, given where we had been, i.e., nearly bankrupt in December. Now, a mere four months later, these same markets were handing us $3 billon. It is astonishing what short memories financial markets have.

Thank goodness.

Love and kisses from your sadder and poorer but wiser "business genius" son,

Bob

Afterword: AES in the intervening years has spent time and money putting into place the systems and procedures that we should have had as we grew the business. This has been a painful process, and included several restatements of previous public earnings reports. And not in a positive direction.

The company has significantly scaled back its development spending, and more importantly, it has reined in the free-wheeling spirit of "any project, any business, any country" that made it successful and a wonderful place to work, but also created an entity that was hard for shareholders and analysts to understand and difficult for the board and the corporate officers to govern effectively.

Many assets have been judged not "core" to the company's business and have been sold off to others who valued them more highly than we did. It remains a major global utility with interesting growth opportunities, but it has far better financial discipline than before and is a much easier "story" to sell to investors. No more telephone companies in Bolivia.

A note on discrepancies in timing: The chapters that follow recount various foreign trips taken during the two year "crash and recovery period" that began on 9/11 and more or less ended by the middle of 2003. But it seemed necessary to place this chapter ahead of these others because of the importance of the period and the tone it sets for the rest of the book. It takes a long time to climb out of a hole as deep as the one the company was in.

chapter three

Tiptoe through the Tulips Wearing Your Triple-Insulated Arctic Ranger Combat Boots

April 2002

Dear Dad,

It is Saturday night in the hot Netherlands town of Lisse, and here in the center of the action is your son, at the Golden Tulip act Naagnagel. This is a small Holiday Inn-type motel on the edge of the bulb fields. There are tulip paintings all over the hotel, including one looming in purple above the chess table where I find myself at this moment. I do not believe that chess and tulips are connected, but it was too smoky in the bar. Besides, the joint was filled with late middle-aged Dutch and other European types who stay in hotels that cost a hundred bucks a night and have thin walls between all the rooms. Mostly the Euros drink red wine and Heinekens and smoke, but they seem harmless enough. Not much Armani, not much black silk, nobody less than forty-five. Not many Americans that we have seen, which is fine. NO disco. The music system is playing "Summertime," "Waltz of the Flowers," "Waltzing Matilda," and "Tennessee Waltz," all in slow tempo, very instrumental versions. No hot chess games going on that the click of my computer keys might be disturbing.

Our party of extended family has just spent the day at the Floriade, which I determined is Dutch for "cold and windy place without hardly any flowers." Dutch seems to be a language completely lacking in English cognates. But what went before this?

Every ten years the Dutch, for whom the flower biz is big business, hold a six-month-long flower show, outdoors mostly, called the Floriade, which is not a sugared drink made from flowers or Dutch for the US state of Florida. I have kind of wanted to go to this event for some time, but missed it in 1992. It is something like the Passion Play at Oberammergau, but instead the focus is on horticulture rather than crucifixion. The motto for this one is See the Art in Nature, which probably sounds better in Dutch. Plus I have always wanted to see the tulip fields in bloom in Holland. We note here as a business matter that 70% of the world's cut flowers still come from the Netherlands— although we suspect that this is because they run such an efficient market, not because they grow all of them—plus probably at least 50% of the world's flower bulbs. They're serious about this. So we checked our schedules and enlisted the Powers family to come along.

The group left the US two days ago for this brief trip, but I had to stay around Arlington for an AES shareholders and board meeting. Given how badly the AES stock has performed in the last six months, I actually would rather have been here. I didn't want to be around when you come to the part of the meeting where the disgruntled shareholders throw tomatoes at us. But such are the requirements of being a director of a Fortune 500 company, a job more admired than its reality dictates.

Lest we forget, on the Monday before the Thursday she left, Linda had major tooth surgery (not really in the plan for this vacation), and so was still not feeling terrific. She hadn't been able to get her prescription refilled before she left, but at least I didn't forget to pick up the refills and bring them along with me. This may explain her warm welcome of "Give me drugs!"

I arrived this a.m., drug transfer was made successfully, and off we went to the Golden Tulip. It wasn't raining. It was just cold and windy. Really windy. You begin to understand why these guys invented windmills.

Probably self-defense.

We had breakfast at the hotel—they had good strong European coffee and tasty but distressingly limp European bacon—everyone rallied, and today was Floriade day. Actually first it was grocery day. One of the few disadvantages of Holiday Inn-quality lodging is that frills like minibars are fewer, so we needed to lay in a supply of fizzy water, beer, Doritos, and dark chocolate.

We finally got to the Floriade about two in the afternoon. It's quite near our hotel, but then this is a small country; I think you can drive around it in about four hours, so everything is near everything else. And if you hit Germany, Belgium, or the sea, you know that you've taken a wrong turn.

The show is set on 160 acres of dedicated tundra. The front gate says WELKOM OP DE FLORIADE 2002, DE LEUKSTE TUIN VAN NEDERLAND and then it flips to English, which says, WELCOME AT FLORIADE 2002, THE GREATEST HORTICULTURAL SHOW OF THE DECADE. Where the "Nederland" went we can't tell, nor can the deconstructionist question of "How do you define the decade?" be effectively answered. However, they expect three million visitors to this thing, and have put up special but not very big road signs on how to get to it, which we manage to do. A fair number of people are buying tickets and going in, all of them heavily clothed. Because we've heard so much about it, because the government has threatened that this may be the last one ever because it costs too much to support, because we're here for nine days and it's a small country, because it's one hundred and sixty acres, we buy "season" tickets. Oh gullible Americans, come visit us again and again.

We enter and wander around—no, we first we have to go to the information building and have our tickets tediously converted into driver license sort of things with our pictures on them, mother's maiden name, sports we played in high school, etc.—so that we can get in again with our season tickets. The use of a computer and digital camera enable this process to be completed by an untrained young woman in no more that 200% of the time it should have taken. But it is done inside, which is a plus. And why they want my phone number I cannot deduce. So it goes. I don't know if they have a formal privacy policy, but if I start getting telemarketing calls in Dutch, I'll know why.

Here is what we find out about the Floriade in three frigid hours:

— Despite all my hopes and experience elsewhere, English is not yet the universal language. None of the signage, repeat none, is in English. Nor, interestingly, is it in French, Spanish, German, or Esperanto. We asked to buy a site guide for three euros, but were told that they hadn't been printed yet. The thing has been open for a month. And as it only comes around once every ten years, there may be sufficient planning time to have the guides translated ahead of time. No. If you were going to have three million international visitors, you might think about making more of an effort on the language front. The whole darn country only has five million people in it, and I doubt that the visitors will be made up exclusively of 60% of the Dutch population.

— One of the most advertised "attractions" is a very large man-made hill, sculpted to look like a Mayan pyramid, covered with grass, steps up the middle, flat on top, but with a fancy mobile sculpture there, resembling nothing identifiable. It is said to give one a wonderful view of the whole exhibition. Note the "is said to." Today it was "closed for maintenance." It is hard to imagine how much maintenance a hill needs, especially only one month into its six-month life-span.

There was a medium-sized exhibit of golf cart-type things, the newest innovation in urban transport that you could rent for a modest five euros and tool around the grounds. Only you couldn't, because it, too, was closed. No further explanation.

It was really cold and really windy. I'll try not to say this too many times again, but you can just add it yourself to each page of this letter. My wife, charitable soul that she is, had called and recommended that I bring much warmer clothing than we had even been contemplating (and another coat of hers), and scarves and hats and gloves. Bless her heart! As I thought about this, I finally concluded that the industrious Dutch had been able to reclaim a fair amount of the North Sea, but we were still basically standing on where the North Sea used to be, and it was now "land" but the weather was still "North Sea." Made me feel smarter, but not warmer.

The refreshment stands sell ice cream but not hot chocolate or hot tea or hot apple cider. Marketing assistance necessary.

It's really not a flower show; it resembles a trade fair/world's fair executed on a principal of undisciplined agglomeration. Each of the Dutch provinces has a pavilion, usually having little or nothing to do with flowers. The Haarlem one prominently featured a broken bicycle painted gold, another one had square cows, and a third had a video of the Internet. There are some national pavilions as well, but usually put up by commercial horticulture folks from that particular country (Japan, Spain, Greece, Thailand) but with no particular rhyme or reason. Sometimes with flowers, sometimes emphasizing other stuff—pots, economic development, the cultivation of mushrooms, and the like. The Netherlands is the third-ranking country worldwide in mushroom production. You probably wouldn't have anticipated learning this useful fact at a flower show.

There were hardly any flowers. There is even a large planting that spells out "Floriade" in big letters on the banks of one of the canals that runs through the exhibit, but the plants used are bushes of various sorts. Not flowers. Green on green.

We wandered into some of the "Floriade stores" only to find the worst collection of awful crap you can imagine, most of it fourth-rate third-world nonsense. African airport stuff, fake Mexican stuff, real junk. And a "blue delft china" booth with blue china in it, all made in Guangdong. No snow globes even. Ai, yi, yi.

So we walked about briskly to keep warm, and took pictures of each other, and spent a lot of time at the indoors stuff. I never tire of exhibits of plants grown hydroponically, or an entire pavilion devoted to the economic potential for the North Holland region (an area of approximately eleven square miles). My favorite for the day, because I was cold and tired and out of sorts, was a pavilion featuring the "man made of manure." This demonstrated, um, what? Modern manure fabrication techniques, we presume. So useful.

The next day was better, in that we saw actual flowers, fields and fields of them, and all tulips, each field a solid color—red, yellow, pink, fringed, striped. The tulips are allowed to bloom, and then shortly after have their heads cut off, but not the flower stems. Their leaves stay undisturbed and the eerily headless plant is allowed to cure. One day a field of black tulips, the next day a field of headless tulips and green leaves. But the bulbs aren't dug until later. I tried to ask where the heads went but was unsuccessful. It was a little disconcerting and led one to muse on the brevity of life, the evanescence of beauty, and how frigging cold it was. Oops, sorry, delete that last part. I am obviously not that good a muser. It was fun to walk along the edges of the fields and take lots of pictures of people with their hair blowing, gorgeous swathes of tulip color in the background.

We went to Aalsmeer, the world's largest flower mart, which is quite something. It is a gigantic warehouse, said to be as long as one hundred football fields under one very large roof. Cut flowers come in one side from all over the world, mostly landing as we did at Schiphol, then are trucked to Aalsmeer, where they are auctioned off and sent back out to Europe, North and South America, and Asia, some in refrigerated trucks and most by cargo plane. The flowers come in and are put on small, automated hand-carts that are running on rails and hooked together in groups of three to five, like trains without engines. The carts carrying batches of flowers are directed in to the many auction rooms where buyers sit in stadium seating. Each auction room is for a different type of flower—roses, peonies, daffodils, etc. Then each cart is auctioned off in, yes, a Dutch auction, a funny kind of commercial proceeding. The carts pass slowly across the front of the stage and the price is represented by a big clocklike thing mounted on the front wall. The price for each cart starts high and goes down and the first party to raise his or her paddle gets the deal. Very efficient, but hard to get used to as you watch. Huge volumes of cut flowers are processed daily through this one giant and very efficient facility. And you watch all this from an elevated walkway where it isn't as cold as outside.

The next day was by far the best part of the trip. We went to the famous tulip garden called the Keukenhof. It is an eighty-acre park of nothing but flower bulbs in bloom, mostly tulips but with the odd muscari (grape hyacinth) and classic hyacinth thrown in. It was too late for the daffodils, but that didn't matter, we were right on time for the tulips. Seven million bulbs are hand planted each year, in designs formal and informal, laid out over the entire park. It was more than breathtaking—it was unbelievable. My father-in-law said it made him feel like he was walking through heaven, and he is not a particularly poetic man. It even made me forget to complain about the cold.

We went other places in Holland since you can only spend so many hours looking at tulips. We found several things:

When the Dutch celebrate the queens' birthday, which they did while we were there, they all go to Amsterdam and clog the streets so completely that you can barely move and are thankful that there are railings on the ever-present canals so you don't get pushed in. The celebrants wear a variety of large orange hats and get roaring drunk and sing songs in Dutch and we presume toast the queen in Dutch as well. It was hard to get close to the many bars, and there was nowhere to sit, and so on. I am glad they like the queen, I suppose, but it wasn't my kind of party.

The Dutch have become a race of giants. Especially the young men and women—they are all tall. They must average six feet in height. Why they don't dominate the European basketball league I cannot tell. They are really, really tall. I am not tall. But I am not short. However, I felt like a damn dwarf in Amsterdam. I should have brought a booster seat.

Maybe it's because they were invaded successfully by the WWII Germans in about a minute and a half. Maybe it's because they used to own a large portion of the world excluding Africa but don't anymore. Maybe it's because they don't really give a rip. It could well be that they would just as soon we all stayed home and didn't bother them, asking repeatedly if they knew Hans Brinker and if they could show us where he stuck his finger in the dike. That, plus the tulips, is about all the average American tourist knows about the place. Whatever it is, for a European country it is not a great tourist destination.

We went to one of the two the best-known castles, the Kasteel de Haar in Utrecht, about forty-five minutes from our hotel. Linda and I went by ourselves first to look at it and look around and make sure it was something nice to see. Then we brought the gang the next day. Silly us, we forgot to check and see if they had any brochures in English explaining it.

r. f. hemphill

Not that there's that much to explain about: it's a big house with a bunch
of pointy round roofs, completely rebuilt in the 1890s on the foundation
of an older "castle." You have so-so late-1890s architecture sitting in the
middle of a small lake and a large garden that is all parterres—patterns of
hedges with no flowers. No king or queen or prince lived in it, and neither
did Snow White or Sleeping Beauty, although the grounds are rented out
every year for the annual Elf Fantasy Festival. We asked to take the tour.
"Fine," said the attendant in very good English, "but it is in Dutch." But
the two of us were the only people on the tour, we noted, how about some
English here? "No," said the resolute guide, "this is how we do it." So we
took the tour in Dutch. Every so often the guide took pity on us and threw
in a phrase or two—"This is where the king slept." Great.

Then we went to see the other famous castle, which looks really like
a big square mansion, the Kasteel Amerongen. It was closed for maintenance. At least that's what we think the sign said.

We went to see the Madurodam. If you like miniature railroads, then
this is for you, only it's not miniature. The place is a replica of a modern
Dutch city, with streetcars and canal boats and a dockyard area. The four-
story buildings come up about to your thigh, although you can't walk down
the small streets. Instead there are a set of overhead walkways and viewing
platforms. So if you want to see a very precise and authentic make-believe
Dutch city in miniature, this is it. If you don't want to, you're probably not
alone. The guidebook notes that it is the seventh most popular attraction
in The Hague. The first six are museums, all of which are out of brochures,
which aren't written in English anyway.

We went back to the Keukenhof, even though we had not bought
season tickets. It was still lovely and breathtaking, and we decided we were
cuckoo for the Keukenhof. Then we went to the park's souvenir shop, and
they told us they were all out of posters.

Love and kisses,
Bob

Afterword: The Keukenhof tulip gardens, which modestly proclaims itself "the most beautiful spring garden in the world," still exists and hosts visitors from late March through mid-May— and after that it shuts down for the rest of the year. I suppose dealing with more than seven million tulips, daffodils, and hyacinths takes some maintenance hours. I have spoken to friends who have visited it subsequent to the date of this letter, and they said nothing about freezing to death. I guess I believe them.

The Floriade was again held in 2012, although the size of the display area was reduced from 161 acres and 30 countries to 66 acres and 25 countries.

It is scheduled to be held again in 2022, although I have my doubts. And I'm not going.

chapter
four

"Island in the Sun" without Harry Belafonte or Much Else Either

February 2003

Dear Dad,

Since we have apparently survived the worst part of the last several years of AES and it's shrunken stock price, and are still employed, we decided we should celebrate, although discretely. And cheaply.

Two numbers: 0330 and 18. The first of these is the time that we got up on Friday. We always like to get a head start on celebrating Valentine's Day. No, actually, we had plans. As you probably remember, we had set up a venture capital company in 2000, funded in large part by the Small Business Administration. The company, Toucan Capital, had then as planned made small investments in a number of biotechnology and pharmaceutical companies.

Linda had been in Boston on Thursday, meeting with a medical foundation that deals with ALS (Lou Gehrig's disease—amyotrophic lateral sclerosis). One of our investments was in a cell therapy company that may be able to treat the disease. No therapies are currently available—the disease attacks the spinal cord, causing it to wither away, and you become by slow and painful steps a quadriplegic, and then you die as nerve functions cease in various vital organs, usually the lungs. It's very unpleasant, untreatable, and invariably fatal. Our company has had wonderful results using its cells as treatment on an "animal model," a fancy research term for mice. Being a mouse, by the way, is not a good occupation to pick in biotech, and if you're one anyway, against my advice, then you don't want to be an "animal model." This ain't Versace and pouty looks and strutting down the runway wearing skimpy clothes. What it means to be an animal model is that you, the animal, are a model for the disease in humans. First the researcher gives you the disease, then tries his treatment on you to see if it works. Sometimes you can create the model physically in the mouse, sometimes you can genetically engineer the mouse to get the disease. This is usually the last step before our guys will go to the FDA and say, "See, this works based on the data from our animal model, so let us try it in or on humans." But if the treatment of the kindly researcher cures the disease, then maybe being the model wasn't so bad, you say. Um, the only really good way to determine how well the treatment has worked is to do an autopsy on the mouse. An animal model is no good; cured or not, you have short life. Well fed, probably. How did we get on this subject?

Let's go back to the first number. We were off to St. Thomas, one of three saints in the US Virgin Islands. There are two others, St. Croix and St. John, and that's about it for US possessions—except St. Puerto Rico, whose status I can no longer keep track of—except that it isn't a state and it isn't an independent country, but it still has its own Olympic team, but no seat in either the UN or Congress, but it does get electoral votes for president, and I think its residents are US citizens. Politics is complicated. And I forgot St. Guantanamo Bay in Cuba, which we either own or lease from Fidel Castro, accommodating guy that he is, given the embargo and all. We don't know what the connection between saints and virgins and Caribbean islands is, and none of the guidebooks are explicit on this matter. It's even more curious as the original discoverers and occupiers (other than the ubiquitous C. Columbus, said to have landed on St. Croix in his second voyage and remarked, "Thank god, Hong Kong at last") were Danes, who made the islands a haven for pirates, Blackbeard among them, and for slavery. And appear to have gotten away clean, since who associates the Danes with any of that stuff? Maybe *The Little Mermaid* and Danny Kaye singing "Wonderful, Wonderful Copenhagen" and *Hamlet* and so forth, but not bloodthirsty guys with eye patches and Super Bowl football teams. Plus I don't think the Danes are much of a Catholic country, so why they would name the islands after saints isn't clear either. We know so little. . . .

The 0330 part is because the best flight leaves from BWI at 0710 and you have to be there two hours ahead of time because we are now in terror threat code Day-Glo yellow, and it's a ways from our house. It's not because I think it's a giggle to get up that early, in fact Linda just never bothered to go to bed, what with getting back late from Boston and then packing, and she still forgot to bring her bathing suit.

The second number was the temperature in degrees Fahrenheit registered at the airport Sheraton at BWI when we drove by it on our way to the parking lot at 0450. This is cold, and the setting wasn't improved by it being also dark and windy. It's been cold like this and snowy all winter. For some reason, this time around we have really gotten an actual winter. I forgot what they were, but now that I see one again, I remember why I dislike them so much. Our mood and external temperatures were not improved by standing around in the satellite lot for twenty minutes, waiting for a bus to show up and take us to the airport. Did I mention the cold, windy, and dark parts? Unfortunately Mr. Good Ideas had said, "Let's not take coats, we're going somewhere warm, we'll get right into the terminal, and lugging them all around the Caribbean will be a pain." The bus shelter did have a charming recording playing over and over, urging us not to forget any of our possessions. If your fingers froze and fell off, you were supposed to pick them up and take them with you, I guess. How you picked up your fingers if they had frozen off and were lying on the pavement was not clear. It didn't really take your mind off how thin your summer-weight blazer was.

Nor were our spirits raised, when we finally got to the airport, by checking in and finding out that the flight was delayed from 7:10 to 10:00 because it didn't have a pilot and they figured that they would use one this time, and he had to come from Boston, which is the only place that American Airlines allows their pilots to live, I presume. It is said that American may be the next carrier to declare bankruptcy. Sadly, this will probably not improve their service, although the next owner may allow pilots to live closer to their jobs. Add to this the fact that there's not so much to do at an airport at 0530 in the a.m. Really there's not that much to do in an airport at any time, but especially in the early morning. Finally Starbucks opened and we were able to fight our way through the hordes and get a cup of coffee—maybe it was a grande or maybe a gigantico or maybe a Cinco de Mayo—I'll be damned if I understand why Starbucks simply can't call the cups small, medium, and large like everyone else who speaks English. But it could be the mystique of it all.

We did finally get on board, and flew four and a half hours to St. Puerto Rico and got off and spent more time in the airport. At least this one was warm. Eventually they let us back on and we flew a massive eighteen minutes to St. Thomas.

It's not a big island. Twenty square miles, fifty thousand people, and a curious system of government that requires each resident to have a car and to be on the road at least 50% of all the hours in the day. It's mountainous, well really the tallest point is probably 1,500 feet above sea level, but there are a lot of such tall points. If there were such a word, you could say that it's hillous. Roads are narrow and very twisty. Traffic is unceasing. I can see the airport from my balcony, I can actually tell when planes land and take off, even without my glasses, so you know that I am not that far away. And there is a road that goes more or less straight to here from the airport except for the switchbacks. Nonetheless, it took us an hour to traverse what must be six or seven straight-line miles. And I only got lost twice, and then once more briefly.

We are staying at the Villa Blanca Hotel. I found it by a combination of a guidebook recommendations, and it has a very nice website. And it is moderately priced. Plus they responded to e-mail. Query: If you identify fifteen hotels and villa rental places, either via the St. Thomas website (which is very good and useful) or the ever helpful Frommer's guidebook, and each of them has an e-mail address listed for you to ask for reservations, and you do in fact send such a query, posed in English, and with the clarity of "Do you have a room for two persons for the period 14–18 Feb?" how many responses would you expect to receive within a reasonable period, e.g., two or three days? Fifteen? Maybe thirteen, allowing for some error rate? How about four? And of those four, zero provided additional detail, as in price, amenities, etc. Ye gods and little fishes. The travel industry wonders why business isn't growing fast …

Villa Blanca did respond, and they also answered their phone (another key piece of guidance from the "how to run a small business" handbook), and they had a garden, a view, and were not expensive. The Ritz-Carlton suggested $500 per day, no meals, but probably extra clean towels, so we figured for the extra $350 it would cost vs. the Villa Blanca, we could buy beach towels and drive to the beach. So we booked them. When we arrived we found a slightly ersatz, large, white clapboard building, which does perch on top of a hill, and we can see all of Charlotte Amalie, not that new Gidget/Audrey Hepburn-like French movie star but instead the capital city and largest city and perhaps only city of St. Thomas from our balcony. All of C. A. ain't that much, but still we got a nice view and can almost look down the smokestacks of the ever-present behemoth cruise ships anchored every day from about 0800 to 1800 in the large harbor. And hear in the distance the honking of the horns of the drivers caught in the traffic jams. Paradise indeed.

As soon as we got here, I went out to find provender. Man, the hunter. Sadly this meant sitting again in traffic. Finally I found a Cost-U-Less store but was only able to buy yogurt, which had been specifically requested, in case lots of 144 units. It was a sort of a Caribe Costco. I got some bananas out of a bin, but I was informed that since they had no tag on them, I couldn't buy them. Most bananas I see don't have tags, including all of the ones in the bin, so I was nonplussed. But you can't argue with an eighteen-year-old indifferent checkout girl. They did sell individual bottles of wine, so I got some, and sought other hunting grounds. Two stops and much traffic farther on I found a real supermarket name of Pueblo, probably Spanish derivation, not named after either the small city in Colorado or the spy ship captured by wily North Koreans. Except, although they had a space for yogurt, they only had one strawberry left. Feast or famine. They also didn't have any real dark chocolate, or any tuna kits, but they were OK on everything else. I returned more or less triumphantly to the hotel, dragging behind me the carcass of the mastodon that I had single-handedly slain, as well as beer and chips, and was warmly welcomed by my spouse with a hand wave meaning "I'm still on the phone." The joys of the warrior and the celebration of the kill. I had a beer and some teriyaki mastodon jerky.

We went out for dinner at a place just down the road, recommended by Eugene, the helpful hotel manager and our new best friend, called "Randy's." It's a bistro sort of place, sells wine and coffee and chocolate during the day, but it had decent food and they took our reservation. I think all these sort of places should be called "Rick's." Unfortunately, no piano player.

Day Two: More numbers: 38, 42, 30, 313. Roads that we drove on as we casually blundered around the island. Better number: 1000—time we got up. This is, after all, a vacation. It is peculiar that none of the island road numbers is lower than 30. No ready explanation for what happened to the 10s and 20s. It is also peculiar that one drives on the left-hand side of the road, although this was never a colony of either the UK or Japan, the only countries whose descendants still adhere to this arcane practice. And all the cars have left-hand drive. Makes it a more interesting game. Fortunately, there is always too much traffic and thus incredibly slow speeds, so the opportunities for mayhem are significantly reduced.

Off we went on our vacation adventure into the tropics—to Kmart. Linda had been so frazzled that she had also forgotten to pack shorts and T-shirts. "My God," I said, "we're going to a resort destination, I can't believe you don't have a T-shirt, it's the one thing we can be sure that won't be available there!"

Successful, we journeyed on to Coral World, sort of a sea life park without much sea life, but didn't go in. Then we tried to find what all our guidebooks said was the best place for island cuisine, Eunice's, but finally were told that it had gone out of business and was now called Glenda's, but that this version was also now closed. It had a handsome sign, however.

So we stopped at another place called Fungi's, advertised to have real island cuisine—callaloo (spinach and crabmeat soup) and jerked chicken and conch fritters and fungi, which is not mushrooms but instead creamy cornmeal pudding—like grits or cornmeal mush. However, it was lunchtime and they only had cheeseburgers and barbecue. So we had some, and Presidente beer brewed in the Dominican Republic, which I decided to count as island cuisine of a sort. We ended up at Magens Bay beach, said to be the best beach on the island. It's kind of like Kailua Beach in Hawaii, where you used to live before the madness seized you and you left, except thinner and not as long. The beach, not you. But very nice, and public—no hotels perched on it keeping one out. The water was warm; most of the cruise people had departed. And the pelicans were diving for fish about twenty feet off the beach. I mentioned that the idea that pelicans hold fish in the pouches under their bills was hogwash. I even recited the Ogden Nash limerick to document the popular belief. And as we watched, sure enough, the pelicans actually swallowed the fish they were catching. My wife seemed rather less than fascinated to hear this piece of natural science mixed with literature. But then a wave came in and splashed her, so there. By the time we had finished a thorough inspection of the beach, the garden we were heading for was closed. More to do for tomorrow.

We had dinner at a place called the Inn at Blackbeard's Castle, and at the same time made reservations for the next night at the Agave Terrace, located at the Bluebeard's Castle Resort. Eating dinner is an important St. Thomas occupation with "many internationally trained chefs" using "only the freshest ingredients," which they have to get flown in because nothing is grown here anymore. And eating is an important focus since there's so little else to do. As far as we have been able to find, "island cuisine" is nonexistent, although if your island doesn't grow anything then it's hard to develop an island cuisine, I suppose, unless you eat sand and hills. Rum actually is said to be made on St. Croix, and some stuff is grown there, but nothing on the other two saints.

Both the Inn at Blackbeard's Castle and the Bluebeard's Castle Resort feature a tall, round stone lookout tower sort of thing. Pirates used to hang out in the islands, looking unsuccessfully for native cuisine, so there are lots of references to them, and lots of Jolly Rogers flying about, decorating T-shirts and car antennae. When you read the fine print, however, you find that there is no evidence that Blackbeard actually ever used his lookout tower (or stayed in the inn, one presumes) and that it was in fact built by the Danes to be used to watch the harbor for something, maybe native cuisine or at least a shipment of Doritos. To make matters even more confusing, Bluebeard isn't even a real pirate, only a piece of French folklore about some guy named Le Barbe bleue ("blue haircutting person"), and why he got transformed into a Caribbean pirate is not clear in translation. There are also no more hotels with the same name, although there is clearly room for Blackbird's Castle, Bluebird's Inn, Larry Bird's Castle, and James Beard's Inn. And maybe Charlie Byrd's Castle and Nightclub.

Day Three: Numbers to contemplate: two million (the number of tourists who visit this island each year); 6,136(4), 4,456(5), 3,490(2), 6,876(3)—according the local newspaper, the *Virgin Islands Daily News*, the number of cruise tourists and the number of cruise ships (in parenthesis) that visited the island each of the four days we were there. If you assume that these visits are mostly concentrated in the six-month winter period, and that at least a few of them stay more than one day, then the base populations is boosted by 40% every day. That's a lot of hotel rooms and shops and rental cars, etc. And yet, there's really not that much here. One can shop and go to the beach, but the best beaches are nowhere near the cruise line docks. We remain baffled by the economics of the place, except it looks clear that it's not a manufacturing mecca, and there's no evidence of a software programming industry.

Because it's there, we take the ferry over to St. John, having arranged to link up with the only "ecotour" hiking folks on that even smaller island. This is not particularly adventurous as the island is clearly visible from the dock, and turns out to be a fifteen-minute ferry ride. We hike through the rather dry forest with Jeff, our guide. The hike takes an hour and a half and has been cleverly arranged to start at the top of a hill (which they also have in St. John in plenty) and end at a beach. All downhill. Two thirds of St. John is national park, and the rest is resorts, private and very expensive houses, and souvenir shops/jeep rental/bars at the beach. The beaches that we see are nicer and more numerous than on St. Thomas, and Cinnamon Bay Beach, where the hike ends, is particularly lovely. But they're all pretty shallow as far as having sand goes. Sugarcane used to be grown and processed on St. John, but now nothing is. Well, tourists are processed. It's sort of a scruffy place, at least the "city" of Cruz Bay—where the ferryboat lands—is, and very Caribbean looking, which means sort of seedy and slightly rundown. We see two mongooses (mongeese?) on the drive to and from the trailheads, and Jeff tells us that they were imported to kill the rats, but it turns out that the rats negotiated a standstill and profit sharing agreement with the mongoose, giving them the day but retaining full rights to the night. So the mongooses have killed all the snakes (not a bad thing) and now are working on wiping out all the native birds and turtles, which is less good. Plans are afoot to trap the mongooses, and then do something with them. Probably drop them in the ocean, but you can't say that or PETA will have a delegation here throwing red paint on your bathing suit. Perhaps they could become animal models, who knows. We take the ferry back to St. Thomas and stop for a slice of pizza and a cold beer to reward ourselves for our exertions. They don't even offer to put pineapple or mango on the pizza. Island cuisine remains elusive, but it probably wasn't pizza anyway.

Day Four: Eleven to fourteen. The amount of inches of snow that fell overnight in the DC area, with the same additional amount expected today. One of our goals for today is to make it to McDonald's for an egg McBagel before they stop serving breakfast at 1030. This proves to be too ambitious. We have also signed up for more ecotouring, this time a kayak trip in a mangrove lagoon. I suspect that lagoon is tropical-ese for swamp. First, however, we go off to St. Peter Great House and Botanical Gardens, an "attraction." For which we have a special map and even a two-for-one coupon. How much better can life get? The sucker is remarkably hard to find, however. We get two sets of directions and even completely drive by it once, which leaves one to wonder just how many tourists, especially those with less devotion to things botanique than we, ever go there. Once we do find it, on the second pass, the fifteen acres of the facility are mostly devoted to a parking lot; a big tropical-style house you can walk around, with couches and chairs all with signs on them marked Do Not Sit; observation decks all around the house so you can look at the other islands; a gift shoppe (natch); and a separate large building that is not a greenhouse, but is rather a big ball room obviously used for functions (weddings, etc.). What there is not so much of is garden. In essence it's a big house that's nicely landscaped. Oh well. We try another nursery that's been recommended to us, but it's closed.

On to the ecotour. We are the only ecotourists for today, which is curious given that this is a nice and interesting thing to do that fits precisely into the cruise ship visiting window. There is a large mangrove-bordered lagoon on the southeastern portion of the island, located conveniently right next to the island landfill and a defunct hilltop asphalt plant painted an eye-catching chartreuse. But setting that aside, we hop into plastic kayaks and, led by our guide, Robert, who also appears to be the eco-owner—a nice guy of fifty plus who came down to the islands eight years ago from Cape Cod—we paddle off into the lagoon. We make several stops and hear about mangroves, the only tree that can live in salt water. This is a pretty neat trick, when you think about it. Somehow the root system filters out the salt and only absorbs the pure H_2O into its system. The explanation of this is unclear, botanically speaking, but it is still an interesting piece of biochemistry. The root system is deep and sturdy, so much so that now the island allows folks to anchor their boats in the lagoon, tied onto the mangroves, in the event of a hurricane. Otherwise it is restricted to Robert and his kayaks. Robert says that during Hugo in 1989, which was the first really big hurricane to hit the island in a very long time, all the boats were in the main harbor. This turned out to be a mistake, as they all ended up on Main Street, including an eighty-five-foot coast guard cutter. The storm surge came in through the widened and deepened channel, and that was that. The lagoon is now preserved, but until twenty years ago it was overfished and slated to become an airport. Good sense prevailed, or else the landfill was the compromise, hard to tell. The current airport looks suspiciously like it's had its runway extended into the ocean, no doubt at some eco-cost.

When we get to the end of the lagoon, there's a coral reef that keeps out the full force of the ocean. We get out and snorkel around, seeing a certain number of small brown fish and lots and lots of odd jellyfish, which are attached to the bottom of the lagoon. I myself think this is a very fine place for jellyfish to be, as opposed to floating around trying to sting me. They are also oddly pulsating. No reason given, frequency cannot be ascertained with precision. Possibly communicating with aliens? Maybe not jellyfish but actually aliens themselves. The water is warm, the sun has come back out, and it is very pleasant with the jellyfish firmly anchored in place. Robert is very apologetic that we don't see any stingrays. Linda is disappointed, I am eco-OK with that.

Day Five: Fifteen minutes, the amount of time I have to wait to connect with American Airlines to find out if we're still going to be able to fly into the teeth of the blizzard and get home. I have my druthers, but since it turns out that the blizzard is over and we are now flying not into its teeth but only into its gums—or maybe esophagus—we can make it. And so we leave St. Thomas, endure one more traffic jam on the way to the airport, and catch our flight home, worrying about whether we'll be able to get up our driveway.

Love and kisses,
Bob

Afterword: When we got back to the Baltimore airport, we found that our car was hard to find since it was sitting in literally four feet of snow. As were approximately ten thousand other cars in the long-term (and cheap) parking lot. All sedans covered with four feet of snow look very much the same. The pickup trucks looked different, but we hadn't brought ours. And I had not been clever enough to write down which shuttle stop we were near. And it was cold and we still didn't have any coats on. Sometimes bad decisions build on each other. And when we found the car we had to dig it out with mostly our hands. This is not a good way to end a tropical vacation.

For some reason I have not been back to the Caribbean since.

chapter
five

How Not to Run a Railroad, or a Utility

September 2003

Dear Dad,

The last time I was in Bulgaria it was 1998, and I had come to pull out
two of our investment fund associates, ones we had hired on the mistaken
notion that they would go to Sofia and find marvelous technologies for
us, ones we could license and take to the West and make into companies and become fabulously wealthy. We had heard that under the Soviet
system Bulgaria was a center for optics and electronics, and for batteries
and genetic research on plants and animals—all areas that intrigued us.
Here's what we found instead:

- "Research institutes" with broken windows, and no money for
  maintenance for the last ten years—dusty, no lighting in the hall-
  ways, no glassware in the labs.
- No one home. Many offices empty and labs unoccupied, like a
  ghost town.
- The people who were still there were only the older scientists; the

young ones had all long since fled to the West and been snapped up by the larger companies in the industry, mostly by Europeans, but in some cases by American companies. The best battery guy had gone to Rayovac.

- The scientists who remained had no idea about the patent status of any of their technologies, and there was no one obvious to discuss this with, even if we could have found something in which we were interested.

Most discouraging was the police harassment, which seemed a fairly prevalent part of Sofia life if you were a Westerner. One of our two guys was a German, and the other Chinese. The Chinese kid, Naidong, turned out to be an especially good target. Not a lot of Chinese with flattops in Sofia. First they wouldn't let him through customs when he arrived; our local real estate lady actually had to go into the customs hall and physically drag him out. She said that they wanted bribes, but since the English of neither party was particularly good, this wasn't coming through clearly. Then a week later, two big, bulky police came to the door of the kids' apartment at midnight, armed of course, and wearing their bulletproof vests. They demanded passports, indicating that the visas were not correct. Christian, our German, argued with them that he was an EU citizen and that certain visa rules didn't apply to him. The police offered to fix these incorrect visas, but the kids refused to pay. Eventually the police went away. A week later, Naidong was accosted in broad daylight, again by police, who demanded 25 lev ($30.00) for his "mistake passport." He asked to be taken to the police station, which they refused, and then he bargained them down to $10.00, and he demanded a receipt. Which they gave him. Bizarre. Since it was in Bulgarian, it might have said "screw you" for all he knew.

We had heard enough. Actually we were afraid that our associates were so dumb and so courageous that they were going to get beaten up or killed, which probably wasn't what they'd signed up for. So we flew to Sofia and pulled them out. This was the weekend of the Fourth of July, and Linda had been scheduled to keynote the First Annual Bulgarian High Technology Investment Forum. Truly. She cancelled her speech, and we met with the deputy prime minister, and with the US ambassador, and explained we were leaving, and that we had several important recommendations for them if they were serious about creating a climate to foster foreign investment. You might be able to guess what they were.

Fast-forward five years. Bulgaria has been accepted into NATO and will join next year. Its national credit rating, thanks to careful fiscal management, is now investment grade. AES has been working on a large power project there for some time, but during our recent troubled period, had decided to cancel the project and write off the rather considerable amount of money spent to date. However, Paul, our CEO, and I, in thinking about it further, came to the conclusion that perhaps the project, although troubled, was salvageable.

Called "Maritsa," or technically Maritsa East 2, it's envisioned as a 600 Mw solid fuel plant in the southeast of Bulgaria. The contract to sell the power from the plant was originally won by a small group of three partners, a US financial person named Bill, a local Bulgarian named Koko, and an Israeli now living in Paris named Jacob. They brought us on to develop the project, as they did not have the skills or the capital to finish it. We have plugged along, spending foolish amounts of money to get to where we are today. Except where we are is not workable. There are two problems:

1. One of the partners, Jacob, appears to be a crazy person. We have had serious partner problems on many of the projects put together by our London office, and this is no exception. We have to get the three minority partners out of the equation, or we can't move ahead.

2. The fuel for the plant is a local lignite, an exceptionally poor grade of coal. US coal runs 8,000 to 11,500 Btus per pound. The Bulgarian stuff is about 7,000, and it's wet. For reference, wood is about 6,000, so we're only a step above that. This means that you have to take elaborate steps to dry the "coal" before it goes into the boiler, and you have to put a lot of pounds of material into the boiler to make the steam, close to twice as much. Electricity does follow some rules, or at least combustion does, and processing twice as much fuel per kWh means equipment that is much

larger—bigger boilers, larger pulverizers, bigger fans and more of them, larger ash-handling equipment, etc. End result: lots of capital cost, in this case over a billion dollars. The fuel is real cheap, but the trade-off is a lot of capital equipment to process it. For the Bulgarians this is a reasonable choice, as their other alternatives are to be dependent on Russian gas, or maybe oil from Kazakhstan, or possibly their old Chernobyl-style nukes. The plant is to be built at the mine, of course, because it makes no sense to move this stuff any farther than you have to.

But . . . we can't finance a billion-dollar plant in Bulgaria. Actually, I don't think we could finance a billion-dollar plant in the US. To my count, there have only been two stand-alone power plants done at a billion dollars or more: the Dabhol plant by Enron in Gujarat, India; and the Paiton plant in Indonesia by Mission Energy, an affiliate of Southern California Edison. Both are now widely considered bad ideas. Not a good precedent, nor a good example to cite for suspicious bankers.

So why are we here, you may ask? To drink fine Bulgarian merlot? Ah, no, but instead to meet with various Bulgarian officials. Not quite as interesting a purpose, depending on what you think of Bulgarian merlot.

We need to explain three things:

1. AES has been through some difficult times recently as you know, but has emerged in decent shape, and we are now moving ahead in building our business. It's interesting to note that the number of Wall Street analysts who still cover us, down to five from our high of sixteen, are no longer asking "Are you gonna make it?" Their questions now focus on "What's next?" or "How are you going to grow the business?" Pleasant change. And in the case of Bulgaria, it means that we aren't going to cancel this project, we are going to proceed and try to get it done.

2. The minority partners are a problem, but it's a problem that we have the power to fix. And we'll either fix it in sixty days, or we will come back to the Ministry of Energy and NEK, the state-owned utility, and tell them that we can't fix it and that they should cancel our contract. No more development money on projects

with screwed up partnership relations. One of the officials asked me what the solution would be and I explained that I was a fairly simple thinker, and the basic solution was that we would give them some money and they would go away.

3. We have to do the project in two 300 Mw stand-alone phases. The first phase will be slightly more expensive, since some shared facilities (the control room, for example) will be built slightly larger than one would if 300 Mw were all you were ever going to build, and the second phase correspondingly less expensive. But it will be financeable; we can do $550 or $600 million in Bulgaria, although it won't be easy. No more development money on projects with a very low probability of ever getting financed. It's interesting to note that the Bulgarian government itself has never done a financing larger than about $800 million. And our project, in the final analysis, will be financed largely on the credit of the contract with the Bulgarian utility to buy the power.

The meetings go well. We met first with the deputy energy minister, then with the woman at NEK with the title of "procurator," a title which may be mis-translated, but she is the person directly in charge of our project. Our last meeting is with the finance minister. All the Bulgarians are young, alert, receptive, wear nice suits, and speak some to very good English. This was not the case five years ago. We also visited the US ambassador and several of his staff to update them. Good English, also nice suits, but not so young. No police asked us for money. This, too, was a pleasant change.

But all that was the easy part. Now we actually have to solve the partner problem, and we have to redo the plant specs, and rebid it, and then work out the change in the electricity price necessary to support a two-phase approach. But the reception was positive, and they didn't tell us to get lost, which they could have, and which probably would have been justified. No one argued that a billion dollars was so doable. I think we may be riding a little on our reputation, and on the fact that the industry is in such a shambles that there aren't people standing in line to do power projects in Bulgaria. OK with me.

Cultural observations: Sofia is not a very big city, and Bulgaria is not a very big country. Our project, if built, will be the largest foreign investment in Bulgaria ever. Hence we are news. In fact, the Energy Ministry notified the press before we arrived about our upcoming visit, and on the day of our first meetings there was a big article in the main Sofia newspaper, front page of the second section above the spread, saying that . . . we were having meetings. Really, our local person, Nadja, read it to me. Nothing about the issues, nothing about the likely outcomes, nothing about how distinguished Paul and I are, just that we were having meetings.

The city itself is a typical old eastern European capital being slowly and erratically rebuilt—some new stuff, some pretty and refurbished old stuff, lot of refurbished seven-story middle-aged stuff. Kind of like me except for the seven stories.

They don't much like the Turks. This is a prevalent feeling in this part of the world, since the Turks seem to have been rapacious occupiers during the period of the Ottoman Empire. According to Nadja, many of the most famous Bulgarian poems, songs, novels, paintings, etc., all celebrate the driving out of the Turks, or say what bad fellows they were, or the like. I don't think they much like the Russians either, hence the Bulgarian drive for NATO and EU membership. They want to be considered Europeans, not something else. And they're even working on making their wine better. However, AOL doesn't work from my hotel or from our office. And my fancy new Blackberry, which is both an e-mail device and a phone (and a GSM phone, the European standard, to boot) turns out to be neither in Bulgaria.

I fly back to London from Bulgaria on Tuesday afternoon to meet with our Moscow office head on Wednesday. He's in from Russia to finalize the sale of all our Georgia businesses, Telassi, and a power plant, to RAO UES, the giant Russian utility. We have spent a lot of wasted time and energy and money on this business, and been unable to make anything of it. Good luck, you Russians. We speculate that they will be delivering the electricity to Georgia with tanks.

On my way in from the train station, I note that things sure are dry. It hasn't rained in the UK for more than a month. Having lived there, I can say without hesitation that this is unusual. All the nice big parks no longer have greens, they now have "browns." It really does look strange. Walking from my hotel to the office, I pass lots of typical English row houses with front gardens. Growing in one is the tallest good-old Kansas sunflower that I have ever seen— it literally must be twenty feet tall. The flower head is about at the middle of the second-story window. I believe that this is the only sunflower that has actually ever grown in the UK, where there is generally no sun. It is certainly having a good time in this temporarily changed climate. No sooner have I observed this than the weather turns gray and cold.

The meeting is useful, as I have never actually met John, our man in Moscow, before. He seems relieved that I do not have horns and a tail. At least not visibly. Paul, the CEO, has recently had a meeting with Anatoly Chubais, the CEO of RAO UES, the giant Russian utility who has expressed an interest in working with us in eastern Europe. This despite the fact that we didn't know squat about Georgia, at least according to the RAO press release they issued when they took over our Georgian businesses (the country not the state—no Russians yet in Atlanta or Macon). John and I agree to proceed carefully on such an alliance, both because we don't know these guys very well, and because we are uncertain politically how such an alliance will play in these locations. These countries just got rid of these Russian guys, how happy will they be to see them back?

Wednesday evening I take the train to Paris for my flight to Cameroon, which leaves Thursday a.m. I am pretty pleased with myself—short cab ride to Richmond station, train in to Waterloo station, then Eurostar to Paris, all for about $200 less than flying would have been. I am also excited to go through the "chunnel." The Eurostar turns out to be nice, a slightly shabby Metroliner, with nowhere to plug in your computer (now standard on all Metroliners so we can all work on our laptops from Washington to NY or Boston without worrying about battery life). Or we can talk annoyingly on our cell phones.

I don't know quite what I was expecting, but here's what it's like going through the Channel Tunnel on a train: it's dark outside so you can't see anything, and the train has lights inside. It takes twenty minutes. There you have it. Not actually so exciting. It's not like taking a train through an aquarium. I suppose I could have anticipated that.

Continuing my campaign to prove that you can travel to Europe for less than a million dollars a trip, I catch the local train from the Gare du Nord in downtown Paris, where the Eurostar arrives, out to CDG. Despite my apprehensions, the train is quite well marked, so my achievement is not quite the same as finding Livingstone in Africa. And I have booked a cheap motel near the airport at 95 euros, rather than the 300 euro Sheraton at the airport that our travel agent recommended.

At the airport, I find the cabstand, but the cab driver points me to a location ten yards away, which is the hotel shuttle location. It's 9:30 at night, it's getting windy and cold, but OK, this is all part of our new economy campaign. Several hotel shuttles do come, but not one for the "Country Inn." I try my Blackberry to see if magically its phone part is working in Paris after it didn't work in London. Nope. After twenty-five minutes, most of the other folks waiting have all been picked up by shuttles. I approach the cab drivers—the exact same ones, still standing around their cabs, going nowhere fast as it's pretty desolate at the airport at this hour— and suggest deferentially that I would actually be able to pay for a ride to the Country Inn. They respond with classic French hospitality: "Non, Paris!" Actually several of them say this same thing, and gesture violently that I should return to my place, so that they can continue smoking evil French cigarettes and complaining about how slow business is.

I note with interest at this point that there are actually four or five hotels right at the airport, not just the expensive Sheraton. I note this because I can see them from where I am standing. No flies on your son. The intellectually challenged travel agent never conveyed this handy information. I give up on the mythical shuttle and walk over to the Novotel. They have a room for 145 euros, and a dining room that is still open. And the young guy at the desk even calls and cancels the Country Inn for me, and writes down the cancellation number. I am amazed. He must not yet have been to "How to Be French" school, or was absent on the day the curriculum focused on "Tourists are Scum, esp. Americans." At dinner I order the largest size bottle of Perrier available to celebrate my good fortune.

Have to take your victories where you find them. I cannot, however, hook up to AOL in the hotel room.

We interrupt this narrative for a brief interjection entitled either "Travel Agents Are Morons" or "The New AES." My borrowed assistant at AES, a smart young woman named Tonya Walker, has worked on the travel arrangements for this trip, and used the company's travel agent. All the flights were business class, the London hotel was 180 pounds, and the hotel at CDG was a five star Sheraton at 300 euros/night, as previously noted. She was pretty surprised when I told her to make it all coach, and get a cheaper hotel, both in London and Paris. The flight difference was more than $4,000 and hotel difference more than $400. I have to admit that there wasn't a hell of a lot of room in the Air France seats, but it was survivable. The travel agent, in retaliation, told Tonya that no seats could be reserved on the coach flights. But when we called the airline directly, wonder of wonders, this was not so. There might be lessons here.

Cameroon is not the Australian contraction for "coconut macaroon," although it could be. Here are the basics: It's between Nigeria on the north and the various Congos on the south. Bad neighborhood. Sixteen million people. German colony until WWI, then split into bits between French and Brits, reunited as one country the size of California at independence, which was about the same time as everybody else: early to mid '60s. Poor but not destitute: gross domestic product per capita of $1,700. Economy is largely agricultural (timber, cocoa, coffee), some minerals, some offshore oil and gas only now beginning to be exploited. Tropical—sits actually on the equator. Got its name because the Portuguese were passing by, noted that the main river was full of shrimp, decided that this was there-fore the River of Shrimp (*Rio dos Camarões* in Portuguese). Perhaps they were having a bad day imagination-wise. The river is now called "Wouri," which was either its original name or means shrimp in Cameroonian or something else, no one can tell me. Ranks 89 out of 102 on Transparency International's list of bribe-worthy states (high numbers are bad); state obligations have a credit rating of single B, also bad, but donor aid makes up only about 5% of the budget. In some African countries, this number is as high as 40%. Heavily in debt—outstanding debt is 95% of GDP;

US numbers range from 40%–60%. One wonders what they did with the money.

The flight from Paris to Douala is basically due south, and takes six hours. We land at an airport with an open-air design, kind of like Hawaii, only more decrepit. In fact the whole place reminds me of the more downscale parts of Hawaii. Or the more upscale parts of tropical India, except there aren't any of those, and there are not as many people here as in any part of India, and they're all African and for some reason they speak French. So much for the India comparison.

The architecture in town is predominantly lots of corrugated metal sheds and shacks, and many small concrete buildings, the tallest no more than six stories, most with brown and black rain and mold stains on the sides. Also many lots with tall grass, and a stream with kids jumping into it naked. There are very serious potholes in the roads. Lots of hibiscus and coral plants and crotons and lantana, and royal palms, coconut palms, traveler's palms, tulip trees, royal poinciana, etc. Warm and damp—the rainy season has just started. Unlike England, lots of green. Lots of advertisements for Orange, the cellular provider, miscellaneous other stuff, all in French. No McDonald's, no 7-Elevens, no Burger King, no KFC. But modern gas stations, Total, Mobil, Elf. Not especially crowded, and almost no Caucasians on the streets, only Africans. Guess that shouldn't be a surprise.

Helen, the head of AES-Sonel, our utility, kindly picked me up and whisked me through customs, etc. She takes me to dinner at a nice French restaurant on the main street, along with her deputy. Not much street lighting or commercial lighting on the main drag. This is assuredly not Hong Kong or Tokyo. I have been sternly warned not to eat the salad. I don't.

A word, or maybe several words, about Sonel. It is a classic integrated national utility. It has as its monopoly territory all of Cameroon, and all the electric generation and distribution therein, or lack of therein. We bought it in a privatization sale about two and a half years ago, for $69 million, which got us 56%, the government of Cameroon retaining the other 44%. There was only one other bidder, the French national utility EDF, who was already running the utility, and knew all about it. They bid less.

We then radically and crazily decentralized everything and destroyed all the centralized systems. This was AES at its brainless, missionary worst: no controls, no checks, centralized anything is bad, including such simple things as centralized information. Or any information. Each business unit leader (and there were thirty-two of them) was given full authority over anything and everything. For example, promotions. About half of them immediately promoted themselves to the top of the salary scale. We didn't murder anyone, but in hearing up close and firsthand all the stories, what happened was a reenactment of the Khmer Rouge purge of everything civilized in Cambodia, except this time in a business context. We are still slowly, painfully recovering. The damage was extensive, and the recovery has been costly.

As if that weren't enough, this is a 90% hydro system, but quite strangely designed. To wit, there are mountains toward the eastern end of the country, and the rivers flow east to west. There are two reasonably big dams with generation capacity on the western end of the river system (we call this a catchment area in hydro land), and several dams on the eastern end, in the mountains, with reservoir capacity. The western dams are all "run of the river," i.e., the water flows right through them, with no real storage. The eastern dams have no generation, and are only for storage. This must be French engineering at its worst. Ever since the forties and TVA, we have always built dams with generation in them, especially if they have storage. And dams at the lower ends of systems always have storage. Perhaps no one told the French. More likely some American told them and they duly ignored the information, given the source.

There are two bad results of this system: During the dry season, all the water is stored way upstream. It takes seven days to get from the storage dams in the east to the generation dams in the west. So you have to guess pretty accurately what your load will be seven days ahead of time, and then release the correct amount of water. And there is very little thermal power plant capacity to throw into the breach if you guess wrong. Second, and in some senses even more stupid, is the fact that much of the annual rainfall falls west of the dams in the mountains. It's a big country, and it's kind of hard to train the rain where to fall. Thus in the wet season you really collect and store very little of the total rain that falls in the catchment area; most of it just rushes down the river to the generation dams that have no storage. And even worse, much of this water is spilled, it goes over the top of the dams, or in spillways around the dams, because we don't have enough generation in these dams to handle the peak flows. Spilling water in a hydro system is throwing away free money. It is Cardinal Sin Number One. We only did it at TVA to prevent floods or some other dire thing, and it was a Big Deal and we did as little of it as we possibly could. In Sonel, during the rainy season, we spill 80% of the water. Holy moly! And it's all because of the system design. You thought the French weren't great at foreign policy . . .

So the French genius at hydrology plus our own Cambodian approach to management have left us a pretty challenging situation for Helen, the new manager, and her team. Our own Pol Pot has moved on but, strangely, he has neither been fired nor sent before a UN war crimes tribunal. In fact, he's running something else at AES.

Collections are poor, losses are around 37%, compared with 3%–5% for a US utility; there is a certain amount of theft and fraud, people steal power; and we can't meet the load in the dry season because of the three-year drought and the annual increase in demand of 7% per year. And ever since our disastrous experience in Georgia, where we funneled in money from AES without plan or purpose, we have been extremely stingy with outside capital. Sonel has had to make do with its own internally generated resources. Add to this some difficult labor laws that make it hard to fire crooked or inefficient employees, and a legal system that makes it slow to prosecute people who steal power, and the problems are interesting, if not formidable. Oh, and I didn't add that the northern part of the country is not connected electrically to the southern part, so we run two different unconnected systems, plus there are about twenty-six freestanding dots of electrical service where we have put in a small diesel power plant in a village, some as small as 80 kW (enough for eight hundred lightbulbs, or six US homes). All of these tiny systems have to be staffed, fuel has to be delivered, and someone has to operate and maintain the equipment. Not a very efficient system.

And just in case you were hoping that that wasn't all the list of problems . . .

» Once we had finished destroying the accounting system, we then went to cash accounting, on the theory that even if you can't figure out depreciation and all that funny stuff that comes with an accrual system, at least you can count the money. We receive money—mostly cash payments—by people bringing their bills and their cash to one of our 110 payment centers. Not a lot of our customers have checking accounts or credit cards. And for some reason, each of the 110 locations has its own bank account to put the money into. And no one was reconciling the accounts—not balancing even the local checkbook. That's the first thing they teach you in Accounting 101.

» As best we can determine from the systems we have slowly reconstructed, most of our customers who get bills actually pay. We have a payment rate of about 95%–97%—except for the government. This is not good. It's hard to cut off the government. The biggest problem customer is the Ministry of Defense, and they are especially hard to cut off. It is said that they have weapons. This is even more irksome as the government still owns 44% of the utility. We are getting even with them for not paying their bills by not paying our taxes. Or at least thinking about it. But it's not a wash, so probably not a viable long-term strategy.

» We lose about 37% of the electricity to theft or technical losses. But we cannot tell precisely how much goes where, since we do not have adequate submetering of the system. This makes it much harder to look for both the theft and the technical losses. Imagine mailing ten letters in NYC addressed to the West Coast, but only receiving six of them in Los Angeles, and having no way to tell how the letters were routed in between, with many, many possible routings. Tracing lost mail in such a system would be nigh on to impossible—you don't know where to start. Same with our electricity system.

» Not so good purchasing system. When we decentralized the purchasing authority, anyone could buy anything with no approvals, etc. A recent sampling by our auditors of bills paid vs. invoices turned up a bigger than trivial number of payees who had no phone number, no bank account, and no commercial address. And it was all paid in cash. Ugh. I do note, in the interests of fairness, that the Washington, DC, school system just discovered they had paid a number of similar invoices. Perhaps also to imaginary folk in Cameroon.

» Who works here, anyway? We have a new and very good security guy who has implemented a revolutionary idea: employees should have ID badges. With pictures on them. He has been at this for forty-five days, and still we haven't been able to track down about 1,400 of the 3,500 persons who are getting paid each month. But we will, and then the number of employees will probably be smaller. But they'll be real.

There's lots to do, but Helen has assembled a very talented set of folks around her, and progress is being made. It's hard, it's slow, it's frustrating, but it is progress.

I spend all day Friday with various managers of the utility. Helen has bravely told them to tell me anything I want to know, and then set me loose. I try to refrain from getting into trouble. All the meetings actually are very helpful and very informative. No one is defensive, no one tries to make things seem better than they are, everyone is honest about the challenges, but upbeat about plans for meeting them. All are eager to see what "Arlington" thinks, and they are interested in my suggestions and reactions. The modeling and rate design guys are especially impressive, including Helen's deputy, a Cameroonian and longtime utility manager named Jean-David Bile. Despite myself, I am impressed.

After dinner with the generation guys, I try to make my Blackberry work, or my cell phone, or AOL, or the AES e-mail system, or AT&T Direct. No dice. Helen has told me that they don't have much better luck at the offices. Plus the hotel business center is closed for refurbishment. The landline phone does work, the water works, and the electricity works, and you can send faxes at the hotel front desk. Fair enough—I can even remember from long, long ago when that was all there was. . . .

Saturday is the main event, the ostensible purpose of my visit. As noted above, we're in the unfortunate position of being an electricity seller without enough product. So we have designed and contracted for a new modest-sized power plant to be built next to the refinery that serves the country, in a town about an hour west of Douala, called Limbe, and today is the day for the groundbreaking. Helen takes me there in her Toyota Land Cruiser, complete with driver and bodyguard. The bodyguard looks like maybe he could take Jerry Lewis on a bad day, but it seems unlikely that we will be accosted by brigands or terrorists. Not a lot here to steal or blow up. I guess I could give up my Blackberry if threatened.

Once we get out of Douala, the drive passes through lots of plantation agriculture that you would recognize—bananas, pineapples, and rubber trees. I even spot a Del Monte sign. The road is good, the traffic is light, and it has stopped raining.

We meet up first with the minister of mines and energy, who has been designated as the "ranking government official" for the ceremony. He is quite young and has no background in either energy or mining. But he is pleasant and supportive. Unlike most of the other senior folk there, he is dressed in traditional African dress, a very handsome blue and white print. We all go to an open-air auditorium near the site, and us dignitaries sit up front facing the audience, which includes a lot of press. Speeches are made. An African singing group sings African songs between each speech, which is pretty cool. Helen, since she is the director general, gets to make a speech, but her staff has given her only half the pages. This seems somehow symbolic.

Speeches over, we move to the actual groundbreaking site, about a thousand yards away. The schedule calls for us to await the arrival of the group of traditional chiefs who will first bless the site before we actually start digging. The chiefs arrive in a bus, then start a processional—slowly and with dignity—walking up the hill toward us. They are led by two young men, also traditionally dressed, except their costumes are hot pink tunics over pale pink trousers. I am not making this up. The one on the right is carrying a spear, which he pounds on the ground with every second step, and the one on the left is sonorously ringing a large bell. Several of the chiefs have really elaborate headgear; I am especially taken by the guy whose hat has about twenty small springy wires coming out of it, each with a couple of beads on the end. I have never seen this in any museum of African art. All of us folks in suits wait attentively, except we take some pictures of the procession. The group of chiefs gets about three-quarters of the way up the hill, and then the spear carrier's cell phone rings. He steps out of the procession, spear and all, to take the call.

The site is blessed with water, palm wine, schnapps, and whiskey. All are variously sprinkled on the ground after much chanting. Then us nontraditional chiefs all stick our shovels into the ground, except it's hard as a brick so not very much ground gets broken. We retire back to a pavilion for a big lunch. Sadly, the food is English as we are in the part of Cameroon that used to be a UK colony. So it goes.

A note on the plant: it's 70 Mw, and will cost $80 million, which is high except that the project includes a transmission line. And we are starting construction without the financing in hand, because if we don't we won't have the power in time for the dry season, and this will be a very bad thing. This is going to be nerve-wracking, and is in general not the way to build a power plant. It's probably not the way to build anything. Or maybe we just have gotten confused and are using the Japanese concept of "just in time" supply chain management in the financial arena. We in "Arlington" have been quite clear that there won't be any money from headquarters riding in like cavalry to save the day, but there are specialized African-focused investment funds evaluating the project. We shall see.

On the drive back to Douala, we pass a bus depot, with many different private carriers all loading or unloading passengers. It's busy and entrepreneurial. Helen points out to me her favorite bus company. She likes the name, and I think it just may characterize the correct approach to our business here. It's called the Patience Express.

Love and kisses,
Bob

Afterword: We did finally get the Bulgarian power plant financed, a financing of $1.2 billion, which remains the largest done in AES to date, although it was quite a struggle.

Then we got it built, another struggle, and brought online in a timely and within-budget fashion. We made and delivered the electricity as promised in our contract.

Bulgaria has had continuing problems doing what they had agreed to, which is pay for the electricity. After much difficulty and negotiation, a new agreement has been put in place in the last year that will allow the state-owned utility to pay for the power at a modified rate, but over a longer contractual period. Let's hope this one works.

The outcome on Cameroon has been less positive. Despite the dedication and selfless efforts of a number of AES people, both from Arlington and from Cameroon, the utility has never really performed as we had hoped that it would, and we have never been able to reduce losses to a rate that would put Cameroon into the positive column of return on investment. The utility was sold to an investment fund specializing in African infrastructure in 2014. Despite decades of talk and analysis, billions of dollars of Western aid, and a continent of stunning natural resources, Africa with few exceptions remains the most challenging place in the world to do business, with the possible exception of North Korea.

chapter
six

Don't Drink the Water Unless You Made It Yourself

October 2003

Dear Dad,

Riyadh is low and tan, or more truly sand colored, with lots of one- and two-story concrete buildings. The capital city of Saudi Arabia is spread out and flat, and the horizon just above the low skyline is a sandy gold. The construction is all concrete and stucco, no wooden buildings. The only two really tall buildings stand out, both for tallness and strangeness: the Kingdom Centre, which tapers to a height of twenty-five stories with an arrowhead-shaped opening of maybe six stories at the top; and the Al Faisaliyah Center, a four-sided narrow pyramid sort of building, a bit like the Transamerica building in San Francisco, except that two-thirds of the way up, the building interrupts itself to house a giant gold glass ball—could be a disco ball about seven thousand times too big. Other than that, there are only a handful of "modern" glass and chrome and marble buildings. Our principal guy in the region, Shahzad, says it's one of those cities still in the first round of modernization. No shacks, no corrugated tin roofing, no piles of trash in the street, all paved roads, lots of cars, several McDonald's and Burger Kings, four million people, and a Dunkin' Donuts two doors down from a House of Donuts. It seems odd to have a donut neighborhood but there you are. It's hot and dry and there are date palms with dates on them (that's how you tell they're not coconut palms) and low evergreen trees and some bougainvillea in the public spaces, principally along the edges of the streets and in the median. Every piece of the shrubbery has its own quarter-inch black irrigation tube running to it. Every piece. I conclude this really is a desert with a city arbitrarily planted on top of it. Insightful, is us.

It takes a while to get here. You leave Friday and fly overnight from Dulles to London, hang around Terminal 4 at Heathrow for three or four hours feeling gritty and out of sorts, then fly another six hours, landing at about ten in the evening. Nothing much to do but go to your hotel and go to sleep. This doesn't appear to be a party town, at least from what you can see driving in from the airport. No bars, clubs, lounges, and not much neon light. No billboards of women in their underwear. Or of women doing anything or advertising anything. A small number of billboards for business stuff—Microsoft, Oracle, ABB, Riyad Bank. I did see a delivery truck for the Al-Arz Automatic Bakery and wondered what it could be; and a shop whose sign declared AL OMRAN HOUSE OF ALUMINUM KITCHENS, which I found equally beguiling.

The next morning, starting immediately as you leave your room for breakfast and continuing, you notice that easily 90% of the people you see—in the hotel, walking down the street, driving cars, working in the office buildings, checking you in at the airport—wear the white dishdasha and the red houndstooth-patterned long triangular scarf with two black circles of cord on top to keep it set on your head. The dishdasha starts out on top as a perfectly traditional long-sleeved white shirt, with a placket front, a pocket, even in some cases cufflinks at the cuffs, then at the waist it turns into a white flowing skirt. The collar is either turtleneck or spread collar. No tie. Some are clearly cotton, some look like a synthetic blend, but they are all startlingly, bleach-me-regularly white. Probably can't get more than a day's worth of wear out of that outfit. I surely have read that this was the case, but you don't really have a good sense of the impact until you see the national garb everywhere on just about everyone.

The other thing you're slower to notice is that there are no women around. None, zero, zip, *nada*, *rien*. I think the whole time I was here I saw maybe three, in serious black abayas. If you didn't know better you'd think it was the kingdom of men (well, it's said to be, actually) and that maybe there was an epidemic and all the women died. It's a touch eerie once you figure it out. The waiters are men, the people who clean the hotel rooms are men, the people who man (correct word) the snack bar counter and newsstand at the airport are men. It's the Man Show.

Sunday we go to a lot of meetings. This passes for work in the executive level of the power biz. The meetings are interesting, if you like electricity. Here are the basics of why we're here and I'm here:

» Of the seven countries in the Arabian Peninsula, the landmass between the Red Sea on the west and the Persian Gulf on the east and formerly unpleasant Iraq on the north, Saudi Arabia is by far the largest, about one-third the size of the United States. Bigger than Texas even. It has the most people, 25 million. It goes without saying that it has the most oil, and the most desert. The other countries run from the northeast corner clockwise around the edge of the peninsula to about the seven o'clock position, in this order: Kuwait on the northeast corner, then Bahrain, Qatar, UAE, Oman, and Yemen bending around the bottom. Saudi Arabia and the first five are all members of the Gulf Cooperation Council, and Yemen is uncooperative. We'll come to Abu Dhabi and Dubai later, please hold your questions.

» Saudi Arabia is growing rapidly: last year's peak electric demand was 10% above the previous year, and the five-year average has been 7%. US comparables are 1%–2%. Water use has been growing even faster. And the Saudis assure us that they have finally, after seven years of to-ing and fro-ing, put in place a program to begin relying on outside power providers, like us. Except in this case we would build and operate a facility that makes both water and electricity. It's a desert, as perhaps you picked up from the earlier references to sand. You can get a long-term contract for the water and the electricity, they pay in dollars, and they need the plants. Equally to the point, the Saudi's, at least, are beginning to be more careful where they spend their money, which they have discovered to their surprise is not unlimited. Better they should use parties like us to finance and build these plants, so that they can use government revenues in places the private sector cannot service. Enough said.

We have a series of conversations with high officials and some midlevel ones, especially the government-owned water and electric utilities. Mostly we are here to sell good intentions and professional capabilities, not specific projects. At our meetings we assure the water utility and the electric utility that we are a serious company, we are quite interested in the region, and we are not retreating to the US, as have those of our competitors who haven't simply gone bankrupt. The chaos in the industry during the last two years, and some fits and starts on our own, have made it important to convey this message.

Some of the conversations are surprising. One official explains his scheme to assure that we get paid for the electricity we're going to sell. It involves creating something that sounds like a funded escrow account we could draw on in the event of nonpayment, although it would still be administered by another unit of the Saudi government. We suggest politely that the letter of credit was invented for just such circumstances, works every bit as well, could be some additional business for the local banks, and would actually be cheaper than a funded reserve account. The good part is the recognition that the Saudi's have a bad reputation for paying on time, and they need to address the problem.

We also spend time with our potential local partner, the Al Zamil Group, a sort of family conglomerate with a number of business and industrial interests in the kingdom. The firm is run by two brothers, one of whom was at one point the chairman of the southern Saudi utility before they were all combined, and the other of whom was recently the energy minister. They both seem professional and serious, and not subject to doing business "the old way." We have already run them through our compliance process and so are comfortable with them, as much as one can be with new partners. And clearly they know their way around a system noted for its opacity. They probably aren't liberal democrats, and they are unlikely to join the Saudi chapter of NOW anytime soon, or invite Israel's current prime minister, Sharon, over for tea. And they do wish the press would be nicer to the Saudi's and that the US would make Israel solve the Palestine problem. In fact, many people made the latter suggestion, while few seemed to care much about Iraq. Maybe in everyone's minds Iraq is already solved.

Another interesting cultural note: the clever observer will have cleverly observed that all of the above took place on Sunday. In Islamic countries, the weekend is Thursday and Friday, with Friday being the holy day. This is not very convenient if you are part of a global enterprise that thinks that the weekend is Saturday and Sunday. A couple of the more forward-looking countries have adjusted things so that they now take the weekend to be Friday and Saturday. This is what we have done in our office and our plants. It's still not a perfect fit, obviously. I feel sort of stupid that I didn't know this before arriving here.

We then flew from Riyadh to Muscat, capital of Oman, but our flight was delayed for some unannounced reason. The Riyadh airport is not a great place to be delayed in—expansive, beautiful, modern, but very, very austere, no place to buy anything except maybe a Coke. Perhaps airports do reflect national culture.

Muscat is Shahzad's favorite city, although arriving at 0130 in the a.m. is not going to endear a city to me no matter what. But in the morning I am less grumpy as I start to look around. The closest analogy I can come up with is the Greek islands. Muscat is on the ocean, in a dramatically rugged setting. The hills are steep and have absolutely no vegetation on them, not a weed or flower or blade of grass or tree or bush or anything. The place is also quite vertical and rocky. Dotted into the valleys between these hills is the city, made up of small houses and buildings, almost all a brilliant white, all with flat roofs, and no development climbing up the sides of the hills. You drive from valley to valley for meetings, and all the valleys run into the sea. It is wonderfully picturesque. The other thing I finally note that convinces me that we are not in Santorini is all the windows are in the Arabian style. The bottoms and sides are square or rectangular, but finished with arches on the top—real arches, plain old triangles, pointed arches, curvy arches, but always arches. It's striking, and gives the setting a certain exotic aspect. I see why Shahzad likes it.

We meet with the appropriate government officials and our local partner, and all are warm and receptive. There is a bid coming up here soon for a second plant in which we are quite interested since we already have one operating, so this is important missionary work. Again, we reassure everyone of our fiscal soundness as a company, and of our commitment to the region. Then we head south to visit our plant at Barka.

How to make drinking water out of salt water, the official secret: boil it and catch the vapor. Well, I wish it were hugely more complicated than that, and I had a heck of a time getting someone to explain it to me before I got here, but that's really it. Both our Middle East plants, and all the ones coming up for bid, are what we now call "IWPPs"—independent water and power plants. They make, yes, both water and power, and as independent operators and owners, we design and build them and sell the output to the local utility, which is usually a government-owned combined water and power entity. This is one dry place, in case I haven't been clear about that before—no lakes or rivers or reservoirs or rainfall of any consequence. All the water they get comes from the ocean. The desal process is called "multistage flash" or MSF, and works something like this: think of a big series of steel boxes, really big, probably ten feet by ten feet on the end, and twenty feet across. The boxes are all connected to each other, broadside to broadside, not like railroad cars. Seawater is brought in and runs back and forth through the top half of the boxes in a series of pipes, several hundred in each box, running long ways through each box. At the output end of the box, a large U-turn pipe takes the water to the next box, and it runs through that box in the other direction. The water makes a series of S's from the ocean side of the system until it finally arrives at the power plant side of the system. There's a point to all this tortuous pathway, just wait.

Once it has made it through all the boxes, the seawater goes into a large cylindrical heat exchanger, where steam from the plant heats the water to about 100°C, which as we all remember from chemistry class is the boiling point of water. The heated ocean water comes out of the heat exchanger, and goes into the bottom of the very same boxes that it flowed through the top of, only this time it's not in pipes, it is just there as if sitting in a giant pan. Given that it's now hot enough, it boils or "flashes." The water vapor rises to the top of the box where it encounters the colder tubes with the cool seawater on its way in. The water vapor condenses on these tubes and then drips back into a pan that is halfway up the box, between the hot salt water on the bottom and the sets of tubes across the top half. Water drips into pan, and runs out into collection system. Hot salt water moves into next box, flowing over the top of a little dam set on the bottom of each box, flowing slightly downhill. A very small amount of sophistication is added to the process by having a pump create a partial vacuum in each box, and this vacuum increases as you move the water in the bottom back toward the sea. This is necessary because as the heated water moves from box to box it loses temperature, but it will continue to flash or boil at a lower temperature if it is under lower pressure. As every cook knows who has tried to hard-boil an egg in the Colorado mountains, water doesn't boil at 212°F when the air pressure is lower. At the low point in the MSF system, you're only down to about 20% of atmospheric pressure, so it's low but this isn't the vacuum of outer space exactly. Eventually the water makes it to the final box, the same one where this trip began. It is collected and unceremoniously dumped back into the ocean. Long description, simple process. As Barry Commoner once remarked about nuclear power, "A hell of a complicated way to boil water."

On the off chance that you are not yet totally bored by all this, here are some additional factoids about making water in the desert:

» Only 12%–14% of the seawater is harvested and becomes drinking water during this process, so you run a lot of water through the system. This ratio is set by efficiencies of capital, steam, etc., but it's still a lot of throughput. But if you took out more water, at some point the remaining stuff would be too gunky with the salt and other stuff that's left behind to continue to process well.

» You have to run some screens and filters in front of the start of the process so you don't get fish and unattractive other stuff (plastic bottles, diapers, cigarette butts, the odd piece of wood) into the system. Guess you could have figured that out. It doesn't have to be a very precise filter as the system is somewhat forgiving.

» The power side is designed to run and produce the right amount of low-pressure steam for the heat exchanger as an integral part of making electricity. It is not designed to use the desal steam to make electricity if the desal system for some reason isn't working. Good thing the systems are relatively simple.

» The plants are designed with little water storage—one or two days— so if there is a problem somewhere downstream and you can't send the water out, you can get backed up pretty quickly. At that point, presuming you still need the electricity, you have to run the desal system and dump the produced water back into the sea. All parties hope that this does not occur frequently. I would add some clever line about rain on the ocean but am suffering from a momentary cleverness gap.

» Before the distilled water is sent out, you have to add minerals back into it. And you have to aerate it somewhat to add dissolved oxygen. The WHO actually has standards for drinking water that include minimum as well as maximum amounts of minerals, including iron, copper, calcium, and magnesium. If you tried to drink non-aerated distilled water, you would find it bitter to the taste. Who knew that? I do now; they made me taste some.

» These systems produce water at a cost of about $5.00/thousand gallons. In the US our retail rates are about one-tenth of that. But if you don't have any other choice, then this is a good deal. Especially if you have a lot of money.

I spend a lot of time walking around the plant, which is very well done and has just gone into service. After about a million questions, I think I finally understand the MSF system, one of the key technical things I wanted to accomplish during the trip here. The plant guys are very patient and helpful, and they are all justifiably proud of their accomplishments. And we have just gotten our first payment from the government for June's power and water, so the system is working. It's good to get paid.

Driving in from the Dubai airport after our early-evening flight from Muscat, I continue to search for city comparisons. Dubai is one of the smaller emirates of the United Arab Emirates. UAE is just up the penin-sula from Oman (see geography lesson above) and is made up of a bunch of emirates, seven actually, who are, uh, united. The one thousand dollar question on *Jeopardy!* is to name all seven. OK, name one or two. Here they are: Abu Dhabi, Dubai, Sharjah, Fujairah, Dopey, Sleepy, and Doc. No, just kidding, I mixed up the emirates with the seven dwarfs. The last three are Ras al-Khaimah, Ajman, and Umm al-Qaiwain. You only hear about the first two because they are the biggest and richest, although Abu Dhabi is bigger and richer than Dubai, and besides it has most of the oil. But Dubai is cosmopolitan and scrappy and has made its way in life by being a trading center, kind of like the Hong Kong of Arabia. Its new commercial district is a single big main street, actually called Sheikh Zayed Road, and many big modern glass and steel buildings are on that street, including two triangular skyscrapers that are called the Emirates Towers and look almost exactly like the Bank of China tower in Hong Kong. Plus there's lots of neon and light and street activity and so forth. And a Hard Rock Cafe and a Planet Hollywood. The place actually looks a bit like Hong Kong, if Hong Kong were in the desert and had only one main street and no vegetation and no Chinese and no harbor. Well, maybe it doesn't look that much like Hong Kong.

On Tuesday morning we have, of course, more meetings. Our regional offices are in Dubai, but the meetings are in Abu Dhabi, which is just down the road about ninety minutes. Once you leave the city, however, there aren't any suburbs, there is just sand and rocks—flat sand and small rocks. You may notice a certain leitmotif to this letter. As we speed down the excellent four-lane divided highway I do, just briefly, see several camels. They don't seem to be doing much, and I cannot spot the associated tents, white-robed Bedouins, oasis, palm trees, genie with a magic lamp, Lawrence of Arabia, etc. I do see lots of Mercedes, but they're on the road, not the sand.

Abu Dhabi has more than one main street, a lot of very modern build-ings, broad roads, and a striking resemblance to Honolulu in the eighties, during the most intense period of Japanese investment, except there aren't any Japanese around. There also are lots of cars and very few places to park.

Just about every fifth building is under construction. This is an economy that appears to be doing well indeed.

The Abu Dhabians (I made that up, I don't think they refer to themselves this way) are seeking a new independent water and power project. This will be their fifth one, and we were all set to bid on the fourth one, then had to pull out at the last minute, due to our temporary loss of cabin pressure. Unfortunately, they remember. As before, my job here is to reassure them that we are serious this time and that we do have the money and the interest, and that they can count on us to bid and be competitive. We meet the head of privatization of the AD utility, who is about thirty-two and, like every government official with whom we have met, is wearing a traditional white robe and headdress. He also has very modern chrome and steel furniture in his beautiful office in his glass and aluminum office building. I refrain from saying "land of contrasts" for the one thousandth time. We reassure him that AES is back in business, and that as a board member I can represent that this is an important market for us, and one on which we are concentrating resources and attention. We later find that this visit has in fact been useful, and that the report of our meeting is already circulating widely. The perceived power of a board member never fails to amaze and occasionally amuse me.

We meet subsequently with our local sponsor from the Abu Dhabi Investment Authority to thank him for his help and assure him as well of our continued interest, and then visit the US Embassy commercial section people, same mission plus asking for their support. Last time around they were more guarded since there were two American companies in the bidding, but now we are the only US guys left standing, so they can be behind us wholeheartedly. It can't hurt. This is a small community, and having the ambassador refer to us positively to the government officials will be a plus.

We drive back to Dubai but the camels are gone. I spend some time at the office with all the AES people there, giving my speech on development, then we celebrate Shahzad's forty-ninth birthday with cake, pasta, and samosas. We are an international bunch indeed.

Venu, Shahzad's head development guy, and I fly from Dubai to Qatar (another thirty-minute flight) later in the evening. Qatar is even more curious geopolitically. It is a peninsula about the size of Connecticut, has 600,000 people (of whom 500,000 live in Doha, the capital, where we are) and sits on 900 million Tcf (trillion cubic feet, the standard "unit" of measure—meant for gas reserves) of gas. This is a humongous amount of gas, especially divided among 600K people, of whom only 200K are native Qatari's, and so the rest really don't count. For comparison, the US annually uses about 18 Tcf, and we use more gas than any other country in the world. There is lots of construction going on here as well, probably one building out of four. The city looks sort of like the French Riviera, only much less dense and no mountains in the background. Perhaps my judgment is clouded by the fact that the seaside boulevard running along the gently curving harbor is called "Al Corniche."

Wednesday morning we go to meet with the Qatar General Electricity and Water Corporation, the government-owned utility referred to as Kahramaa. We already have a big project here, called Ras Laffan. Mr. Janahi, the head planning person for the government utility, informs us that they have decided to start the process for the next project, news we did not expect, and that they intend to limit it to two bidders, us and the local IPP company, Qatar Electricity and Water Company, really news we did not expect. It is interesting to note that QEWC is also a partner in our first project. And the general manager of QEWC sits on the board of the government utility. We visit this gentleman next, thank him for being a good partner, and generally exchange information about AES and the Qatar system. He explains to us that Qatar is not Saudi Arabia. Actually many of the people we have visited are interested in explaining to us that wherever we are is not Saudi Arabia, except, reasonably enough, the ones in Saudi Arabia. Our final visit is with the CEO of Qatar National Bank. They are a big participant in the Ras Laffan financing, and he sits on the board of the QEWC. This is really a small country.

We leave to drive out to our Ras Laffan plant, about one and a half hours north of the capital, located on the tip of the peninsula, which is also where all the gas infrastructure is, since the gas is all out under the ocean. I review the basics: Qatar already has 2,400 Mw of power, and the need for another 700 Mw could be questioned. Rule of thumb: in the US and other developed countries, 1 million people require 3,000 Mw, so in some senses Qatar is already oversupplied. Except that they used the full 2,400 this summer and electric demand is growing at 9% per year. And they can certainly pay for it. I put off worrying and concentrate on the drive along a very nice highway, bordered by (you will have a hard time believing this) absolutely flat terrain of rocks and sand. Ahmer, the plant manager who is graciously heading this expedition, says that this is a dangerous highway. I ask if this could be because you run into camels, although I don't see any. He says it's actually because the highway is so straight and flat—and it is—with nothing to see—and there isn't—and so people fall asleep. He points out that many of the short poles protecting the median are squashed down flat, having been run over by sleeping drivers. And the road is only a little more than a year old.

Our plant is very large, and it sits in the middle of what is called "Ras Laffan Industrial City," which is an accurate descriptive statement. Lots of LNG facilities, gas processing, desalination, etc. Very industrial in a chemical plant/petroleum refinery sort of way. Our facility is sized at 750 Mw and 40 MIGD (million imperial gallons per day). Note for compatibility fans, an imperial gallon is 1.2 US gallons, and has nothing to do with the metric system, which doesn't have gallons of any sort, only liters. There is undoubtedly some peculiar history here, probably something to do with Henry VIII, but we don't know what. The imperial gallon does seem to be the unit of convention in desal land. This is a very big plant, bigger than Barka in Oman, bigger than a breadbox. Lots of the folks managing it are Pakistani, some UK, some US, a Sudani, a guy from Kazakhstan, several Indians, and about eleven Qataris. The government's mandated goal is to have 50% Qatari employment in all industrial enterprises in five years. Given the extreme youth of the population, that will be a very tough goal to meet unless we can hire ten-year-olds. ENEL, the Italian utility, is constructing this plant, and is doing a mixed job. They did get the first units online in time for the summer peak, as required, but there is still a lot of work to do and a number of mistakes to be corrected. But the AES folks seem to have it under at least reasonable control. I have a good time tramping all over the plant, which is still in construction with only part in service. Later I meet with everyone available and discuss with them our development strategy, the latest gossip from Arlington, etc. It's a very attentive and well-qualified group, and they ask good questions.

Ahmer and I drive back to Doha, avoiding falling asleep on the long, straight, and now very dark road, and have dinner at the Marriott with his team leaders. They are a capable and enthusiastic bunch, not awed by talking to a director, and they, too, have good questions and suggestions so it's fun to meet with them.

Ahmer drops me off at the airport about 9:30 in the evening, and I prepare for the long flight home, in coach. I have been in five countries in four days and am thus now a Middle East expert. I have even figured out desalination. My only real remaining question is, where are all the camels?

Love and kisses,
Bob

Afterword: Get in early, get out early. We were able to ride the wave of the "privatization" of power plants in the Middle East and had two marvelous early successes with our plants in Oman and Qatar. But there are smart people everywhere in the world, and the governments of all these countries quickly figured out how to construct bidding procedures that got the Japanese and the Europeans and the Americans to all compete against one another. This ended up favoring those who were construction companies first and power plant operators only as a sideline. AES was not that, and was not successful in any further development efforts in any of these countries, including Saudi Arabia.

We came to our senses and sold our two Middle Eastern plants at a very good price and shut down all development efforts in the area about four years ago. Given the rise of ISIS and the disintegration of Syria and the chaos in Yemen, we look like at least minor geniuses.

chapter seven

We Get to Know a Real Russian Oligarch, and He Doesn't Shoot Us

June 2004

Dear Dad,

My expertise increases by leaps and bounds. Am now an expert on Russia, having visited Moscow for two and a half days. And read a twelve-page report on Russia in the latest issue of the *Economist*. The latter was more difficult than the former. *Da, nyet,* and *placebo,* which means "thank you."

Why go visit our former enemy who has turned into colleague in the war on terrorism, as long as terrorism is defined as Chechens and other folks trying to blow up the Moscow subway, theater, and the odd apartment block? (I've seen those apartment buildings, a well-placed explosion or two could help their aesthetics, he said, completely forgoing political correctness.) Because they're growing like crazy, helped by $40.00 oil, which they sell to everyone, and $6.00 gas, which they sell to Europe. And they have decided, against all odds and possibly against common sense, to take their 197,000 Mw integrated electric utility that serves the whole blooming country and bust it into smithereens, hopefully smithereens that are well designed and will still work. This is the largest "utility" in the world, so there should be many smithereens. We are a potential smithereen purchaser.

It has taken the US twenty-five years to liberalize/reform its electric system, and one could argue that we haven't quite gotten it right yet. The Russians plan to do it all in two or three years. The most interesting thing is that they acknowledge that they haven't written all the rules or designed all the systems and institutions that will be necessary for the new creation to work, but they're going ahead anyway. One of the folks we met with characterized it as driving the train as fast as possible down the track, in the dark with no headlamp, with some folks madly laying the track ahead as fast as they could, hoping the train didn't outrun the track and that they all ended up wherever it was they wanted to go. Another said charitably that this was "just in time" policy making, and there wasn't any sense in trying to solve all the problems in advance, as you'd just make a lot of mistakes you'd have to fix later. This is a bit circular; sometimes it really is useful to have a plan, even if it changes as it's implemented. We have lost sight of our objectives but have redoubled our efforts.

One important reason for going was to see if it was just me who was skeptical. If we are to make a significant commitment to this market, then I don't mind not knowing things that are not knowable and that no one else knows either (what will the price of power be once a free wholesale market is established?), but I don't want to not know what other folks *do* know. It's a conservative stance, admittedly, and up to recently the difference between the "don't knows" and the "can't knows" hasn't been clear to me. I feel better now.

Here is what the utility system is planned to be at this point in Russia:
»   A "federal system" in which are gathered all the nuclear plants (22,000 Mw, not as much as I would have thought given all the bad press on Chernobyl, which turns out actually to be in Ukraine), and all the hydro (45,000 Mw, again a small number for a country so darn large and with so many rivers), and a big portion of the thermal plants (36,000 Mw), and all the transmission and a very large number of the bureaucrats. As

you probably remember from previous letters, in order to confuse you, we members of the power brotherhood say "thermal" when we really mean oil/gas/coal. Nuclear plants also work on "thermal" principles. As in, they use heat to make steam, etc.

» A bunch of regional utilities, seventy-three to be exact, neatly covering the whole country in an orderly patchwork, each with some modest portion of the remaining 94,000 Mw of thermal plants. The regionals also own 27,000 Mw of hydro, which somehow escaped from the federal system. The thermal plants are generally combined heat and power (CHP), sited at or near major cities, and supplying hot water to the cities for district heating, as well as electricity. This is very widespread in Russia, more than anywhere else I have seen in the world. Of course, it may be colder in Russia than anywhere else in the world. This is also where the retail distribution takes place and where the bills are sent out and collected. These guys buy the power the federal system generates.

» An organization called RAO UES (Russian Unified Electrical System) owns all the federal assets except the nukes, which are in a different company, and is a publicly traded company, EXCEPT that the state owns 52% of the shares. I cannot think of any US analogue. It was set up this way in 1992 as a three-year temporary structure on the way from Ministry of Power status to full privatization. Well, these things take time.

» The regional systems are all also "private," but RAO generally owns 50% of each, although there are a couple of curious exceptions that we will ignore as we cannot spell them.

» Power is sold at a regulated rate set by the government, with a fair amount of regional variation depending on something that no one can explain clearly. The RAO plants sell to the regional utilities, who also run their own plants, and sell both sources of power to the ultimate customers. What everyone agrees with is that the price signals are wrong in two ways. First, they are overall too low—the system barely recovers its operating costs, and almost no return on capital. So you can run what you got, but you can't pay for new plants to replace the aging equipment, nor can you even pay for much capital to upgrade or expand the existing system. This hasn't mattered until recently for an interesting reason: in 1990, the peak year, the system generated and consumed about 1,100 gigawatt hours (roughly one-fourth of US consumption). Then the economy cratered, and as late as last year consumption was about 880 GWh. Hence there has been little need to add new generating or transmission capacity. You already had it all there fifteen years ago and, unlike computers, the technology doesn't change much and the product, kWh, is still exactly the same. The equipment has gotten a bunch older, however. Unlike you or I. And none of the old stuff has been replaced.

General practice in the utility biz is to charge customers roughly what it costs to serve them, and industrial customers are far cheaper to serve than residential customers, mostly due to higher capital needed per residential customer, and much less volume using the same capital. Everywhere in the world, residential customers pay two to four times per kWh what industrial customers pay. In Russia, this appears to be reversed—residential customers pay about $0.02 per kWh, industrials up to $0.04. Bad economics, although maybe good Bolshevik policy.

OK, that's the system. But what you're probably asking is: What about the shoes? I don't care about a bunch of electricity dudes, what do their shoes look like? The hot fashion in Moscow is for the shoes to end in long points. I noticed this first on the women's shoes. Please believe that this is not just your normal pointed toes that you see on a standard pair of Bruno Maglis or Ferragamos, these are shoe extensions, a couple of inches long. Very peculiar. And it's not just a mistake, because when you walk down the street and tire of looking at everyone's feet, and look instead in the shop windows of the shoe stores, there are the same shoes. Well, not the same shoes that were just on the feet of the people walking down the street whose feet you were scrutinizing, but the same style of shoe with the same pointed extension. And on men's shoes too, except sort of flattened and chopped off. This is not a good style, unless you are auditioning to star in the remake of *Elf*.

We return to our fascinating electricity story. The reform plan, in summary terms, is:

» Bust up RAO itself, organizing it into separate generating, transmission, and system operations companies.

» Suborganize the generation into six thermal generation companies and four hydro companies and one nuke company, and sell off the six generation companies.

» Keep the transmission, system ops, and hydro and nuke companies as entirely or majority state owned, but have the thermal generation now be entirely private.

» Let the regional utilities bid for power from the new generating companies, with no more locked-in buyer/seller relationships, and the market setting the price.

» Bust up and reorganize all seventy-three regional utilities, creating private generating companies and government-owned transmission and distribution companies.

Whew. And do it all in two and a half years, starting at the beginning of next year. Double whew.

You gotta love central planners, they're nothing if not ambitious.

I won't even try to tell you how many questions this raises, just suggest one confusing example: Let's say you and a bunch of your vodka-drinking buddies have carefully accumulated 50% of the shares of a regional utility company called Kraptogorskenergo. They're all called "something-energos," which makes it a tiny bit easier. Right now you, in some senses as a shareholder, "own" your slice of the generation, the transmission, and the distribution that serves the Kraptogorsk area and makes up the company. But soon (timing not yet set precisely) a government-mandated swap will take place and you will trade your slice of the transmission and distribution for the proportionate piece of the generation owned by RAO and the state. Remember that RAO owns 50% of the shares, but the state owns 52% of RAO, so in essence the state owns 26% of K'gorskenergo. Fine. But what if poor old Kraptogorsk only has one moth-eaten power plant but lots of very nice transmission and distribution? What if the power plant is worth only 33% of the asset value of the energo, and the T&D is worth 67%? The RAO/state combo will still get it all, and give up its 50% of the generation to you and the other owners. But then RAO/state owns 67% of the assets (by value) and you and your buddies own 33% when you used to own 50%. Not so good a deal. What happens? Do you get compensated in some way? By whom and with what money? And who determines what that asset value was in the first place, since if there is to be a system to remedy the two-thirds/one-third disparity above, it's critically dependent on who decides the value of the assets in the first place. Maybe the generation really wasn't 33% of the value, maybe it was 60%—if so, the private guys get a great deal, as RAO/state trades 50% of the overall ownership for only 40% of the assets. Children, do we really think that Mr. Putin will be happy in this situation? Anyone know what "fat chance" means? And what about the fact that RAO owns any of this—where does that leave RAO shareholders? My head hurts from just writing it down, let alone thinking about it.

And when my head hurts, I find relief by trying to see Red Square. Not that it has much to do with electricity, but we tried. We (Paul, the CEO and I) did drive back and forth past the Kremlin what seemed like constantly. And it's yellow. I had a vision of a dim, gray, forbidding building, but instead it's very colorful, sits next to a bunch of churches that are also very brightly painted and do in fact have the round-domed tops, as advertised. It's a nice location, on a small hill next to the Moscow River, surrounded by a couple of two-story brick walls, painted a nice brick red. But the Kremlin rises several more stories above the wall, which explains how you can tell it's yellow. Very attractive, but when we walked up from our hotel to actually get in to Red Square, we found that it was closed off at ten o'clock on Friday night, because Saturday was Russian independence day. We inquired about this, as I always thought that May 1 was the big day, but now find that it's not. It was patiently explained that June 12 is the day Yeltsin was elected president and the Soviet Union officially broke up, so Paul and I decide it's "independence from ourselves" day. We also noted that Red Square is nice, but it isn't nearly as big as Tiananmen. We politely didn't say that either. We didn't get to go in because the soldiers suggested that we not disregard the fences. Paul asked if anyone knew how to say "maybe next time" in Chechen, but fortunately this was beyond us. We thus did not see Lenin's tomb, but during one of our drives to a meeting we did see the big statue of Lenin in Lenin Square, Lenin looking all determined and metallic and much larger than life, leading workers boldly forward in best socialist realist style, except now he appears to be leading them forward toward a three-story poster graphically advertising and displaying women's thong underwear. Economy in transition, all right.

But say, what about this really interesting question of electricity sector reform? No one we have met can explain clearly how the above transactions (not Lenin and the girl in the underwear, more above than that) will take place, except they are clear that they will. Or take the interesting issue, also noted above the underwear, of the cross-subsidies between industrial users and residential customers. The plan is clear: "Cross subsidies will be gradually eliminated." How? How gradually? And by the way, who defines just exactly what it "costs" to serve someone? There is a whole industry of consultants in the US that focuses on this, as it is a recurring and contentious issue in utility rate design. Probably they have all opened offices in Moscow long since.

Enough already. You get the point. And you're much more concerned about the state of the average Russian soldier, anyway. According to the Wednesday *Moscow Times*, twenty-nine soldiers were taken to the hospital because of contact with a hazardous chemical that they discovered in a dump. The "contact" came because several soldiers ingested it, others put it into their tobacco and smoked it, and a couple put it into their boots as foot powder. That's all the detail there was in the article. One does wonder why they were doing soldierly things in a dump, what they thought this stuff really was, and what sort of packaging would lead some to consider it a food item, others tobacco, and a few to think it a new version of Desenex. I conclude that the state of the Russian military is still low.

As you can tell, there will be much change and dislocation in the electricity industry, if not in the military, and therefore probably much opportunity to make or lose significant money. But lots and lots of power plants are going to be sold, so we are interested. It's what we do.

Interestingly, so are many of the local Russian "economic groups," popularly called "oligarchs." This has not been a good thing to be called ever since Oligarch #1, Mikhael Khodorkovsky, got thrown in the slammer for (take your pick): (1) threatening to run for prez vs. Putin; (2) declaring that he was more popular than Putin (although not more popular than the Beatles or Jesus); (3) offering to sell a big piece of his oil company, Yukos, to the Americans; (4) funding newspapers that said Putin had stinky feet thus partially explaining mysterious foot powder incident of the twenty-nine soldiers; (5) failing to pay his taxes (the official explanation).

But they are still around, and many of them have many rubles. Many of them also have significant power-consuming businesses—aluminum, nickel, manganese, steel—or sell to the power industry, principally gas and coal. These guys have all indicated over the last year an interest in buying some of these plants that will be for sale in order to protect their other businesses. This may seem superficially sensible, but are not if one thinks at a more careful and analytical level. Electricity is a networked good, we note, and actually buying a power plant, in a modern electric system, doesn't guarantee you much of anything except that you own a power plant and can take your chances on selling into the system like anyone else. Buying electricity is not connected to making electricity. Another oddity—most of the ones we talked to are convinced that the price will go up, and they have all made lots of money by purchasing stuff on the cheap, running it better than it was run under the Bolshevik system (this is not hard: reduce staffing by 75%, cut all other costs by 50%, increase quality by 2,000%, provide customer service one day a week) and then watching their boats rise along with all the others. The arguments we heard, over and over, are:

» the plants will sell for $100–$150 per kW, and it costs $1,000 to $1,500 per kW to build new ones;

» many of the plants are old so they must be retired;

» prices are too low so they will go up.

We began to refer to this latter as the "prices will go up because we think they will go up" argument. But remember, this is a system with a lot of overcapacity. And one that is converting overnight into a bare-knuckled, hourly bid-and-ask, lowest price clears the market sort of beast. In these

situations, the economically rational player bids his or her fuel plus operating cost, with no return on capital, because you need to stay alive and
wait for the shortage times when you can make a bucket of money. Hence
for an undeterminable period of years, there may be no return on capital
and $100/kW will have been too high a price to pay. It is useful to note
that the "must be retired" argument also doesn't work, since power is not
an industry with a high rate of technological change, and forty- or fifty-
year-old plants can still work just fine. Even though their "design life" is
less than that. And nobody who buys one of these plants is spending the
money just so he can retire it.

The good news is that if you ever tire of talking about electricity, you
can get a decent meal in the town. We ate at a restaurant called Market
one evening, with Asian fusion cuisine and fish and vegetables you pick out
yourself from a display counter, South Sea island decorations, and balalaika
music playing. Fortunately there were no native touristic dancers. And
their idea of Asian fusion is to cook your selection, then give you a bowl of
sauce to dip it in. But the fish was fresh. We also ate at a very good French
restaurant called White Square, where the plates were, um, white squares
except with wavy edges and raised circles in the middle so they looked
like they were upside down sitting there in front of you. We ate lunch at a
restaurant named Pushkin, decorated to resemble a house the famous poet
might have lived in when he was alive, if he had been fabulously wealthy,
which he was not. The principal decoration was a bunch of tall bookshelves
with old books in them, generally not by him. But good food.

Our favorite oligarch is a guy named Vladimir Potanin. I am relieved
in our meetings to find that Russians actually do have names like Vladimir
and Sergei and Andrei and even Igor. It is also interesting to note that Mr.
Potanin runs a group called Interros, which has as one of its components
Norilsk Nickel, Russia's biggest nickel producer. This smelting and such
takes electricity, hence the interest. It is also interesting to note that he
sought us out, first meeting with us in Arlington. It was sort of a "I have
chosen you to be my foreign partner so I am coming over to meet you"
kind of thing. We were all atwitter with excitement, since one so infre-
quently meets a real-life oligarch. And the best part is he really looked a

bit frightening—short, thinning, blond hair in a crew cut; Slavic features; thick fingers; a scar along his hairline. One would not want to meet him in a dark alley. He is, however, quite nice and came unaccompanied by bodyguards carrying AK-47s, so we have gotten more comfortable. In fact, during the whole time in Moscow I saw not one bodyguard armed with an AK-47. A little disappointing.

Just for fun and because we spent a lot of time sitting in traffic, I tried to read the words on the signs, but the Russians have not yet changed back their alphabet. They changed it during the Cold War, adding secret letters to confuse visiting Americans who were all, they thought, spies intent on their destruction, when in fact only half were. It's quite tricky, and very inconvenient. For example, the denizens of the Kremlin changed R to P and N became H. You see a sign saying PECTOPAH on about every third commercial establishment, and only when someone tells you the code do you realize that this actually is RESTORAN, and you can get food there. To make things even more secret, they threw in the odd Greek letter, even though few of them had been in fraternities. Thus you see a sign on every third place that isn't a pectopah, saying KA[Greek letter for phi)E." Well, that's really KAFE and you can get coffee there. The language isn't so hard except for the obvious deception involved. Just use a few Greek letters—pi means P, you had to have something to replace P since it got used for R— and turn around a few others, like the backwards R and the backwards N, and there you go.

One final note: don't bring a car. Probably you wouldn't anyway since you'd be flying in from Seattle, but the traffic is really truly awful. Many boast that the traffic of *their* city is bad, but in Moscow it really does suck. We spent about half of each working day sitting in traffic on the way from meeting two to meeting three. Perversely this is because: (1) the economy is actually working and thus everyone has been able to afford a car, and (2) the Germans didn't get to Moscow during the war. The city is reasonably attractive, especially compared to some of the former Eastern bloc capitals, because it has many nineteenth- and early twentieth-century buildings still standing, almost all of them cleaned up and painted, and it does not have many skyscrapers, and it has broad avenues, albeit car clogged, so the scale is attractive. But given when all the buildings were built, none of them have parking, and certainly not the Stalin-era ones, so the cars all park on the streets, alleys, boulevards, and it's a jammed-up mess. And the laws have been changed so that you can no longer tow illegally parked vehicles. This human rights stuff may have gone a bit too far.

Economy in transition, final final note: The morning we leave I am up early for no useful reason and walk around near the hotel. I notice two busloads of slightly bored-looking young women, all dressed in identical white outfits that, except for the red scarves around their necks, would make you think they were Muslim nurses in training, and deduce that they are headed for the Red Square parade, and further decide that it ain't starting very early. I go to the local kafe place to see if you can get coffee to go, an important test of economic development. Answer, no. Later at the hotel, Paul and I try this same test in the lobby coffee shop, and the answer is yes. For $5.00 per cup, and it isn't particularly good coffee. Someone call Starbucks, there's work to be done.

Love and kisses,
Bob

Afterword: A famous but now long-dead senator was asked late in his career by a reporter what his most significant accomplishment had been. The senator thought carefully, then said, "I stopped a lot of stupid shit from getting passed into law."

I spent about two years going back and forth to Moscow, cheering on the efforts of our development team there, meeting with battalions of mid to upper-mid level bureaucrats and peculiar (that's charitable) business people and lots of "helpers," none of whom we hired. The opportunity seemed so enormous, so attractive, and so similar to what we had done in other countries. The power system was a mess, no maintenance for the last ten years, decrepit grid connections, an economy beginning to grow, a commitment to privatization, a reform plan that could probably be made to work, etc. It looked great on paper and in the speeches. And the food was even pretty good, although the weather was wretched.

Besides that, the key to successful development is optimism and perseverance.

But this wasn't my first rodeo. After the third time we came to and blew past the "deadline" for the privatizations to begin, and the starting date was rescheduled to yet another six months in the future, I began to suspect that this was an expensive waste of time. So after many internal discussions, we crossed Russia off the list, shut down the office, fired the locals, and brought the one or two expats home.

As of the middle of 2015, the Russian power system has not yet been privatized or reformed, and the role of the domestic but anemic private sector in electricity remains close to zero.

Peru Is Discovered by Yale, but without Hiram Bingham to Assist

August 2004

Dear Dad,

I had always wanted to go to Peru and see what it was like to be an Inca, so when this brochure from the Yale Alumni Association comes across my desk advertising an economical trip to said location in the last two weeks of August, when—as we all know—nothing much happens in the business world as everyone in Europe is at the beach in the Mediterranean, and all of Russia is at Odessa or in their dachas in the countryside, and all of China (or at least the three thousand people who actually run China) are at Bei Da He, the exclusive Party-only coastal resort city, and all of the US is at Disneyworld or on a Carnival cruise eating six meals a day, I thought, "Let's go!" No, not really, I thought, "How in the world can I convince my darling wife to take a group trip with thirty folks whom she has never met, to a country that is not Nordic Germanic, sponsored by a university she did not attend, and for a period of time that makes her nervous, which is longer than a long weekend basically, to see ruins in which she is not too interested in the first place?" But somehow, I caught her in an off moment in mid-January, probably in the middle of a snowstorm, and she agreed, but only with the proviso that I didn't try to sneak any power plants into the trip. Which was hard for me, but I agreed.

So here we are in Lima. I asked about the beans several times and how come they pronounce the name wrong—everybody knows it's a long *I*, but all I get are the *"no comprendo, gringo loco"* looks, so I have desisted. It's hard to find them in the US anymore, anyway; I think you fed us kids the whole country's supply while we were growing up. And I'm no longer sure they even came from Peru.

So far we have met all our fellow tour mates who are in fact almost all from Yale, having graduated in various parts of the second half of the twentieth century. Also several widows of Yale persons who graduated in the same time period. One single guy, at least I think single, same approximate age, and one Harvard guy from Europe who seems to have wandered in by mistake, dragging along his late teenage son but leaving his wife at home. She's at the beach at Cannes, no doubt. These Euros are so modern. Linda has agreed to wear her name tag, which is good, but declined to carry her small tote with the Yale University logo prominently displayed. Seems fair for a Princeton graduate.

Day One—Lima (the city not the bean)

Our first day has started with breakfast, which is useful, and then segued into our first lecture by the Yale professor traveling with us, an academic but otherwise normal person named Richard Burger, an archaeologist who headed the Anthropology Department at Yale (where archaeology was kept), then ran the Peabody Museum, and is now back to just being a professor. Rather than talk about all the ruins to come, he gave his own views of the country, making the point that it's different than perceived in the US popular press. This may not surprise you, and is an observation that could be accurately applied to any country in the world.

He mentioned that, for example, US history books make no reference to the War of the Pacific. I thought idly to myself that it was in fact pretty well covered, including the heroics of a certain Major Robert F. Hemphill flying P-47s in the Marshall Islands. Turns out he meant the one fought between Peru plus Bolivia vs. Chile plus Ecuador, in the late1870s. If I were choosing teams for a baseball game, I can't say as to which two of these four countries I would favor, nor can I explain how the Peruvians had the bad fortune to choose the Bolivians, or what exactly the Chileans have in common with the Ecuadorians, but never mind. The Chile/Ecuador combo kicked bootie, the Bolivians lost their access to the sea, thus becoming the only landlocked country in all of South America except for Paraguay, who no one much cares about anyway, and Peru lost all of the Atacama Desert, which may not have seemed like much at the time but turns out to have especially valuable deposits of copper and nitrates that the Chileans have been digging up and selling profitably to the Chinese for a good long while now. And the best news—Nobody Has Forgotten! Especially not the Peruvians. It's not all sweetness and Andean brother-hood down here. In fact, the Peruvians fought a nice little war vs. Ecuador just twenty years ago. They also refer to the Ecuadorians as *monos*, which means monkeys, allegedly because during the war the Ecuadorians ran out of munitions and began using their air force to throw coconuts down on the Peruvians. As an old air warfare tactician, I suspect you will realize that this is unlikely, for many reasons, including the fact that open cockpits no longer predominate in warplanes. And we thought just us US folks were guilty of stereotyping.

So why is this important, except as not so interesting background for something not clear in the trip itinerary? And why isn't it actually called the War of the Pathetic, which is sort of what it sounds like? We're coming to that.

Obligatory First Day in Country Bus Tour: large bus, enthusiastic Peruvian tour guide named Kika takes us through the variously named "suburbs" of Lima, a town of a discreet 8 million souls. These suburbs actu-ally appear to be political jurisdictions since each one has a mayor, and as Kika tells us, some have nice names like Miraflores ("see the flowers" or maybe "wonderful flowers," can't find my dictionary) and La Isleta ("small island") but my two favorites are the Jesus and Mary suburb, and Pollo Libre ("free chicken"). And somewhere in Free Chicken is the first major military statue, this one of General Francisco Bolognesi, "hero of the War of the Pacific" and "father of the Peruvian Army," although given the war's outcome one wonders if he wouldn't prefer to be remembered for inventing the pasta sauce that bears his name. But even better, in the Jesus and Mary suburb, right on Christopher Columbus Blvd, is a truly huge statue of bronze and marble, with ocean waves, sailors, cannons and whatnot dedicated to Admiral Miguel Grau, also a Hero of the War of the Pacific. We don't know what battle he lost. It stands directly across the street from the Center for Military Historical Studies. Which is a very small building.

We had dinner at a restaurant right next to the Huaca Pucllana, a pretty large pre-Colombian three-level pyramid that is being reconstructed by the city of Lima, after a mayor in the sixties bulldozed a road through the middle of it. It is made entirely of adobe bricks and given that the site is 5.7 hectares (2.4 acres per hectare) in dimension, there are quite a lot of bricks. The terrace of the restaurant looks out on the reconstruction work, and after dinner we walked along the edge of the lighted area. One of our group remarked, "It looks like it's made of bricks." Hmm.

Day Two—Outside Lima

Our fears about group tours, i.e., it's like a combination of prison, basic training, and being in a bad sorority, begin to be realized. Wake-up call is at 0645. As Linda sees it, "If I wanted to be hauled out of bed, exhausted, in the predawn darkness, I could do that without flying several thousand miles to 'vacation.'" She has a point. We have to be on the bus at 0800, and then after touring around, we are to go direct from bus to airplane to Chiclayo in the late afternoon, without coming back to the hotel. To make matters more confusing, we will only be in Chiclayo one night, then return to Lima, so we are to pack only a small overnight bag and leave the rest of the luggage checked at the hotel, to which we will return the next day. But naturally we have not unpacked everything and we have not packed in layers envisioning this eventuality. Also Linda has employed her usual mission-to-Mars approach to travel, which I of course applaud so long as I do not have to carry the suitcases, and brought a number of what some puritans might call "extraneous" items along—a large box of Cheerios, ten tuna kits, two boxes of chocolate covered almonds, one box of chocolate mints, eight cans of salted almonds (two smoked), two Starbucks travel thermoses, two bunches of radishes, three bunches of celery, and four cucumbers. Actually I'm kidding about the cucumbers, we did buy them but there wasn't room. I wonder why no cheese doodles, but maybe they don't travel well. Good thing we're not trying to enter the US, we would surely be accused of novel means of smuggling cocaine into the country, probably secreted inside each radish or cheerio. And we're too tired to stay up after dinner and unpack/repack, so we have to get up at 0600 to make it all work. Which we do in varying hues of humor. I discover that I have brilliantly come to Peru in midwinter with no warm jacket, so I begin cajoling and negotiating to borrow Polartec and a windbreaker from Linda. Turns out her mission-to-Mars approach to packing has some merit, since she packed two of each of these.

Off to our first site, Mina Perdida, located south of Lima in the Lurin Valley, and excavated by our Yale professor and his wife, Lucy, who is conveniently also an archeologist. It rises above the valley only seventy-five feet and does resemble somewhat a big pile of dirt. It is a pre-Inca site dating from about 1000 BC, and has the odd set of stone walls running in short bursts through it. Some looting has already long since occurred but this wasn't a big deal site; only about one thousand families lived in the area and were probably too busy farming to make a lot of cute pots with images of sharks, guys in funny headdresses, jaguars, snakes, etc., on them. It has also suffered the curse of the bulldozer as a road has been run through a big part of it, and at least one wing has been leveled and a monastery built on it. But probably not consciously to prove religious dominance, but more because the site is near the canal and river. And it was one of ten equivalent sites in just this small river valley about six miles from the coast. This is a many-sited country.

Then we go to Pachacamac, which is much grander. It sits on about four square miles about half a mile from the ocean, and at its highest point is easily 1200 feet above the base terrain. The archaeological record indicates that this was a ceremonial center much like Delphi in Greece, with a

long-running set of priests who dispensed advice and accumulated treasure
in return from locations all around Peru. It was sufficiently important that
Atahualpa, the last Inca emperor, thought it necessary to come here in
person as he sought to unify the empire and ask the blessing of the priests/
oracles. Apparently they said OK, fine with us, and in return he built a big
temple/pyramid on the site, right next to the one in which he had made
his visit to the priests—only his was bigger and about a hundred feet taller.
And blocked their view of the ocean. Had Atahualpa been born later and
in New York he might have given Donald Trump a run for his money.

Very early in their conquest of Peru, the ever-lovable Spaniards, while
holding Atahualpa prisoner, asked, as they were wont to do with every other
sentence, where they could find some gold. He suggested Pachacamac,
which was a long way from where he then was. Off went some Spaniards,
but word got there first and the priests are said to have hid all the gold,
which then no one has ever subsequently found. I myself believe that it is
in the Lost Dutchman Mine in Arizona.

On the way out of the site, which is massive and sandy (yes, it's those
adobe bricks again; no one discovered lime plaster, which is fortunate
because they didn't have the trees to burn to make it in the first place),
we stop at the small museum. I learn that "Pachacamac" was not only the
name of the place but the name of the god, and that translated it means
the "god who animates the universe," also known in academic circles as the
Walt Disney God.

We have lunch at a nice horse farm where the owner raises horses
with a fancy gait (the horses not the owner), shows them off for gringos,
and feeds them a nice lunch (the gringos not the horses). It is named the
Hacienda Santa Rosa, which a lot of nice places are, as well as an excellent Chilean wine, but I am not sure who Saint Rose was. You never let
me read *Lives of the Saints* when I was growing up is probably why. Then
again, we were Protestants of a sort. It was a very pleasant location with a
large, grassy corral, beautiful gardens, and there was also a round of Native
Touristic Dances but in this case the horse dances, too. Once this silliness
was completed, they let me ride one of the dancing horses, carefully, but it
refused to tell me where the gold was buried.

Off we go to the Lima airport and fly to Chiclayo on the northern coast. Basically the entire coastal area of Peru is a desert and is generally anywhere from ten to sixty miles deep, except for where the approximately fifty rivers run down from the very high mountains and form little valleys and small plains where people can actually live. But these rivers are also very seasonal, relying as they do exclusively on snowmelt. The coastal areas do not get much rainfall, so water management is a big deal. Hence there was lots of emphasis on canalizing and controlling the rivers early on. Hence the need for lots of labor in the public interest, civic or political organization, etc. Many of the earliest Peruvian cultures grew up along these coastal valleys, starting with the Chavin, then the Moche. The highlands cultures didn't become much of a factor until about AD 800.

Day Three—Chiclayo

We arise at a semireasonable hour and pile on the buses for a visit to our first museum, a new one which houses the impressive Moche material found at a pyramid/ceremonial site called Sican, and excavated from two grave sites thereat by a clever Japanese archeologist named Izumi Shimada. He discovered the grave sites by using ground-penetrating radar (cesium magnetometer, no further details available) that peers into the ground for a depth of up to ten feet and is good at picking up anomalies—original dirt vs. fill vs. empty space. The Sican site had already been pretty worked over but he found an intact royal burial, and then he found the burial of what appears to be a priest, both unlooted. The museum does a very nice job of both displaying the objects and explaining the archaeology of how they were found and what information was conveyed. Then on to Sipan. Yes, almost same name. Actually the Sican site was originally named Lambayeque and is still so noted in older texts, but once Shimada found the graves he started calling it "Sican." Given that there was no Moche written language (and if there were one, how in the world would we know how the words were pronounced?) he probably could have called the site Pecan or Cinnamon Bear and who could have argued. Looks to me like whoever finds the most stuff at a site gets to decide its name.

Probably different in China. Anyway, Sipan is quite famous as well, since they have found *nine* burials including the Lord of Sipan, complete and unlooted with all his stuff, which includes much gold, some not so impressive ceramics, and quite a quantity of jewelry. Walter Alva is the Peruvian archeologist who did the work, protecting the site from looters scrounging for money, etc., and it was impressive to tour the site and see all the graves, all large and quite deep down. Of course, had they not been so deeply buried, they would have all been long since looted. Then we go to Walter's newly opened museum, perhaps just a tiny bit competitive with Shimada's newly opened museum in the same province. Once we had experienced it, we decided it should not be the Museum of the Royal Tombs of the Lord of Sipan but the Museum of Squashed Skeletons. Too much emphasis and way too much exhibit space on each of the careful steps of excavating, preserving, and analyzing, and not nearly enough on showing off the items. This may be what happens when you let archeologists design museums rather than designers or historians.

Final stop is a giant local market in Chiclayo, the *curandero* ("curer" or maybe "sorcerer") section. Not clear what this has to do with archeology. All thirty of us dutifully troop through it, where you can buy charms to cure specific sicknesses, make someone love you, cure hangnails, etc. I was looking for one for peace in the Middle East, but all they had was ending world hunger. I also asked our guide if the young children of Chiclayo were called "Chiclets" but got an indistinct reply. We got back on the bus, to the airport, to Lima, to the hotel, to sleep.

Day Four—Yucay

Wake-up call at 0430, followed by very early morning flight to Cuzco, up in the Andean mountains, and then an hour and a half drive to Yucay in the Sacred Valley (Urubamba Valley). We are now in Inca land. Along the way, our new guide assures us that the Inca referred to Cuzco as "the navel of the universe," or alternatively "the belly button of the universe." I ponder this, especially as, on the flight in, the attendant prepared us for landing by asking us to keep eyes clear and not use loud toys. I asked Linda what she thought of this and she patiently explained it was aisles clear and not use lavatories.

We are staying at the Sonesta Posada Del Incas. Well, I don't think any Incas have actually stayed there but the name is used rather a lot in the highlands. I don't think any Incas have eaten at the two hundred Inca cafés, either. We are smack in the middle of the Urubamba Valley, also called the Sacred Valley of the Incas, although for no real reason. It could quite legitimately be called the Inca Heartland but that doesn't have as much zing, one supposes. We had basically a travel day to acclimatize ourselves to the drastic change in altitude—sea level to ten thousand feet.

In the afternoon, I elected to find one of the hotel folks to take us on a hike up into the mountains just a little bit, along the Inca terraces and through the fields, instead of going shopping with the group. It was exceptionally pleasant, all the peach trees were in bloom, the paths were negotiable, we saw women out harvesting herbs then carrying enormously large bundles on their backs, etc. The hotel gardens are also lovely to include a large white camelid (alpaca maybe) grazing on the grass, but see "mysteries" below. And when we get back, lo and behold, there are women who appear to be local Andeans with nice displays of textiles laid out in one of the courtyards—for sale. We fall in love with a rug with a large headdress god figure of some sort in the middle, surrounded by four other symbolic *leones*. Linda bargains hard, buys it, and as she walks away the woman is seen making the sign of the cross. Later we find out that the guy with the big hat is Tumi, god of medicine (and here I thought it was Hippocrates or Caduceus or someone like that) and both he and the *leones* are from the Ayacucho culture which is a good one hundred and fifty miles away from where we are. Oh well.

Day Five—Urubamba Valley to Cuzco—Ollantaytambo, Pisac, Pisac Market

A day of driving around the valley, which is rural and agricultural, not a big surprise when one considers that the largest Andean city is Cuzco and it's only 400,000 persons. As this is essentially the end of winter so the landscape is brown or straw colored; the houses are all of adobe brick construction, the wealthier ones plastered and painted, usually white. No brick, no block, no wood, but then there are precious few trees here. The predominant vegetation is eucalyptus (imported from Australia but thriving), and Scotch broom, also nonnative and also doing just fine, thank you. The mountainsides host large colonies of bromeliads, although none are in flower at this time of year. Major crops are potatoes, barley, beans, chilies, and some limited corn. We visit two sites—Ollantaytambo and Pisac, and both are impressive and somewhat similar, although at opposite ends of the valley. Each is a series of terraces with the classic Inca stone-work running up a very steep mountainside, with a series of buildings at the top. Some of the buildings have what for simplicity we shall refer to as class A quality stonework (generally known as "can't get a knife blade between the joints"), although the terraces are all class B work, where no joint fitting is involved—you just fit whatever stones you have into the best pattern and closest fit you can. This has been good enough to last six hundred years, so it's not chopped liver, as stonework goes. To give you some idea of how steep this stuff is, the terrace walls average eight to ten feet in height, then you get level surface of about two-thirds this depth, then another terrace. I can't do the geometry or trig in my head but that's probably fifty to sixty degree slopes. These are not the rice terraces of Japan. They are also generally straight and geometrically regular—none of this fitting the contours of the hillside. And their purpose is agricultural. When you excavate a core sample, you find large rock at the bottom, smaller rock in the middle, and about two feet of good quality soil from the valley floor on top—the soil has been carried all the way up these steep hillsides. This is again all about water management, which has to be one of the Inca's major accomplishments. Hard to irrigate on a sixty degree slope.

Right now you are no doubt asking yourself, "But what about electricity reform in Peru?" Nope, this is not an electricity letter. What you should be asking yourself is how the Incas actually built this stuff. This is especially interesting because the class A stonework is generally at the top of the mountain and uses big, big stones. And it's not thin or decorative facing; the stone projects through the wall and is the basic material of construction. As we have been told, the Incas did not have the wheel, had

no beasts of burden more powerful than the llama (which is so un-pow-
erful that you can't ride one), and of course were short on steel chisels,
grinders, pulleys, cranes, Kubota tractors, and heavy lift helicopters.

The answers are rather simple: first, you can use stones to chip and
break other stones, although it is tedious and you run through a lot of
rocks. Not a shortage around here, however. Second, you can tie these
stones up with ropes and, given enough humans, actually pull them along
the Inca roads and across the rivers and up the hills. It does take a rather
large number of persons. An architect and an archeologist from Berkeley
did some experiments and in fact showed how, using stones from Inca
quarry sites, you can make very decent joints. More impressive, they actually marshaled the entire population of Ollantaytambo, got permission
from the government, and moved one of the giant ten- ton stones (called
"lost stones" in Quechua, they appear to have been prepared for the OTT
Summit but never got there) down the main street of town. It took a lot of
ropes, several offerings of cane alcohol, and 250 people, but they did it. This
was all in a very interesting video we saw that evening.

Where did they get the people? Taxes to the Inca administration were
paid solely in labor, so they appear to have had enough over time to build
really impressive stone structures. I would also argue that although the
Incas continued to expand their area of domination, it was a period of relative prosperity and peace, and thus folks were available for stone moving
rather than killing one another.

At our final stop of the day, we went to a local market in Pisac, a weekly
affair known for yards around, full of crafts, mostly textiles, and the usual
assortment of knickknacks— jewelry, pottery, carved gourds, etc. Once you
have looked at roughly 150 stalls, been assured that it is all local and all
hand woven by the dedicated weavers of the Sacred Valley, you do ask,
"How come all the patterns look the same?" There's a god, there's a lion,
there's a llama, there's an eagle, there's a couple of others. And especially
why all the rugs with images of house cats are the *same* image—cat sitting
upright on its haunches, no arms or legs, tail curving up in the air. What
part of Inca or Quechua iconography is that? And I admit that when the
local native artisan pulls out a calculator to negotiate a price with you, and

can rapidly translate back and forth between soles, the Peruvian currency, and dollars (and probably euros and yen and possibly RMB—soon they'll have cell phones and be calling up their banks and wiring in the money), I begin to wonder if all this stuff didn't come out of the same forty-foot container from Hong Kong or Shanghai. The other explanation that I tried out with Dr. Burger is that the cat images came from the Egyptians—it wasn't the aliens that built Machu Picchu, although that is one school of thought—but in fact it was the folks from Cairo who, after they finished the pyramids, came over and showed the Incas how to do it. And everyone knows they considered the cat a deity. There is the small matter of a two thousand-year mismatch in timing, between the pyramids and Machu Picchu, but those are just details, and I have the cat rugs as evidence.

During the day our local guide delivered the following remarkable bits of "information":

» "We use cactus juice to make our adobe bricks, it makes them stronger." Note: there must be a billion bricks in the valley and about eleven cacti. And getting "juice" out of a cactus is no mean feat. We have passed several folks making bricks, with nary a squeezed cactus in site. . . .

» "The Incas used bromeliads as lubrication for transporting their stones to the building sites." Note: absolutely no indication this is true in any document.

» "The Spanish took the water system of Cuzco that delivered pure water and turned it into a sewer." Note: much evidence obtained from analysis of Inca-era skeletons that parasites were a big problem, which doesn't say much for the pure water or public hygiene theory, plus, why would they? Part of a larger "blame the Spanish" theme to which we could subscribe if it were only changed to "blame the French," but they don't seem to have been in charge here.

» "To cook a guinea pig just dip him in simmering water by his tail and his fur comes off." Note: doubtful, but who cares. One of our party lived in Peru at several different times during his career, even studying Andean nutrition, and never ate a guinea pig—"Too close to rat for me."

Day Six—Cuzco: Inca Museum, the Pre-Colombian Art Museum, and the Weavers of Chinchero

We started with an altitude headache and a long bus ride, uphill for good-ness' sake, as if Cuzco weren't high enough, to Chinchero—12,343 feet, only 45 feet short of the summit of Mount Fuji-- to visit local native weavers in their local native weaving habitat, which turned out to be a courtyard in an adobe building. Some of us, having been to perhaps one too many exhibits of local native weavers or potters or carvers or metalsmiths, began grumpily referring to this as the visit to Chinchilla. It was about what you would expect—a bunch of solid and in some cases grizzled Andean women demonstrating weaving (they use yarn and looms, surprise) all explained by a younger and not grizzled woman who is the organizer of the group and, unlike the weavers, was not dressed in the traditional Andean costume of a black square dance skirt, a red embroidered bartender's vest, and a flat black hat like a sombrero, but thicker and with no crown. And, wonder of wonders, when the very long discussion and demonstration was complete, there were woven textiles for sale. I was shocked. They all had calculators. But no cell phones that I could see. Subsequently Richard's wife, Lucy, who besides being an archeologist is a native Peruvian, told us that the local weavers are only using the traditional stuff for dyes—bark of this, flower of that—because the tourists demand it. If you go to a really local festival, you find nothing but fabrics of bright colors, made with aniline dyes imported from the US. The gringos get the brown stuff.

Back to Cuzco, to the Inca Museum that confirmed my shorthand analysis of Inca artistic capabilities: great stonework; arresting architecture, especially site selection; good hydraulic management; and lousy pottery—on exhibit were either pretty pedestrian drinking goblets or really big pots for making corn beer. We don't know about their metalwork because the Spaniards vacuumed up all the gold. The museum does have the six remaining pieces not found and melted down by Pizarro. One is a llama, or maybe a guanaco.

In the late afternoon Linda was looking for a new camera (Cuzco, photographic navel of the universe?) because hers broke. She had declined my gallant offer of advice and assistance ("Hey, don't get that one, it's too expensive."), so I roamed around the main square, looking for an Inca belt buckle. My wants are few. Note that there is a lot of—I mean a lot of—silver jewelry for sale in Cuzco, much of it very nice. But try asking for a *hebilla por una correa* as I was instructed to do after pointing to my own, and you won't find any. Big commercial loss, hard to believe the Navajos are ahead of the Peruvians, but it's true. Later when I looked up the phrase in my own Spanish dictionary, I found that *hebilla* does mean buckle, but *correa* means belt in the industrial sense, as in conveyor belt, so God knows what the shop attendants thought I was looking for. Surprising they didn't send me to a hardware store.

Guantanamera Index (a scientific measure similar to Richter scale, measured by number of times one hears a local set of musicians play said song, used to denote level of non-authenticity of any tourist visit to South America. Index is cumulative and when it reaches five in any fourteen-day period it is important to return to the United States immediately): the index reaches one today at lunch in the Inca Café where we are served native Peruvian food of broiled trout and poached pears. Band plays "Guantanamera" on Andean pipes and guitar, also sings.

Day Seven—Train to Machu Picchu and First Visit

"In Xanadu did Kubla Khan / A stately pleasure dome decree . . ." The same could be said of Machu Picchu except for the stately. The archaeological record now seems quite clear: Machu Picchu was constructed by the first Inca emperor, Pachacuti, in about 1440 to 1460. It sits on the top of a mountain, and has the requisite terracing and distinct areas for the ruler, for the sacred/worship functions, and for the retainers and servants who accompanied the emperor when he came here. And he tended to come here in the winter, on vacation, when Cuzco is at its coldest and brownest. Cuzco is at around11,000 feet, and MP is only 7,900 and sits on the edge of the Amazon. The vegetation includes orchids, cannas, perennial begonias, caladiums, passionflowers, and other plants we would think of as tropicals—all things you don't see in Cuzco. The site, however, is not large and was not self-sustaining—hard to put in enough terraces and crops on the top of a rather pointy mountain, no matter how good your skill at terracing.

Walking around Machu Picchu the late morning of the first day, we were told by our guide:

» The Inca used concave golden mirrors to start fires.

» Hiram Bingham promised to return the artifacts from his first expedition and never did so.

» The famous gnomon (called the *intiwatana*, which I now understand means in Quechua "carved rock that no one understands the purpose of") was:

   a. sundial, and indicator to the Inca that nights were getting longer (when it cast a longer shadow during the day);

   b. somehow oriented toward Ecuador and thus pointed thirteen degrees south;

   c. a worship stone that pointed to the sacred mountains (*apu* in Quechua—at first I thought he was talking about Steve Jobs and Apple although it seemed unlikely that the sacred stone would have foretold the iPod) surrounding the site.

The truth is, according to Richard:

While some *convex* mirrors have been found—concave mirrors just make your nose look big—they were not designed for focusing the sun's rays enough to start a fire, as this requires a fairly precise construction and 360 degree radial symmetry.

Hiram Bingham made no such commitment on his 1912 expedition, although he did do so on his 1915 expedition, and honored it.

   a. The small, carved hunk of boulder has been studied by real archaeologists and "does not cast a useful shadow." Of course, casting a longer shadow means the nights are getting longer. Um, OK, probably so. Could also be a weather-telling stone—when wet, indicates that it's raining.

   b. Ecuador is a big place, so thirteen degrees might hit part of it, but it would probably be north.

    c. Pointing to the "sacred mountains" on all sides isn't hard if they're on all sides. Which they are.

Yeesh.

Yale history professor Hiram Bingham discovered Machu Picchu, or "rediscovered" it, depending on your degree of political correctness, in 1911 on a mission here financed in part by Yale. He also had a letter from President Taft (another Yale man) and both good judgment and incredible good luck. Essentially, he went to Cuzco and, on the strength of a letter from the prez of Peru, which he had received based on his letter from Taft, the governor of the province convened a meeting of all the experts in the area on the issue of "Any lost cities around here?" and they pointed him in this direction. When he got to Aguas Calientes, the little town at the bottom of the mountain, he asked the locals if they had seen any lost cities recently and they said, basically, sure, you must mean that bunch of rocks at the top of the mountain, but it's a tough climb. He got one to lead him and, about two-thirds of the way up, came across a shepherding family, who dispatched their son to take him the rest of the way. So did he "discover" it? In any event he gets the credit, which in many ways he earned. He came back several more times, this time much better financed by *National Geographic* (before the war started in Europe—when it did, he signed up as a fighter pilot), and cleared and mapped the site, which was a not small task. He excavated parts of it as well but found little in the way of artifacts. The general explanation is that when the Inca emperor was here in residence he brought his stuff, and when he went back to Cuzco he took it back with him. Bingham wrote a trip report with a lot of pictures that was published in *National Geographic* and took up two hundred pages. So, no complaining about long letters from me.

The site is impressive for the quality of its stonework, much although not all of it of the class A type. It is impressive for the sheer physical labor that had to go into hauling all that rock up this very steep mountain, and then chipping it so that the joints all fit. It is impressive that, in a land of relatively high earthquake risk, it is still standing six hundred years later.

Several other specifics are noteworthy. First, it's all essentially single-story architecture, or at most two rather squatty stories. The buildings are individually small, like bedrooms in cheap subdivisions. Hence, to accommodate the several hundred persons that would have been here with the emperor, you had to go out rather than up. Of course, on a mountain, going out to some extent means going up. Second, the palace is small and its rooms are small. Not so much a palace as a ranch house. Maybe the site says it all, but there is no sort of "statement" made by Pachacuti's residence. It's just set apart from the others and therefore more private, but essentially no different in design. Finally, and most remarkable to my eyes, is the complete and utter absence of ornamentation. With two modest and somewhat enigmatic exceptions, the *intiwantana* being one, none of the stone is carved or decorated. And it wasn't like they didn't know how to work stone, they dragged the darn things up here and then carved huge blocks to fit very small tolerances, so they certainly could have ornamented the stone if they had taken a mind to. Compare Angkor Wat, where every temple complex is elaborately ornamented, and the ornamentation as well as the architecture is part of the allure and the mystery. I find it very surprising that Pachacuti didn't at least have his stone masons carve something that would say, in effect, "This is my place, I am the ruler of the Andes, and the fact that I had this built should impress you with what a powerful guy I am."

Guantanamera Index reaches two on the train ride from Cuzco to MP. At least no one has as of yet played "My Way."

Day Eight—More Machu Picchu

Our second day is "free," but we are encouraged to get up and see sunrise at Machu Picchu. It turns out that the sun comes up about six thirty but at 5:45 it's getting light out. So like good troopers, we get up and go out on the small terrace of our very nice rooms at the Machu Picchu Sanctuary Lodge, and I notice without consulting the Inca weather-telling stone that it is raining. This modifies my enthusiasm to go hiking up the park and sit on some wet rocks and see the sun rise, especially as it just rises over the mountains that surround the place, not illuminating any special location like the Plaza of the Sun or some equivalent.

After breakfast, the sun being up and the rain being stopped, we join up with two trip mates, Herb and his companion, Ann, a photographer. Herb is a medical researcher at Columbia, specializing in addiction; he was the number two guy in the Drug Office in the first Bush administration, so he has stories from his time in Washington. He is smart and funny, and Ann is as well. They refrain from mentioning Yale in every third sentence, which is also fine with us. We hike up part of the way to the Sun Gates, which, as with most of this, may or may not be what the Incas called it. We are on the Inca trail and were we to keep going, we could get back to Cuzco, but it would be a slog. However, we have now "hiked the Inca trail" so we can buy the T-shirt. What is especially nice about it is the tropical vegetation, including a wide variety of orchids, some literally arching over the trail, and in blossom. None of the guidebooks remark about this, but the flowers in the area are really quite magnificent. Ann gets special credit for coming along, as she is not comfortable with heights and exposure, and there is some of this, but she grits her teeth and makes it.

Interesting note: No one in the administration of Machu Picchu seems to have thought about guardrails; there are many places in the park including Machu Picchu itself where you can go down a flight of stairs and with no warning plummet into several hundred feet of nothingness. This would not be good for the tourist trade, including of course the original tourist taking the header. As Americans accustomed to vigorous efforts to avoid at least obvious liabilities, we are amazed that there are no barriers, ropes, or even warning signs of any kind on all these stairs to nowhere.

We are told that Machu Picchu in Quechua means "manly peak," but sitting beside it is another even more manly mountain called Wayna Picchu, which was also part of the Inca resort and has a few stone buildings on its summit. I do not think its name translates as "Wayne Newton Peak," but maybe.

In the later afternoon—the day-trip tourists all leave about two-thirty and only those staying at the lodge are left, and that is quite nice—we explore the area where the less royal folks stayed, and it looks pretty much like the Inca's residence—small stone houses with small windows if any, and no decoration. Many pictures are taken to remind us of this. Then we see that they have let out the medium-size hairy animals—llamas, guanacos, alpacas, but not sheep—to eat the grass, so we go over there and take pictures to confirm that we have in fact seen some.

Day Nine—Machu Picchu and Train Back to Cuzco

We awake (again) to rain, only this time it doesn't seem likely to stop. One can imagine the following scene: Mrs. Cuti, wife of the Inca emperor, confronts her husband Pachacuti on their third day of their winter vacation here: "You call this a tropical royal retreat? It rains all the time, it's cold, it took forever to get here 'cause we had to walk from Cuzco, it's at the top of a mountain, the rooms are small, there's no air-conditioning when the sun does come out, there's all these steps and no elevators, and you're the only one with a private bathroom. You're the ruler of the world, so how about some better weather? And by the way, the next time you suggest this, bring Wife #43—I'm going to the Four Seasons."

While we wait for the train at Aguas Calientes at the base of the mountain, we browse through yet another "local artisan handicraft market." I have remarked that at least we haven't seen any howling coyotes or slumbering Mexicans, two quite popular southwestern motifs, and sure enough, there's a rug with sleeping Andeans woven into it. They look somewhat more bulky than the classic sleeping Mexican but the cross-cultural borrowing is unmistakable. And there were lots more rugs with cats. It's as if someone went around to all the weavers and said, "Tourists really like cats, so we're going to be pushing cat rugs this year."

Day Ten—Cuzco with Inca Sites, Cathedral

It is really raining this morning, but we are intrepid and have been counseled to bring rain gear. Linda, being methodical, has brought two pieces of gear and I, being the grasshopper, have brought none, although I do have a nice rain hat. Fortunately, we have not yet run into a situation where she has to wear both rain jackets simultaneously, so she graciously loans me one. We tour the Koricancha—Inca Temple of the Sun (somehow they all seem to be called that) with great class A Inca stonework that the Spanish built a big convent on top of, then the real cathedral (large religious edifice full of altars and very large religious pictures made by little-known Spanish or Peruvian artists), then to the sites outside of Cuzco. We got to the best one, Sacsayhuaman, last, and of course had spent so much time at the other less impressive ones that we were rushed. Too bad—this was both a ceremonial center and a military post guarding the entrance to Cuzco, and it is large and impressive. Again wonderful stonework, only this time some of the boulders weigh as much as one hundred tons, or three hundred tons depending on which guide/guidebook you believe. Richard Burger notes that these are generally agreed to be the largest stones ever moved anywhere in prehistory. Fortunately for the movers, they only had to come one and a half miles from the quarry, and up a gentle hill, but a hundred tons is a bunch of rock to haul. There is also an open plaza, sawtooth construction of the walls rather than long flat expanse, narrow doorways up to the various levels, and a number of other things that set the place apart. Very interesting and impressive, even in the cold and the rain.

During the endless cathedral visit we were inspired to begin singing, softly, to the tune of "Maria" from *West Side Story*, "*Salida, Salida*, I just saw a door named *Salida* . . ." *Salida* is Spanish for exit—tour group fatigue is beginning to set in.

The afternoon is free so I spend it in the traditional fashion—trying to get onto the Internet. After three hours, two experts, and much frustration, I give up in disgust and we go out to wander the streets of Cuzco looking for snow globes and Inca key chains. We find alpaca sweaters and Machu Picchu refrigerator magnets.

Day Eleven—Flight from Cuzco to Lima

Another early morning wake-up. The winter fog that had the Cuzco airport locked in the day before has lifted and we are able to get out. It is surprising that an airport that large, with that many flights, would be VFR only. In Lima we visit the Larco Museum in the afternoon. Despite a large helping of museum fatigue, this one is quite interesting. For one thing, they have some forty thousand pieces of Moche pottery, and all are on "display" in a manner of speaking—in glass-fronted cases that look like bookcases, with shelves going all the way up to the twenty-foot ceiling of the storage room. Not just one pot representing a crab, but fifteen of them, all grouped together; not just one head of a nobleman, but 450 of them. It's quite neat.

Day Twelve—The Mysterious Nazca Lines

We fly to Ica in the south, and land in an oasis in the middle of desert, complete with large sand dunes. One is reminded again that, except for the mountain-fed rivers, the coast is a desert, and here once again is proof. This is an "optional extension" of the tour but personally I would not have missed it. We are fewer now in number (ten vs. thirty-four) so we fit nicely in a single engine, high-wing monoplane, which flies over the Nazca line figures, found on a plateau south of Ica. These things are tracings or line drawings of recognizable figures, and include a monkey, a hummingbird, a tree, etc. They are large—the largest is about 800 feet at its greatest point-to-point distance—and can only be discerned from the air. This actually does qualify as a mystery—not who did them (the Nazca, the designs are also found on their pottery) or when (AD 200–600), but why?

That evening we elect to eat dinner at the restaurant on top of the hotel, and find that when they bring us the bill there is a 10% cover charge. Peculiar—not listed on the menu. I don't think I've ever been to a restaurant that had a cover charge.

Day Thirteen—Lima and Flight Home

The not-so-good hotel confuses us with others in our dwindling group who need to go to the airport for early flights, and thus gives us a wake-up call at 0330, even though our plane does not leave until late evening. I am not amused, especially since the phone is on the other side of the bed. If anyone we know ever comes to Lima, we strongly recommend *against* staying at the Hotel Las Americas, despite its five star designation. They lose faxes, there is no Internet connection in the room, the rooms are poorly lit, there are mysterious cover charges, and they call you at 3:30

in the morning. Enough said. But we soldier on, valiantly visiting various Indian markets and one really nice gallery, helping President Toledo to make his numbers for this month.

The Yale brochure advertises this trip as "Machu Picchu and the Mysteries of Peru." We won't stop to speculate on whether this means that Machu Picchu is not a "Mystery of Peru," but rather a solved mystery or never was a mystery. But there are mysteries. For example . . .

» One of the specialties of Andean Peru is the alpaca sweater woven from the stomach hair of the alpaca, and only from alpacas (alpacae?) that are one or two years old. In Cuzco, the Navel of the Alpaca Sweater Universe, there are many, many stores featuring alpaca sweaters. And even one at Machu Picchu. And no doubt other locations, we just didn't stop there. If we posit two sweaters from the stomach of each alpaca each season, presuming that the alpacas don't run around with naked stomachs forever, and if we further assume each store has an inventory of four hundred sweaters, then that's two hundred alpacas per store. There seem to me to be at least a hundred such stores in Cuzco, which comes out to twenty thousand alpacas, not counting the alpaca retirees. We have driven up and down the Urubamba Valley three times and taken the train through it two times, so we are pretty familiar with the somewhat limited landscape in the general vicinity. We have seen dogs, cats, pigs, horses, chickens, ducks, donkeys, guinea pigs, and lots of cows. Except for the five or six alpacas we saw grazing Sunday evening at Machu Picchu as a more efficient and certainly more picturesque way to keep the grass down than a riding mower, and easier to move between terraces, we haven't seen a single alpaca.

» How do you tell the four camelids apart—llama, alpaca, vicuna, and guanaco? There was a less than helpful picture of all four animals, each carefully labeled, in a brochure handed out at the "fashion show" Sunday evening at the MP Sanctuary Lodge. One of the participants was an outfit called Alpaca 111, which owns retail stores that sell alpaca sweaters, coats, scarves, hats, gloves, etc. Shows how desperate we were for entertainment that we all went. As best you can tell from the picture, alpacas have slightly fatter faces and a tendency to look directly at the camera; the rest of the group looks pretty much the same. No help there.

» Do mysteries one and two actually matter? Polartec has arrived and is everywhere in the highlands, and not just on the rich gringos. No one has yet alleged that this is locally grown plastic or recycled from the water bottles and knit by the Andean women, but that will probably come. Such garments will have to be died brown, of course. My favorite: a blue Polartec pullover with the "Machu Picchu—Land of the Inca" legend on front, sold without shame in the gift shop of the Posada Del Inca. I present this as conclusive evidence that plastic will ultimately triumph, and have slowed my efforts to tell a guanaco from a guayabera.

» To get to Machu Picchu you take the train from Cuzco, which you board quite early in the morning, early enough that it represses one's natural urge to break into song when seeing the railcars. The song being, of course, "Pardon me, boy, is that the Machu Picchu Choo Choo?" It makes stops at a couple of places and you can get off and walk the Inca Trail to Machu Picchu from Ollantaytambo. The train is run by the Orient Express people but nonetheless its seats are hard and they arrange to pipe some of the diesel engine smoke into the passenger compartments so you arrive feeling somewhat queasy. The final destination is Aguas Calientes, the tiny and touristy town at the base of Machu Picchu Mountain on the very top of which sits—the Leaning Tower of Pisa! No, just kidding, the ruins of Machu Picchu. The road from Cuzco, which has been more or less paralleling the train tracks, runs out and ends a little past Ollantaytambo, so the train is the only way to get to Aguas Calientes and hence to MP. The train tracks follow the Urubamba River through an increasingly dramatic and narrow canyon, and just before Aguas Calientes there is a modest but hardly inconsequential power dam in the river. I excitedly pointed this out to Linda, but she seemed strangely unmoved. At the train station one transfers to a small bus (thirty-four passengers, so not that small) that takes you up the 117 switchbacks on a dusty and steep road to the top of the mountain. It is but one of a fleet of dozens, all of the remainder of which insist on coming down the mountain while you are going up, thus forcing you to the edge of the no-guardrail, very narrow dirt and gravel road. Great views of the other mountains, the river far below, and your impending death. Anyway, if there's no road to get here, where did the buses come from? And how did the material to build the dam get here? All on flat cars? This is, we were told, a narrow gauge railroad, so I doubt specialized rolling stock is plentiful. Mystery.

» Why did the Nazca make those figures on the San Juan plateau anyway? Truly nutty theories have been advanced ever since they were "discovered," although "recognized" might be a better word. Signals to aliens, flying saucer landing fields, something or other to do with the solstice or the change of seasons (this seems to be the all-purpose archaeological explanation for everything, or perhaps it's the thesis that you try out first), something to do with worship and deities—but no evidence of ceremonies. One idea is that the religious celebration could have been folks trudging along the path of the design. Doesn't sound like a terrific ceremony to me, and still doesn't explain why these particular designs? The real answer seems to be—beats the heck out of us. It really is a mystery. But the designs are pretty cool, even elaborate.

» How come it's so hard to find a snow globe in Cuzco or Lima or anywhere we went? Another missed commercial opportunity. We did, however, find Nazca Lines refrigerator magnets, and we're sending you one. Be careful, it may send out a beacon to aliens and attract them to your fridge. I don't know if they will like Omaha Steaks as much as you do.

Love and kisses,
Bob

Afterword: For reasons that I cannot recall, I have left out one of the few good pieces of advice that should have been included in this letter. I have always been subject to altitude sickness, usually setting in above ten thousand feet. Altitude sickness is ugly, being a rancid combination of a splitting headache and a very bad-feeling stomach that makes one quite nauseous. Only diarrhea has been left out. And it can actually lead to serious debilitation.

Much of Peru is above ten thousand feet. I knew this ahead of time because the trip material said so, and I read it. "Ugh," I thought. I then tried to read something about altitude sickness, but most of the popular discussion says that the remedy is to descend to a lower altitude. But that doesn't really work if what you're there to see is the stuff at the higher altitude.

So I gave up and actually checked with a real-life doctor. "Oh, that's easy," he said, "Diamox." This is a relatively new medicine used for treating glaucoma, certain types of epilepsy, neither of which I had as far as I could tell, and (yeah!) mountain sickness. Side effects are trivial.

I got my prescription filled, I took it every day we were at altitude, and it worked beautifully. And yet in early June of 2015, the Wall Street Journal ran a two-page article on altitude sickness and never once mentioned this very friendly member of the carbonic anhydrase inhibitors family. Goodness, if you can't trust the Journal for medical advice, who can you trust?

Remember this, the next time you decide to climb Mount Kilimanjaro: DIAMOX.

chapter nine

Life on the Eleventh Floor, Where the High-Paid Executives Live and Play

November 2005

Dear Dad,

 I have been collecting small bits of happenings here at AES, and thought I would pull them all together in a couple of letters. This one is from things that went on at the top floor of our fancy new offices in Arlington, largely in 2005. You'll be amused or appalled or both. I was.

A Half Day in the Life of a Big 'Xecutive

This morning I arose at four a.m. in our house in Potomac, and found that it was still dark and cold outside, something I could not have otherwise known, since I have a long-standing personal policy never to arise at four a.m. when I find myself located in either hemisphere, north or south of the Arctic and Antarctic Circles, respectively. The second part of the policy is never to go north of the Arctic Circle or south of the Antarctic Circle. I had found that US Airways has, annoyingly, put in a flight to NYC that leaves at 6:00 a.m. In the good old days, the flights it's offering never left before seven. I had been asked to go to an Important Breakfast Meeting with His Excellency Shaukat Aziz, prime minister of the Islamic Republic of Pakistan. The goal was to convey to the PM the importance of having Pakistan provide us at AES an allocation of natural gas, so that we can, as the Pakistan government itself has requested, develop an additional power plant at the site of our two existing oil-fired units at Lal Pir in the Muzaffargarh area. I needed to arrive early, at eight o'clock, as we were warned that security would be tight, and, short of going the night before, this was the only way to do so. Hence Good Soldier Hemphill is tooling down the GW Parkway, heading toward National Airport, at 4:45 in the morning. Traffic was light.

The airplane took off, flew uneventfully through the air, and landed safely—always a good thing for an airplane to do—especially one carrying me. The taxi deposited me at the Regency Hotel in midtown Manhattan at about seven-thirty. There were lots of NYPD cops standing around on the sidewalk outside the hotel, hands in pockets, furry little hats on their heads, talking to one another. Perhaps they were adroitly surveilling me and others, but they were very discrete about it. To further confuse evil-doers, many of NY's finest were drinking coffee, probably with the plan of throwing it on miscreants, should any be detected. I felt secure.

Then I felt less secure as I noticed that the central coat button of my serious, go-to-meeting-with-prime-minister charcoal-striped suit was dangling by one thread, about an inch below its proper location, swinging back and forth like an imitation pocket watch. Made it hard to button my jacket and look properly executive-like. I found the small sundries store at the hotel, bought a sewing kit, but then I couldn't find any place to sit down and look like a seamstress. This is a very fancy hotel and it has a lobby about the size of a sandwich. "Well screw it," I thought, "maybe they won't look at my stomach. Let's go through security."

The meeting was to be held in the Regency Room, to which I was directed by going, curiously, through the middle of the dining room, where many high-powered executives were clearly having high-power breakfasts. Their jackets were all buttoned. If this had been Washington, it would have been lobbyists, except that there aren't any left in town due to Mr.

Abramoff and his associated lobbying scandal.

A large, college football-looking sort of white guy was standing at the unmarked door to the Regency Room, at the back end of the restaurant. When I finally got up to him, dodging waiters and diners, he said, "Go around to the Sixty-first street entrance." The hotel is on the corner of Park Ave and 61st, with its major entrance and awning and cluster of cops on Park, so this didn't seem intrinsically bad advice. I went back out into the cold, walked around the corner, walked down the block, and found what was clearly an entrance. I am smart, so I observed that this entrance, which had metal-covered, swinging double doors, was currently being used by small but energetic men pushing through large rolling carts of supplies— bread, milk, meat, etc.—which they had taken from delivery trucks. It seemed possible that this was the entrance to a fancy meeting, but maybe not likely. Unless the Regency Room turned out to also be the kitchen. I went back inside and asked the concierge where the damn door was. He was very kind and walked me back around to 61st street, where the door was carefully disguised as a window panel. No doorknob, no PLEASE COME IN sign, nothing. And it was locked. Very tight security.

We went back inside. The concierge suggested I wait in the lobby and have a cup of coffee, but did not specify a subsequent event. I suspected delaying tactics. However, I no sooner got a small cup of coffee, wondering idly if I now looked like a cop, than the concierge came back with another big guy, who was bouncer sort of big, which is about a third broader than college football big, but no taller, and thus has a different aspect ratio. Think plasma TV wide versus normal TV. He also had a round head with a buzz cut, and was wearing a suit with luminous white stripes. "Security," the concierge said. Security walked me again through the restaurant, this time causing waiters to press themselves tightly against the walls, and up to the door guard. Security said the magic words, "This guy is coming to the meeting." Door guard immediately let me in. Apparently it only works if you know the right words—not if you goof up, show up by yourself, and say, "I am coming to the meeting."

Finally inside, I then encountered the tight security, which was, um, nothing. A couple of the women from the meeting organizer were there, looking well dressed rather than dangerous. There was the standard really long and large table, set with lots of nice breakfast looking things, and a TV guy was playing with his camera and microphone. I walked around the table for twenty minutes and found my place card, which was not next to, nor even particularly close to, that of H. E. Aziz.

I looked around. Another guy had already made it through the many checkpoints previously described and was sitting at the table assiduously reading his *Wall Street Journal*. According to the seating chart that had been put at each place, he seemed to be Mr. Kenney from Merrill Lynch, but he also seemed in no mood to chat. "I'll show you who's important," I thought, and took out my blackberry and read the messages that I had already read before in the cab on the way in. They hadn't changed.

A less off-putting person came in through the outside door, now unlocked. He turned out to be a Lockheed Martin VP for Business Development, former naval aviator and Annapolis grad, class of '76. Since he had no *Wall Street Journal* and we were still the only two friendly people in the room, we chatted, and he told me in great detail the virtues of the F-22. Undetectable, computing power of three Crays on board, cruising speed of Mach 1.5, operates easily above sixty thousand feet, power plant of a 747, etc. Actually it was pretty interesting and he was a nice guy, but as far as I could tell he wasn't going to be much help in getting gas in Pakistan, since he lived in Dallas.

More people came in through the tight security by opening the door to the outside and walking in. No ID check, no name cards, no "Who the heck are you?", no guest-by-guest greeting by the staff, no nothing. If you were a homeless person in a nice suit, you could have had yourself a free breakfast while listening to a speech by a high-ranking Pakistani.

The room mostly was full by eight twenty, when a large delegation of Pakistanis came in through the magic door. No one asked for their IDs either. The prime minister was third; one could tell which one he was by the way the others cleared a path through the crowd for him. He is a distinguished looking silver-haired guy, who for most of his career ran Asia for Citibank. Not a lightweight. Since 2001 he has been part of the Musharraf government, first as finance minister and more recently as prime minister.

He slowly worked halfway around the room, shaking hands, but didn't get to me.

We all sat down, me and forty-two others of the "small group of senior executives." The sponsor, managing director of Coke for Pakistan, Afghanistan, and Tajikistan (and you think you have a bad region?) made a nice introduction, welcoming us, whoever we were, and suggesting that we eat our fruit cups. I introduced myself to my seatmates, a Liz Claiborne vice president on my left and a Citibank global risk management guy on my right. I told the Citibank guy that we were a big and happy customer and were even paying back some of the large amounts of money we had borrowed. He grunted appreciatively and immediately turned to the person on his right and conducted an animated conversation with him for the rest of the breakfast. I checked my deodorant.

The Liz Claiborne person was chatting up the textile minister to her left, so I ate my fruit cup and spilled several raspberries on the floor. Eventually she turned to me, so I told her I thought they made nice clothes. I don't think this is a good pickup line. She was polite, however, and noted that she had just come back from Vietnam. Enthusiastically, I allowed as how we might build a power plant there.

Conversation lagged, as we had used up all our commonality.

Fortunately, it was time for Aziz to speak. He was eloquent and persuasive. Theme: Pakistan is better than you think. Subtheme: we're doing fine and will soon do better, come on down. Actually his remarks were well delivered and convincing, and even useful if you had never been there. He did not mention the "earthquake relief entrance fee" for investment that I had been led to expect, nor did he say, "Hey, Bob, good to see you, thanks for the power plants." Next, former secretary of state Madeleine Albright, who was seated next to Aziz, made some considered remarks, although why she was there we know not. She noted that her connection with Pakistan began with her father, who was on the original Kashmir Commission that examined the problem and opined on it long ago i.e., 1945. She concluded, succinctly, "He's dead, I'm old, and it's still a problem." I kind of liked that.

After she finished, Mr. Coca-Cola invited questions. I considered asking, "Hey, Your Excellency, can we have some gas?" but suspected that was not the sort of question they were interested in. Instead people made complex geopolitical points like, "What about those crazy al-Qaeda guys?" and "You folks think Iran is a problem?"

Then the questions and the pleasant and judicious answers were over, and His Excellency and his entourage of gray-suited Pakistanis and big security guys swept out of the room, pleading a meeting with outsourcing companies. I exchanged cards with the Liz Claiborne woman and the fighter pilot, promising to call them should we ever need madras shirt-waists or F-22s, and headed for Penn Station and the office.

It Is Possible to Know Too Much

Andres, our very smart and capable COO, and I were sitting around his office, looking out the window at the view of a very similar office building to ours, just across the street. Of course, we could have been in the CEO's office, in which case we would have had an excellent view of a used car lot. Andres was mildly complaining about all the problems of leading our businesses in Latin America, where there is a decided leftist/populist swing in the political leadership emerging—Lula in Brazil, Kirchner defaulting on Argentina's debt, Chavez running around with the demonstrators when Bush attended the Summit of the Americas in Buenos Aires, etc. The newest problem, he said, is the recent election of Evo Morales, the radical Indian leader in Bolivia.

"Yeah," I answered, "unless you're Bloomingdale's."

"Huh?" Andres responded acutely.

"Well, he wears that damn sweater everywhere and now people want to buy a copy. Probably just New York liberals and Hilary Clinton, of course."

"You know what his campaign slogan was?" Andres asked me.

"No, what?"

"'I want to be President Bush's worst nightmare.'"

"Well, given that Bolivia is the poorest country in South America, and only has a bunch of natural gas and some coca growers as its natural resource base, and thanks to the Chileans has no seaport or access to the ocean, I don't see what he can do that's annoying. Maybe he gets mad at the US and cuts off the gas to Brazil? 'Take that, President Bush!'" I thought about it some more. "Besides," I said, "I think he's too late."

"Too late for what?" asked Andres, who seemed to be rapidly losing interest in the conversation.

"Well, I actually think that Bush's worst nightmare could be Kim Il-sung in North Korea, or if not that, then Chavez certainly has a claim for 'worst nightmare.' And then, there's that newcomer in Iran coming on strong, President Mahmoud Ahmadinejad, who, by the way, definitely gets the prize for most unpronounceable name, and doesn't believe in either the Holocaust or in Israel's right to exist, and probably really is working on a nuclear weapon and may be crazy enough to use it."

"So you're saying . . ."

"Right, I'd argue that the best that Morales can do is be Bush's fourth worst nightmare— all the top slots are already taken."

He nodded, looked out the window, and started shuffling the papers on his desk.

"Wait, there's more. Did you know that Evo Morales has a twin brother who moved to Japan and became an innovator in the field of consumer electronics?"

"You're kidding, right?"

"Yes, he's the well-known Bolivio-Japanese inventor, TiVo Morale . . ."

"Get out of my office," Andres responded cheerfully.

How to Deal with Stock Market Analysts

During our weekly executive office meeting that Paul the CEO chairs, we reviewed the tentative numbers for the first quarter. We have been worried about the numbers as some preliminary looks in January and February seemed to say that we were already running maybe $80 million behind budget—$0.07 on a $0.95 per share guidance to investors. However, what we seem to have for Q1 is $0.42 vs. budget of $0.22, and street expectations of $0.23 to $0.27.

Now the interesting part is that we're not quite sure what this is all made of—some of it is one-time events, some is currencies doing better than we had forecast, some of it is a 30% tax rate vs. the 36% we had used in the budget, some of it is timing (selling some environmental offsets in this quarter vs. selling them next quarter as projected), some is operational improvement. It is not quite resolved.

The downside of course is that we also forecast doing worse than budget for the following three quarters, but even so it looks like we will end up comfortably above the $0.95 per share we have told everyone we would hit by year-end. Besides us, who will this make happy? One would hope our investors, but it will make our analysts all mad.

"Why?" you may ask. Shouldn't they share in our joy? Well, no, what they want is to be *right*, they don't really give much of a rat's ass about us, and this will not make them look right or smart. Perhaps they will take it out on us by sharply raising their estimates for the year, so that we will end up in that dreaded "missed analyst estimates" category, usually mischaracterized as "they didn't make their earnings targets" when the targets were not ours in the first place. This will need to be handled with some subtlety and sophistication. Which is not always our strong suit.

Nonetheless, it is an interesting sort of problem to have. Would we rather be twice as good as estimates for the quarter or half as good? Both are problems, but the first is better.

At the end of the discussion, Paul said, "I know how to handle this. I'll just say, 'We had a great first quarter, but we have the rest of the year to recover.'"

And You Thought That YOU Worked with Idiots

> **Sent:**   Thursday, November 15, 2005 3:51 PM
> **To:**   Arlington People
> **Subject:**   Very Important International Dialing Instructions
>
> Good afternoon, everyone.
> Please, make sure you dial 9-011 before making all international calls. It is very easy to forget and dial 911, please double check before dialing. We have been contacted by the Arlington Police Department concerning three calls from our location. Please forward to all contractors working in our building.

Thank you, and have a good day.
Thank you,
Front Desk Coordinator

Subsequent e-mail several days later:

Subject: AES has placed 24 calls to 911 today

AES will be the recipient of fines of up to $500 per call if this continues to be an issue. The local police department has requested that if you do mistakenly dial 911, you stay on the line and confirm that there is not an emergency that requires police response.

Please ensure that you are dialing outbound calls properly to avoid placing a 911 call.

Dialing Instructions:
Local calls: 9 + 1 + area code + phone number
International Calls: 9 + 011 + country code + phone number

We finally gave up and arranged to use "7" on our phones as the access to get an outside line. There was no "7-1-1" number to screw us up.

Sell Everyone in China a Pencil so They Can Write Down our Hot Line Number

Today one of our international AES board members decided that we were not getting enough calls on our hotline, which we have set up for the purposes everyone sets them up, to allow our employees to make anonymous calls to the general counsel and the chief compliance officer, and rat out their fellow workers for fraud, waste, abuse, corruption, and all manner of wrongdoing.

We get around two hundred calls per year. We have checked and that is more than either GE or BP gets, and these are both paragons in the arcane world of "compliance" and "governance." But it was decided it wasn't enough.

"That's not enough calls!" the board member said with some agitation, although to whom the agitation was directed was hard to discern. Paul almost, he told me later, said, "Well, what do you want us to do to stimulate more calls—have more fraud?" but instead wisely held his tongue.

The board member continued in a troubled tone of voice, "How many calls did you get from China last year?" Keep in mind that we have six small plants in China, each with maybe fifty people, and in three cases we are the minority partner so the employees really aren't "ours" anyhow and are not under our compliance system, nor do we tell them what to do.

Brian, the general counsel, said, "We received one call that we followed up on."

"Well," said the board member, "there's 1.3 billion people in China. You guys just don't know what's going on." We hung our heads and resolved to try and get a much larger fraction of the total Chinese population to call us one of these days.

Are There Any Phones in Cameroon?

Today we all had on our schedules a telephone conference call with our problem child, Sonel, the national utility serving Cameroon, of which we own 56% and manage. This is all made more important because we are about to sign a renewed concession deal with the government, and the IFC, in its infinite wisdom, wants to loan our guys $350 million dollars.

The utility does have a lot of capital needs, including the fact that they serve only about 25% of the citizens of the country. However, running lines out to people who will then use one lightbulb six times a month is expensive business with long capital recovery times. Especially as they don't pay their bills all that regularly.

For comparative purposes, the current book equity of the utility is about $75 million, and they have already $60 mil of debt, so if someone gives them another $350 mil, then they will be leveraged out the kazoo, more than five to one. This is not in the rest of the world considered "best practice" for corporate finance. Does the IFC know better? Probably, but they are under a lot of pressure to throw money at Africa, and Sonel, believe it or not, is one of the more likely institutions they have found. So there you are.

Our Sonel guys had arranged the call and sent around the call in numbers. Paul was to be on the call with me and the CFO, all to discuss their plans to remedy their "material weakness" status with regard to accounting controls, a Sarbanes-Oxley thing that, as you can perhaps tell from the language, is not considered to be "good." In fact, we might even call it "bad" as in, do you know how much money you have, do you know who has it, do you know what they are doing with it, etc. Hard business concepts like that.

It is interesting to note, for the language scholars in the crowd, that there are actually two levels of "badness" in the Sarbanes accounting and controls world. "Material weakness" is the worst designation (I guess beyond that you are assumed to be Somalia, where you have no business at all so forget reporting anything), and we are trying to get Sonel to move up the chain to the level of less badness, which is called "significant deficiency."

Now that we have been dealing with this stuff for a while, we use only initials, like SD and MW This causes a tiny bit of confusion, since when we say internally that such and such a business has MWs, I always have to stop and remember that in this context we don't mean megawatts, another part of the lingua franca that is equivalently abbreviated.

So much for background. We are all hunched over our phones at the appropriate hour, trying to call in to the number provided. This proves not easy. Finally I succeed, only to find that the Sonel people have given us not the number of a conference call service, but the 800 number of a dating service. We are promised intriguing conversations with charming people. Personally, I am tempted for at least thirty seconds. I suspect that such conversations might actually be more interesting than a discussion of the accounting procedures and transaction controls of a poorly run central African utility.

But duty calls, so I run around and finally get the correct number. Sure enough, the discussion with Sonel is vague and, despite pushing from us, seems about twenty-five degrees off true north. I console myself by noting that at least the Sonel folks hadn't given us a 900 number by mistake.

After the wonderful success of the call, Paul said to me, "You should go over there early in July and see what's going on, before I go there and sign the agreements for all the money."

"Of course," I responded dutifully. "Maybe I can just skip the Fourth and go in the hottest time of year, and thus not miss any real working days. . . . I love this game."

Perhaps It Is Good That We're Not in the Security Business

We have an annual shareholders meeting every year, which is open to all shareholders and really open to the public. And also required by law. Almost no one comes because all we say is the same information that we have already said a bunch of times in numerous public documents. It is a leftover requirement from earlier, gentler times.

But we have an ex-employee who has become something of a crackpot, named Dwayne. For this meeting we were worried about Dwayne showing up and doing something weird, and therefore we had hired two security people, one said to be an ex-Navy SEAL. They both showed up early, both wearing blue blazers and ties. They were briefed and given a picture of Dwayne.

They proceeded into the meeting prepared to be inconspicuous but eagle-eyed. However, you could keep track of who the security guys were in the meeting as they were the only two persons chewing gum. This is a future security tip.

When the meeting was about ready to begin, Brian, our general counsel, went in to ask them if they had Dwayne spotted and under surveillance. He is bald and undistinguished looking (Dwayne not Brian). They each, separately, said yes, we got him, we're looking right at him. This was not reassuring as Dwayne was not in the room.

One security professional had identified and was carefully surveilling Scott, our investor relations head, and the other had picked out a member of our board of directors. We did not believe either man constituted a threat. I hope that we did not pay much for this assistance.

And so it goes.

Love and kisses,

Bob

*Afterword: In the second half of the decade beginning in 2001, we
sold all our Chinese plants and our two plants in Pakistan, for just
about opposite reasons.*

*We had first gone to China in 1991. There was only one ring
road in Beijing, and only two "Western" hotels, the Great Wall
Sheraton Hotel and a Kempinski. At least every third person still
wore Mao jackets, the heat wasn't turned on until late November
in any government buildings, and Beijing was a sea of bicycles
with very few private cars. But the country grew and prospered
and began building 300 Mw coal plant after 300 Mw coal plant,
using the same design and Chinese-made equipment. And getting
very cheap financing from the government-owned banks. At one
point they were bringing one new power plant online every week.
They simply no longer needed us, they had learned enough, and
we couldn't compete. But we made a very nice return when we let
a Chinese private firm acquire our 1,100 Mws of plants.*

*We went to Pakistan in the mid 1990s. The country was a mess,
there was a military government, the tribal areas were beyond
the reach of the government, there was insufficient electric power,
financing for new infrastructure of any kind was incredibly
difficult and largely reliant on the international lending agencies,
and there was neither domestic coal nor natural gas available.
Corruption was a big problem, as was local security. Nonetheless,
we built two very nice 300 Mw oil burning plants and made very
reasonable returns.*

*Today, well, go back and read the paragraph above. The country
is little changed, except for more security threats and increased
political instability. It is not a good place to do business, but there
was enough money in the country that we got a reasonable price
for our assets. Thank goodness.*

chapter ten

So You Think Snakes in a Plane Are Bad?

April 2006

Dear Dad,

This Dubai is a strange place. I am attending a three-day conference reviewing all our AES businesses in Asia and the Middle East. I got up this morning at 5:30 after a relatively sleepless night and went out on the beach, Jumeirah Beach to be exact, to run, since it was clear I wasn't going to sleep anymore. Usually I am better than this with jet lag, but not this time. You may not be surprised to hear that there are not a lot of folks around at this time of the day, but it was plenty light out. Jumeirah Beach starts, as far as I can tell, at that oddity and wonderful accomplishment of the dredging and filling profession, the Palm Islands the group of islands artificially plunked into the gulf in the shape of a palm, as seen from a high-flying airplane. It is constructed entirely of ocean bottom dredged up and deposited to form these not-so-small islands. And then there have been houses and such built on them. From my window on the 15th floor of the hotel you can't really see the palm shape, it just looks like a bunch of rows of houses. You cannot, by the way, go visit the island and walk around and gawk and buy the Palm T-shirts, as you cannot get on the island unless you are a resident. So there. Anyway the beach starts there, or rather it starts after the jetty-protected marina next to it, filled with big white James Bond yachts. It runs for, I estimate, probably two miles, ending in another long stone jetty and then you have the ten stacks for power plants, arranged two, two, four and four, with the twos being the older plants. Several were on this morning, emitting a discernible plume from the oil that they burn. Did I mention this beach is on the Arabian Gulf? The area where all the oil in the world lives? I presume these are both desal water and power plants.

On the stretch of beach between the jetties you can find a nice array of shells when you stop running. Or if you are running in bare feet you can find them by stepping on them, which is not as good a plan. The water is bathtub warm and the beach slope is very, very shallow, so the waves are nothing. I didn't see any sharks or other dangerous animals, but then I stayed on the beach. Our hotel has a maze of swimming pools and outdoor entertainment restaurants and such that you must thread your way through to finally see the sand. This pool complex includes a nice artificial rock feature with a two-story waterslide. Almost no one seems to use the pool, and I checked at midday when we took our lunch break. Maybe everyone here is business nerds like me and is in meetings all day. It's also hot and sweaty and sunny. We are, don't forget, in the desert.

I ran as far down the beach as I could, which was pretty far, then I stopped and turned around and sweated and walked back. Since I am a counter, I started counting buildings under construction along this stretch of beach. There are seven existing buildings, all of which seem to be hotels, a Sheraton, a Hilton, a Ritz-Carlton, an Oasis Hotel, the two buildings of this hotel, the oddly named Habtoor Grand Beach Resort and Spa (trying to spell "harbor" and missing?). There are forty-one buildings in construction along the beach in addition to these existing seven. Yes, forty-one. And this is not small construction, not your two-bedroom beach bungalow. No building is smaller than twenty stories, and most are forty or more. And almost all are close to complete, at least they sure are big and tall and just right there. Some are condominiums or such, and a couple of the seven existing buildings seem to be beach clubs/sales offices for the buildings behind them. Can they really possibly fill all those buildings? This place is going to be drowning in tourists or vacation travelers or oil-rich Arabs or rock stars or Russian mafia or a combination of all of the above. And there is not any smaller infrastructure—no supermarkets, no 7-Elevens, no delis, none of what would, in a normal place, have grown up first, then been slowly replaced by the larger, more grandiose buildings. Of course there are the big, Cartier/Gucci/Fendi shopping malls and the famous indoor ski slope. I don't think you can eat scarves and shoes, however.

I do note for the record that, about half way down the beach (our hotel is at the eastern end), in front of a construction site, I saw a man in typical Arab dress, with three rather confused looking camels. What in God's name he, and they, were doing there I cannot guess. He wasn't close to any of the existing buildings, he didn't have a sign in front of him saying CAMEL RIDES $5, and it was a quarter to six in the a.m., not a good time for having somebody come along and ask to have his or her picture taken with the slightly mangy animals. Very peculiar. Maybe they were looking for the Oasis Hotel and got lost. It could happen.

I got back to the hotel and walked through the lobby and out the front door. It's not just on the beach. Standing where the cars come in, and looking across the horizon, I counted sixty-four construction cranes. And once again, they are not working on single-family dwellings, it's all big stuff. "I guess they're here to stay," I said to myself. Looks like Miami Beach, only more garish, if that is possible.

As an integral part of the conference, we had scheduled a "dinner cruise with Arabic entertainment." My sense of dread immediately went into high gear. However, because I am (sometimes) a good sport, despite my trepidations, I went. I do know better than this, I hate being held prisoner on boats, I get seasick, and doing a cruise at night means you can't see anything anyway. I am sorry to report that I was right.

I am now safely back in the Habtoor Grand Beach Resort, having been rescued by a special ops team, rappelling from a black helicopter down onto the deck of the notorious Cleopatra Dhow (I know she lived in

Egypt, I don't know why the Dubaians don't know that) and winching me up and away from the gay bamboo dancer, the large snake he was wearing on his head, the bad wine and the worse food.

I made up the part about the rappelling. But let's say this again—the dancer had a damn cobra around his neck. On a small boat!

Oh yeah, the electricity went out on the boat, so the AC went off for the voyage "home" and we weren't allowed on the top deck (where it would have been cooler) as one of these boats tipped over in Bahrain several months ago (where is our safety team?), so now you have to all sit downstairs and drown sweating. What fun.

NO MORE BOATS. Especially no more boats with snakes on them. Double especially no more boats with snakes on them, boats that leave from a dock that take an hour and a half bus ride to get to. Could I make this up? I won't even complain any more about the opera singers.

Love and kisses, your not-Arabic son (despite the tahini and olives and beetroot and ginger juice for breakfast),
Bob

chapter
eleven

Ho Chi Minh Wouldn't
Recognize the Place

June 2006

Dear Dad,

The trip started off with a visit to Las Vegas, truly one of the strangest of all American cities. There's no city to it, it's all big and bigger hotels, each complete with internal shopping malls and restaurants and, oh yes, did I mention gambling? The last time I went there it was pretty remarkable and this time I was truly astonished. I was to be the speaker (one of three on the keynote panel) at the most highly attended annual meeting of people in the IPP (independent power producer) business. We at AES are this, although we are now other things as well.

The conference was at the Bellagio, a relatively new hotel that is approximately the size of the Louvre but more confusing and with fewer statues. There are big signs hanging down from the ceiling at each hallway junction, with arrows telling you where the front desk is, where various restaurants are, where this or that set of guest elevators are, etc. There are no signs for the gambling as it is all around you. What's three card poker, by the way? There was a table with a little sign indicating that's what was going on there. I guess you can't have four aces in that game. I have so much to learn. . . .

I wandered next door to the Caesars Palace establishment, which is once again not one simple hotel, but a bunch of them clumped together. It has an indoor shopping and restaurant area laid out as a faux European set of streets, complete with a large arched ceiling about three floors up, painted blue to look like the sky and then lit with changing lights to represent sunset or something, including the passing of time. But I guess not too much time, as they really don't want you to go to bed, they want you to gamble. You've seen the slogan—"What happens in Vegas, stays in Vegas"—and what happens is you lose your money and yes, it sure enough does stay there. But all kinds of people come here; the places were really full of people, young old, all colors, mostly in shorts and short sleeve shirts, many gambling, some families with kids. I wondered to myself just what kind of a family vacation coming to Vegas to play the slots would be, but then I stopped wondering. Some parts of America are odd.

I gave my presentation on Monday morning to an attentive conference audience of six hundred. Everyone is here at this conference to hear what some of the industry leaders and wannabe leaders are doing or, more interesting, are going to do. And a lot of times, the speakers say just that. I have never understood why you would tell a room full of your competitors what your plans are, but maybe the ego in it all just overcomes one. Generally speaking, I don't do this. It's a wonder I get invited to speak. In my presentation, one of the early slides was our official "forward-looking statement" slide which, in legal language and very small print, lays out the current regulatory position of public companies, which I explained thusly: *You are viewing on this slide an arcane dialect called "the language of the lawyers." What our slide says, in real English, is that, number one, I am not allowed to tell you anything that isn't already public information, disseminated equally and simultaneously to every man, woman, and child on the planet, so don't be expecting any of this to be new; and, number two, if by chance I do slip and say something interesting, that wasn't my plan, and you are not allowed to rely on it for anything, and I probably didn't mean it anyway.* The audience laughs ruefully.

The other two persons on the panel, both of whom have gone before me, have dutifully tried to address the issue suggested by the panel organizer, to wit: What is the future of competition? Since my thoughtful answer to this would be "there will be some," I decide instead to give my standard, "this is AES, isn't that interesting" speech.

After all three of us finish, the moderator asks the audience for questions. There aren't any. I have a question, why did I agree to do this, but feel it would be in bad taste to ask it. The moderator asks all of us some questions that, fortunately, he has prepared ahead of time. We answer. Finally the presentation is over and the coffee break starts. I note with interest that, although we big-time speakers (and, of course, important industry leaders) have done this entirely on our own nickel, the moderator/conference organizer doesn't give us squat in the way of a memento, a thank you, etc. Well, how many Cross pens does a person need, anyway?

I leave Las Vegas, pleased that what has happened there, i.e., my speech, will in fact stay there.

To get to Vietnam from Nevada is not easy or quick. My route takes me through LA, with a change of planes, to Taipei (a twelve-hour flight, whew). I arrive too late in the evening in Taipei to connect to Hanoi until the next morning, so Dora, my assistant, has arranged for me to stay at a fancy downtown hotel called the Landis. I get there, I check in, I notice they have a bottle of champagne and not one but two personalized letters of welcome from the hotel manager, and some nice stationary with the letterhead "R. Hemphill," just in case during the six hours I am there I decide to dash off a note to someone, maybe the manager or Prince Philip. As I go into the bathroom to brush my teeth I also notice that the lovely marble floor in the bathroom is raised about one inch above the carpeted floor in the bedroom. I notice this by kicking the marble threshold hard with my bare toes, then confirm this subtle change in elevations by hopping around on one foot in the bathroom, going "Ow, ow, ow." I limp to bed. But first I set my alarm for four a.m. local, compared to the then current time of about eleven at night. I asked the desk person when I checked in what time I should leave to catch a 7:30 flight. She said that getting to the airport in the morning would take "more than one hour." I asked why, since it had taken me twenty minutes coming in. "Holiday," she explained precisely. I asked if it were really true that there was more early morning traffic on a holiday than on a normal day. "Yes," she confirmed. "Some weird sort of early morning Chinese thing," I muttered to myself, glad that I had connected with someone so knowledgeable.

At four I pound on various buttons on the alarm until it succumbs, and then I stagger into the bathroom to take a shower and carefully kick the marble threshold again. Other foot, however. I hate walking with a limp, better to be totally crippled. Then for five minutes I cannot figure out how to make the gosh-darned hot water in the shower come on. It finally turns out that the temperature indicator on the dial is written in some strange Chinese numbering system: "40" turns out to be hot, and "60" turns out to be cold. Never mind that "40" is written in blue and "60" in red on the shower dial. Checking out at 4:30, I see not so many people on the street, and not so many cars. No one appears to be in the holiday spirit yet. Getting into the hotel car, I see only one car on the street, mine. Driving to the airport in fifteen minutes, I see on the street two motorbikes and one other car. I see a number of 7-Elevens that are open, thus belying the name. No Starbucks. Almost no bicycles but lots of motorcycles . All the motorcycles are parked. It's a holiday, for god's sake. I arrive at the airport so early that the check-in window for Air Vietnam is not even open. I mull over this brief experience and conclude that in fact Taiwan is a part of China—the Chinese in Beijing are correct. My stay at the "five star" hotel has mimicked almost every hotel stay that I ever had on the mainland. I remember nostalgically the lack of hot water in Qingdao, stubbing my toes in Shanghai, and the fact that "yes" spoken by a Chinese hotel person means "I do not understand," or, for the truly cynical, means "Go away, big nose."

The flight from Taipei, once enough time has passed and they let me on, is not full, not even half. The flight attendant offers me either Vietnamese or Western breakfast. Since the former has dim sum and chili sauce, I choose it, and am not disappointed. She asks me if I want coffee, tea, or Vietnamese tea. I take the latter. She brings me the tea, and then comes around immediately with the bar cart, and asks if I would like some whiskey. At about 0815 in the morning. I suddenly have the urge to say to her, "You buy me one Saigon tea?" the opening line that all the bar girls on Tu Do Street in Saigon say to the American soldiers. "Saigon tea" was supposedly an alcoholic drink, although I never knew anyone who had actually tasted it. We all, us GIs that is, figured out that it was diluted Coca-Cola or something equally innocuous, but it cost five dollars and bought you the company of the bar girl for the period of time it took her to drink it—twenty to thirty minutes. Fortunately, a rare instance of good judgment kicks in, and I refrain from asking the flight attendant. Also she's way too young to understand what the hell I would be talking about.

Customs and immigration and baggage claim are uneventful. The uniforms of the Vietnamese do look familiar, but I don't have any flash-backs and no one seems the least bit interested in me. I guess a former infantry first lieutenant long past combat age is no longer on anyone's watch list. Our AES driver, Mr. Hai, meets me as planned, and leaves me at the curb while he goes to get the car. It is hot and sunny and muggy. Squatting beside me in that classic Vietnamese squat are several old men, most wearing cheap cotton shorts, not really doing anything, although one is smoking a small cigarette. This part looks the same as 1968.

The drive in to Hanoi from the airport is fascinating. It is a four-lane road, although hardly a superhighway, but there isn't much traffic. Along both sides of the road, right up to the edge, is agricultural land actively being worked by farmers, most wearing the conical straw hat that is an Asian cliché, except here they really do wear them. All the work—hoeing, transferring water into each separate paddy from the small irrigation canal, transplanting—is being done by hand. Women in loose pajamas carry two part loads, one container on each end of poles suspended on their shoulders. There is no farm machinery or mechanized anything, not even the small two-wheel tractors. The fields are the emerald green of new rice plants, so bright it's almost flashy. Occasionally the rice gives way to soybeans or in several plots squash and tomatoes. Small concrete mausoleums appear randomly in the middle of the fields, just as I remember from the south. From time to time a water buffalo appears, not working nearly as hard as the humans. Everyone I see is working for a living, not just doing Asian

Disneyland for the tourists. And it's still hot and humid and there are royal palm trees and red hibiscus bushes in flower and traveler's palms and plumeria trees, although it isn't their season to bloom. There are poinsettias grown as tall as a Christmas tree and as lanky as a small forward drafted right out of high school. "Dang," I think, "this really is Vietnam. Just as I remember it."

Except . . . except that growing out of the middle of the rice fields, held up on large concrete posts or supported by iron scaffolding, are big billboards, obviously aimed at the travelers driving in on the airport road. Some of the companies and products advertised are predictable: Panasonic flat screen TVs, LG cell phones, Thai Silk Cut tobacco, baby formula fed by a pan-Asian mother to an entirely raceless baby, Visa cards, Sanyo, Toshiba, Ricoh copiers, Nokia, Erickson, Siemens, Honda—lots of banks—ANZ, HSBC, Seabank, ABN AMRO ("twenty-four-hour ATMs!"), and all this mostly in English, which last time I checked was not the national language, at least not yet. Also there are comprehensible but less global ones: VG Pipe (with a helpful picture of a bunch of metal pipes); Viettel Mobile; Maxxis tires; Lady Dutch clothing; Tiger Beer, but no Ba Muoi Ba or "33 Beer," a war-era GI staple when we couldn't get American beer, but this may be only sold in the south. My two favorites were Vietcombank, which I initially misread as "Vietcong Bank" and thought, "Golly, would Uncle Ho approve?"; and a big billboard for the Suzuki Smash motorbike—maybe not the best choice of names. Perhaps it sounds better translated.

Eventually we get closer to the city, and light industrial buildings start appearing behind the rice fields. The Than Long Industrial Park has buildings devoted to Yamaha, Canon, Komatsu, Sakurai. I wonder if this could be *sakura*, the Japanese word for cherry blossom, only misspelled? No, this company, Google tells me later, makes automated offset printing presses—this could be the five hundred-dollar question on *Jeopardy!*— good to know. There are other stand-alone industrial buildings with signs like FINNISH TECHNOLOGY GLASS FABRICATION or ZAMIL STEEL, but no refineries or chemical plants or power plants.

Economic growth doesn't always follow a smooth path. Just on the outskirts of the city stands a large and imposing white marble structure, about the size and shape of two Arc de Triomphes. The big metal letters rolling across the lintel say something in Vietnamese and boldly, in English, INTERNATIONAL CITY. There are on the top of the arch are about a dozen stylized horses that appear to be doing aerobics, manes flying. This is quite an imposing entrance for . . . nothing. The street stops just after one goes through the arch. And then the rice fields start again. It might have been better to build at least a couple of model buildings first before putting up the imposing entranceway, but real estate development is no doubt new to Hanoi.

We go to the AES office rather than checking in to the hotel. We're tough, we don't need sleep. I meet with the staff, a young group who has put together a remarkable project. Warning: some Btu talk follows. Norman Mailer, or maybe Susan Sontag (I get them confused a lot) at one point in his or her career wrote an antiwar tract called "Why Are We in Vietnam?" We are here because they think they need some power plants and some money to build them.

Do they really need the power? The place has 83 million people, the economy is growing at 7%, and they have only 12,000 megawatts of generation. Here are the rules of thumb: Western countries, fully industrialized and with air-conditioning and hot water heaters and hair dryers and toaster ovens and all that have, at a minimum, 1,000 Mw per million people, an easy to remember one-to-one ratio. That is the UK ratio, for example: 60 million people, 58,000 Mw. The US and Australia have more like 3,000 Mw per million people. Rapidly developing countries like China have about a third of this one-to-one average—400,000 Mw for 1.2 billion people. Vietnam is sitting at not a third, but less than 15%. And if you don't believe that, then one of the embassy people remarks to me at one of our meetings, "Well, summer is coming, it's time for the blackouts to start," with the tone of one resigned to the inevitable. We love it when people talk like that.

It is still early in the development cycle. We haven't bought the dancing metal horses for the top of our arch yet. We have just completed the detailed feasibility study; the plant is to be located near Ha Long Bay in the north. Since we have been coming to Vietnam for maybe ten years now, just dropping by when we're in the neighborhood, stopping for a cup of tea, making polite conversation such as, "Say, need any power plants today?" the Vietnamese government has finally taken pity on us and offered us a negotiated, not competed, opportunity to build one. The study is over and we are now about to get into the important part of the transaction, which is negotiating the power purchase agreement, or PPA, the document that says who buys the power, under what terms and conditions, what they pay for it, and so on. It is obviously key to everything else, and we may or may not be successful here. One hopes yes, as we know how to do this, and we know what they're paying for imported power from China, and we can beat that. And we think that we have figured out an important potential advantage, which is to use Chinese manufactured equipment, but manufactured to international designs and standards by Chinese licensees of Western technology. The only small trick in this clever idea is that no one has ever done this before. It's not that the Chinese don't have the manufacturing capability; they have been making power plants like crazy and throwing them up inside China for years now, in standard 600 Mw sizes. But not using international technology, or at least we don't think so. Maybe they have just been "borrowing" the technology, hard to tell. But the cost per kW, which is the way we measure these things, could be in the $600 to $900 range. The alternative, using Western equipment manufactured in Western shops, comes in at $1,200 to as much as $1,800 dollars/kW, even defining "Western shops" to include Korea, Poland, Malaysia, etc. Should we be able to do this, we can apply this new skill in many places and have a real competitive advantage.

We pause now for lesson number two in comparative power plant economics: while the cost of the capital equipment is important, it's not everything. There is the fuel that you burn in the darned thing, and then there is the efficiency of converting that fuel into power. Coal plants cost more per kW, and are a bit less efficient than modern gas-fired plants, but coal costs, on a dollars/Btu basis, about one-fourth what gas costs. Generally accepted costs today for gas in the US are $5.00 to $7.00 per million Btus, and coal is $1.50 to $2.00. Gas plants cost $500 to $800 dollars/kW, and are about 25% more efficient, but the high price of gas means that today no one is building new ones unless they have no access to coal. Just to be honest, I should note that the price of natural gas has been all over the place since I first began working in energy—as high as $9.00/mm Btu and as low as $1.50—and all of it completely unpredictable. Forget oil—current prices are in the $10.00 per million Btu, although it too has jumped around a great deal. No one anywhere in the world is building oil-burning power plants in any quantities. I could also discuss nuclear and hydro and potential CO_2 costs, but you will be thankful to find that will have to be for another letter. You can't have all your treats at once. But that should explain why we are so keen to do this plant with Chinese manufactured equipment, although since this is our business we would be keen to do it anyway, even without the spin-off effects.

I ask our team about any site concerns. Well . . . the plant's exact location is determined by the Vietnamese, who have sensibly placed it near the coal mine. Vietnam has a decent amount of coal, some better quality and some less good. The wily Vietnamese have decided to export the good coal to China, to keep feeding all those 400,000 Mw of Chinese power plants, and to keep the crumby coal and burn it in their own plants. Coal being a high-bulk, low-value commodity, transporting it is always a good idea to minimize, so this makes sense. Plus if you know what coal you are going to burn, you can design the boiler and the fuel handling equipment—stacker, conveyers, pulverizers, environmental clean-up equipment, etc.—to handle that specific type of coal. Coals vary by Btu content per ton (more is good), moisture (more is bad), hardness (more is good), sulfur content (more is bad), and other stuff that we won't go into and I forget. The particular type of boiler we are planning here is called a down-fired boiler, which does not mean that it burns the feathers of aquatic birds. It means that the coal is blown into the boiler shooting downward, and then, as it gets into the combustion zone, reverses direction, and thus has a longer residence period in the hot insides, and a better chance to burn completely, which is good. Like so many power plant trade-offs, this is a slightly more expensive design, but it enables you to use a worse, and thus cheaper, coal. I point out to my colleagues that this is the exact design of our first plant ever, Deepwater in Texas, which came online in the early eighties and thus prevented us from going bankrupt. They are suitably respectful. I feel suitably old.

OK, the site, I didn't forget. The Vietnamese state-owned power company, Electricité de Vietnam, or EVN (well, yes, the name's a hold-over from the French colonial days, I wonder why they didn't change it) is building their own 1,000 Mw plant at the site, at the same time we are to build ours. We will be, technically, Mong Duong #2, while they will be Mong Duong #1. Most of the facilities are not shared, which is a good thing as sharing arrangements are very difficult to work out on paper, and then not easy to operate with. However, they are in charge of the site preparation. In general this means getting rid of the vegetation, doing the grading, etc. "How hard can this be?" one asks. Oh, um, in this case the site is sort of in a river and on a mountain. Odd place to put one, I suggest, but our crew agrees with the Vietnamese engineers that this is really the only feasible location. Now we do have to dig into the side of the mountain, but fortunately we can take the fill from the mountain and dump it into the river, and thus end up with a nice flat site. Oh, did I mention rerouting the river slightly? I note carefully that both plants will be constructed and operated in accordance with World Bank environmental standards, which are in fact quite strict, and as good or better as any in OECD countries. But, me oh my, this amount of civil work is not something that we could easily do anymore in the US, or Europe, or anywhere Greenpeace hangs out. We also probably couldn't build TVA or the Hoover Dam again. Nice to be working in a developing country with clear goals. Also about twen-ty-five families will have to be relocated, but again that is a small problem, we have been assured. I guess there is not a chapter of Friends of the Rivers at work here.

As you can perhaps tell, there are challenges. But it wouldn't be fun without them. I guess.

By now it is relatively late in the day. I have had breakfast on the plane and then lots of coffee and no lunch. It is suggested that I go back to my hotel, then they will send Mr. Hai to pick me up and we will all go out for a Vietnamese dinner. Sounds great to me, but I ask that they just let me walk back to the hotel from the office—it is four or five blocks, but not hard to find. So I set off.

It is absolutely fascinating to be here. I kept saying to myself, both on the drive in and while walking around, "My God, this is really Asia, it's not Hong Kong or Taipei or Bangkok or Shanghai or god forbid Singapore, all cities that could now comfortably be neighbors of Dubai—same big glass skyscrapers, same salary men pacing the streets purposefully and talking into their cells, same impossible lots of traffic, same cleanliness, and the occasional ethnic remnant of a structure—this is really, no kidding, not cleaned up yet, not rich yet Asia." There are many, many motorbikes on the streets, and they probably outnumber the cars by ten to one, but despite this there is really not much traffic. Large, old plane trees still line the major streets (thank you, France), and the buildings with few exceptions are one or two stories, and many look like they have been here a long time—that sort of Euro colonial architecture that prevailed and you still find all over Asia. It is a significantly horizontal city, with countable tall buildings of probably fewer than six—a couple of office buildings, a couple of hotel buildings. I am surprised at all the older buildings. I rather thought that we had bombed Hanoi flat during the war, but that is clearly not the case.

It is always harder to see what is not in the picture than what is. As I walk back I suddenly realize the absence of American commercial culture: No McDonald's, no 7-Elevens, no KFC, no Starbucks. There is very little global brand penetration as far as facilities. Food vendors have carts or small storefronts, and people squat on the sidewalk, eating out of bowls.

I am staying at the Metropole Hotel, one of the two or three Western-style hotels in the city. It was, however, built before the turn of the century, the last century, and has a magnificent dark wood bar with polished wooden floor, open architecture with shutters to keep out the rain when it comes, and slowly revolving ceiling fans. I expect to see Graham Greene sitting in the bar or maybe Somerset Maugham, but then realize that they are both dead. Shucks. It is a neat and atmospheric place. It also has an exercise room with shiny equipment and loud disco music, and high-speed Internet service in the rooms. So there.

Eight of us eat dinner that evening at a wonderful Vietnamese restaurant called the Emperor, where we sit in the courtyard in the middle of the building with several large trees providing shade above us. The food is exquisite, nothing weird as in China, even including what is explained as "morning glory spinach," which I sense is different than morning glories in the US, or else I will go home and plant some. Two of the office staff are Vietnamese women, both of whom function as translators and one as office manager. The latter, Ms. Khanh, is sitting on my right and explains to Haresh, our regional president for Asia, and me what the dishes are. I ask her where she's from. She explains that she is a farm girl and that her father is a teacher in the village about fifty miles from Hanoi, and that he was away for several years during the war, fighting in the south. I note that so was I, and I am glad I never saw him, and the conversation moves on. Seems to be a simple factual matter, with much more interest in the food, and in the fact that Ms. Khanh is worried that she will never find a husband, as her skin is too dark. I am amazed but both the women say that this is an important consideration, and that skin color varies among Vietnamese. You couldn't prove it by me, so I evince modest disbelief. As evidence, they ask if I have noted the many young women on motorbikes, and I agree that I have seen a lot, not only as passengers but just as often as drivers. "What were they wearing?" asks Ms. Huong, the other young woman.

"Well, mostly Western clothes and almost no one was wearing helmets. And they were all wearing face masks or kerchiefs to protect against the dust," I reply. Actually I had noticed this and thought it was pretty funny that some of them looked like outlaws in Western movies.

"Those weren't for the dust," they both say, almost in unison. "Those were to keep their skin from getting tanned so they would look whiter!"

The next morning, the team and I meet for breakfast in the hotel. It is the typical buffet breakfast, except that they have Chinese dim sum and chili paste and black vinegar, and really crispy croissants, and excellent cheeses, and pretty decent sausages with French mustard, and fresh squeezed orange and grapefruit and pineapple juice and good strong French roast coffee. OK, stop that. I do wonder if I shouldn't just hang out here all day and have a lot more breakfast.

But no, serious business stuff calls. Our major local consultant, a very sharp young Vietnamese man named Hoai, is there to discuss the reception for the evening, and the meetings they have arranged for Haresh and I for the day. Mr. Hoai is young, a Harvard Business School grad, and quite capable. Good English and very likable. He apparently not only runs Galaxy Ltd., his consulting and "help the foreigners" company, but now owns several restaurants and a computer business. Lots of room in Vietnam for the young and business trained. We discuss the reception scheduled for the evening in some detail. It becomes clear that our problem is we have not one, but two vice ministers who have agreed to come to our Official Office Opening, one from the Ministry of Industry and one from the Ministry of Planning and Investment. And we are not sure which guy is of higher status, and thus who should speak first at the inevitable "remarks that no one really wants to listen to" part of the program, e.g., "Glad to be here, great day for the company, solidarity with the noble Vietnamese people, high-priority project, pledge our best efforts, blah blah blah" in two or three languages. The guys in our office have already written my speech for me, and it sounds much like that, except I am making up the part about solidarity. So we worry a while about status and rank and local politics and then decide, in the finest tradition of large organizations everywhere, not to decide right now. It is, I will admit, not an issue upon which I believe the future of the project will turn, but everyone else is fretting about it, so I feel the need to show solidarity with our noble project team and fret as well.

Having now been fully briefed and sufficiently fretted, we roll into Being Externally Visible by setting off for a series of meetings. My role here is threefold: to get a better feel for the project, its characteristics and status, and the quality of our team on the ground; to visibly make the rounds of the ministries and assure them—speaking as a high-ranking official of AES—that we are serious about this project and dedicated to carrying it out; and finally, and most importantly, to be the AES high-ranking representative at the Official Office Opening in Hanoi.

Perhaps a small diversion for explanatory purposes is useful. The Vietnamese have been after us for some time to have an Official Office Opening. First we said, "OK, we now have opened an office and there are six people there, and it's official. We'll show you the lease if you want."

Expecting us to have a local office was a reasonable demand, and in fact the only way to do this. Energy project development is a contact sport. You cannot do it from a distance.

"No," they said politely, thinking to themselves, *No, you stupid Americans.* "You must have a ribbon cutting." We were nonplussed. We understood groundbreakings at a plant site, we understood ribbon cuttings when a plant is finished and goes into operation, but for renting some space in an office building? "Yes, surely," they explained, "and you must have a senior person come for the opening and ribbon cutting."

"Can we use the office that we have already rented in the meantime?" we asked. With some exasperation our advisers said that was not the point and of course we could. And besides, the Official Office Opening was not actually held at the offices, it was to be a big reception held at a fancy hotel. Well, naturally. "OK," we said, "we can do it any time, and we can send our regional president to preside, name a date."

"No," they said, "we need an American." Finally we began to get it. Although the president, Haresh, is an American, as is his wife, the lovely and talented Flora, both of whom we hired from the University of Maryland grad school, Haresh was born in India and Flora in China. They wanted someone born in South Carolina. They needed an old white guy—and who better than yours truly? Jeez, finally I am politically correct, except it's in Vietnam.

So off we go. The meetings are typical—most are held in what I think of as "Chinese style" conference rooms—rooms with a series of varying armchairs, usually not very comfortable, set in an open rectangle. The chairs are arranged in clear sets of pairs, and there is frequently a small end table between each set. The two most important persons sit in the two chairs at the end of the room, and the rest of the participants sit as close as possible. There is nothing in the middle of the room except, usually, rug. Now I may be culturally insensitive despite being—for the moment—politically correct, but this is a lousy arrangement for a meeting. Or for anything else except maybe watching the image of Princess Leia appearing in the empty middle of the room to warn us of the approach of the Death Star. You can't really see the person you are there to meet without turning unnaturally sideways in your chair, and the interpreters can't hear, and you can't hear them. But we soldier on.

We meet with our partner, the Vietnamese coal company, or Vinacomin, which sounds like some sort of health tonic but at least isn't French, and with high-level folks from the Ministry of Industry, the Ministry of Planning and Investment, and the Ministry of Foreign Affairs, all of whom have some role in the approval of the project. Remarkably, in only one of the meetings, that with the coal company, is there a picture of Uncle Ho displayed. I am surprised.

The only real "issue" discussed is a request/demand that the US Trade and Development Agency (TDA), an American bit of the Commerce Department which supports foreign trade by giving grants to folks, provide a grant to the Vietnamese so they can hire international project finance lawyers and be represented by same as we negotiate the PPA with them. The number $2.5 million is thrown about, but we suggest that it is not likely to be that large, although we will try. Internally I blanch at the very idea of using up that much money and therefore legal time on the other guys' lawyers, and having my tax dollars fund it. This is strange. However, the Vietnamese clearly are positioning this as a question of support from the US for this project. It would be OK with me if they were going to use the money to help move the river or dig up the mountain, but for lawyers!! Yeesh. Nonetheless, we agree to continue pursuing this important matter.

Later that day we meet with the ambassador, a very nice guy and career Foreign Service Officer named Michael Marine. He is in fact a former marine, and I somehow suspect he had no choice in the matter. I cannot imagine how hard a time he must have had at boot camp with that name, but it would have been worse if he had been in the army. Although he and I are roughly the same age, he was never sent to Vietnam, closest he came was Okinawa. He is knowledgeable, and agrees to send his own message supporting the Vietnamese request through State Department channels to the TDA organization, which is actually located in the US Department of Commerce.

At around noontime all the ministries close down for two hours, another interesting hangover from the days when Parisians ruled. Haresh

wants to make sure I see the Military History Museum, a famous stop
on the tourist loop of Hanoi. I have seen only one tourist group here—
Americans in Bermuda shorts, size large, and no Japanese or Germans.
The president is right: all Americans need to lose thirty pounds. We go
to the museum only to find that it, too, is closed from noon to one-thirty.
OK, they got a few things to learn about dealing with tourists. We wander
around the outside courtyard, looking at the Huey helicopter and the
French tanks and the F-105s captured from our gutless South Vietnamese
allies, and whatnot. Toward the back of the grounds there is a big sculpture
of sorts that is in the image of a fighter plane crashing headfirst into the
ground, and is made of bits of shot down American airplanes. Not particularly subtle, but then we were on the dropping-bombs end, not the being-
dropped-on end of the system. We do find that two small souvenir shops
are open, and while they do not have coffee mugs or refrigerator magnets
or snow globes, they have interesting, inexpensive replicas of propaganda
posters, mostly of the heroic Vietnamese either building the country or
shooting down the American airplanes, as they needed aluminum for their
sculpture industry.

Finally it is time for the Official Office Opening, which is being held
in our very own Metropole Hotel. I must say, in all honesty, I had a bit
of free-floating dread about this, but it is a hell of a party. I have been to
more than a few equivalent functions, some ours, some of politicians or
suppliers, and this is one of the very best. The good Mr. Hoai has organized things to a fare-thee-well. There is a wonderful sign across the back
about AES and the office opening, in flawless English and (I hope) flawless Vietnamese. We have name tags for all of us and for all the guests, and
the letters are, for a change, big enough to read. Each guest gets not only
a name tag, but a small red rose pinned to his coat, or her dress. Mr. Hoai
has arranged for a flock of six or seven, yes, I did notice, model-quality
beautiful Vietnamese young women to serve as hostesses, checking people
in, pinning on name tags, etc. They are all wearing bright red silk ao dais
so they stand out, but they would be hard to miss if they were wearing
Siberian prison garb. But it is all absolutely innocent and straightforward.
The hotel has done an exceptional job with the food and drink, there are

more than enough bars plus waiters circulating with water and juice and wine, the food is a mixture of Western and Chinese and Vietnamese all exquisitely displayed, and everything is in small enough sizes that you don't have to cut anything up—another frequent problem with cocktail receptions. I am very impressed, and I don't impress easily. Our local folks are busy working the crowd and introducing me to the right people and it is all quite well done. There are lots and lots of people in attendance, some of whom have come from as far away as Singapore and Indonesia. Many Westerners, local reps of suppliers, law firms, accounting firms, and the like, but also regional presidents and office heads. I am surprised and impressed. This is quite a high-quality group. And then . . .

Paul, our CEO, and I have a running joke that no one else seems to have tumbled to. Almost anytime he goes anywhere, to an out-of-US AES function or someone else's function, if there is food and drink, there is "entertainment," and we use quotation marks advisedly. The entertainment is almost always what we have taken to referring to as "native touristic dancers." Sure enough, in the middle of this really nice party, with really interesting people to talk to, there is the sound of beating drums and the master of ceremonies announces that it is time for the Drum Dancers of Quang Ninh. I try hard not to laugh. "Quang Ninh," I think coincidentally, "is the province where the plant will be located." Onto the stage leap six nice young Vietnamese men, each carrying an Asian (Quang Ninh?) version of conga drums. They are wearing yellow silk pants and open silk vests—no doubt the native costume of Quang Ninh. They beat on the drums for a while. They flip their drumsticks, which are really just sticks, into the air and catch them eight times out of ten and go back to pounding. It's loud. Finally the dancers appear on the small stage. So we have young men beating on drums, young women clad in yellow satin pajamas with bright red trim doing dance routines that probably wouldn't have made it past round one on *Dancing with the Stars*, complete with much swishing of long black hair. In essence it's the Dallas Cowboys Cheerleaders do Hanoi. I am bemused. When there has been enough hair tossing to give one a stiff neck for a week, the dancers and drummers leave the stage. To prolonged applause.

But now it is time for the dreaded Official Office Opening speeches. Ambassador Marine speaks excellently, telling the Vietnamese that the feasibility study is complete, we have determined we can do the project competitively and they need the power, so let's get on with it. The "problem" with having too many vice ministers has resolved itself, as one after another they came up with conflicts, so now we have only office directors present, but that's fine. The woman from Foreign Affairs gives a nice speech, the head of the coal company gives a nice speech, the Ministry of Industry guy gives a nice speech, all carefully translated into English for us gringos. Then it's my turn.

I have been worrying about this. I really dislike canned speeches (probably that's the ego in me), and I discussed this with Haresh and Ravi, who is our local project director, and Mr. Hoai: How do we handle the Vietnam veteran part of this? I surely cannot just deny I was ever here before. After some temporizing we come up with a plan, and now it's showtime. I make all the obligatory acknowledgements and remarks. About halfway through the "glad to be here, important project for the company" stuff, I pause, look carefully out at the audience, and say, "It is important for me to add a personal note to all this. Many people have politely asked me if this was my first trip to Hanoi, and it is. But it is not my first trip to Vietnam. I first came here thirty-eight years ago. I was wearing a different suit of clothes, I was working for a different organization, and I had a different business plan. That plan was not successful. I believe that our current business plan is a much better one, and one that will provide more benefits for my company, for the United States, and for the Vietnamese people."

The remarks were well received. We all stayed until all the food was eaten and the last guest left. It was a great party.

Friday morning I got up, had a final breakfast—dim sum (bao and shumai) and an almond croissant and salami and cheese and olives. And coffee. If that ain't international, what is? The ever-faithful Mr. Hoai took me to the airport for the long flight home.

Love and kisses,
Bob

Afterword: AES had an excellent team working on the Mong Duong plant in Hanoi, as I indicated above. It was eventually successfully financed and constructed. The construction process was one of the best in the history of the company, especially as far as safety is concerned. The plant, at 1,240 Mw, is the largest thermal plant in the AES portfolio, and began commercial operation in May of 2015, a mere nine years after my visit there.

chapter
twelve

Why You Need or Don't Need a Personnel Department

March 2007

Dear Dad,
Herein a second collection of vignettes from Arlington, as we go about our daily business. Strangely.

How to Hire People, Version 1
Our executive office meeting yesterday morning started without all the players, as Brian, the general counsel and Jay, our head of human resources, were busy firing our assistant controller who had been on board for two weeks. His background check revealed he had lied on his application about a company he worked at for six years (we could find no evidence that it had ever existed), and his residence, and possibly his name. Also one of his previous employers—listed as a reference!—had issued a press release in 2003 stating that he was being terminated for failing to disclose a previous criminal conviction on his job application.

Hey, do we know how to pick 'em or what? One might ask why we brought him on board before the background check was complete, or why someone didn't do a simple Google search on his name. Did I mention there was a PRESS RELEASE? We need smarter hiring practices or people.

At least we didn't wait until he knifed someone or ran down the hall naked or stole all the money (what little there is). Life sure is interesting is these here big companies.

How to Hire People, Version 2

We attempted to hire a retired admiral, three stars, someone that Paul had at one point actually worked for and liked a lot. But we forgot that we were not the Defense Department. Silly us.

David, a skillful and smart manager and our head of North American operations, was the executive trying to bring the admiral on board, using exactly the ideas and processes and expectations that we use for everyone. Note also that finding a high-level job in private industry in a company that is both established and growing, in a hot area, is something most serious out-of-work executives would kill for, and isn't that easy. That said, you won't believe the message—an actual excerpt—about the guy and his reasons for quitting after five days on the job:

- *It is not going to be a fit. AES is too "flexible," "ambiguous," "unstructured" for him. We went thru the entire issue of why I thought he would be a good fit because he will help move AES towards more structure and process (which we need) without overdoing it.*
- *He feels overwhelmed at the amount of information we have dropped on him in a short period of time.*
- *He is tired and should have taken more time off between change of command and starting. He feels that sending him the prereads before he started exacerbated this. He feels tired from having to fly here and hit the ground running after no real interim time off and that while he feels we pressured him a bit, he should not have agreed to the schedule/ start date.*
- *He would have preferred to have had an orientation that had meetings in the morning and left the p.m. free to assimilate the information.*

- *He is frustrated at the lack of "infrastructure" to support him (e.g., IT, travel, an AA) and concerned about the prospect of starting the Houston office on his own (although he volunteered that some of these are in the "whine" category). He said each admin step of getting started has been "painful," from IT to HR paperwork to Amex card. He also felt like the travel schedule expected of him was tough.*
- *He alluded to the fact that he feels like we shorted him a bit on the $ offer relative to his friend who went to Florida Power & Light (and I suspect his friend got more infrastructure) and the relocation policy (which does not cover his house closing costs at this end as he is currently a renter and not an owner).*
- *The ambiguity over the precise role during the recruiting process concerned him. He also felt we imposed on him to have to fly to Denver for the shrink (and in some other minor ways as well).*

David carefully and reasonably told said admiral that the issues sounded like near-term ones that we can fix. He apologized for the onboarding process flaws (which many others have survived just fine), and politely suggested that his reaction feels disproportionate. If he needs a reset we offered to just have a time-out for a month so he can get the needed time off. He said he felt like the issues are indicators of how AES is overall and he is not at all comfortable at all with the fit, hence still wanted to quit. He told his wife that he dreaded coming to work today and she said she had never heard him ever say that before.

The next time you have personnel problems at a start-up company, just note that you are not alone. . . . You have only been on board five days and you "dread" coming to work? Give me a break . . . some of us wondered how in the world this guy ever got to be an admiral.

At least he wasn't a felon.

How to Hire a Consultant

Since we had so much fun with star-rank ex-military people, it was suggested to us by one of our board members that we meet with General Wesley Clark, since he could be helpful to us in Kosovo, where we were interested in doing power plant business. Thus when I ran into one of his key aides at a Renaissance Weekend in Utah in August, the idea was reborn.

The theory of the case was simple: the leadership of Kosovo, under the meddlesome tutelage of the United Nations, supplemented by the thoroughly unrealistic kibitzing of the World Bank, had figured out that they didn't have much going for them other than a large supply of really lousy lignite, a fuel we laughingly designate as "coal," but which is really about halfway between real coal and wood. But it's cheap, they have a lot of it, and the Kosovars wanted someone to come and build a big mine, rehabilitate their two lousy old power plants, and build them a shiny new big one to use the lignite and sell all the new power into the EU.

There were some shortcomings to this idea. First, this is a very costly and ambitious project, probably on the order of 2–3 billion euros or more. No project of this size has ever been done anywhere in eastern Europe. There is very little market for the power in Kosovo itself, and you can be pretty sure that the Serbs aren't likely to buy any of it, as they are still quite hacked off at the EU and the US for bombing the crap out of them and in essence liberating Kosovo, formerly a nicely repressed province of Serbia.

And there is the annoying geopolitical reality that Kosovo is not a country yet, so any guarantees by the government of Kosovo, which would be necessary to support the whole entity, would be made by, um, who exactly? Full faith and credit of the UN? With their budget deficit? And who would guarantee that any permits issued by—who exactly?—would be valid once the place became a real country? And can you get political risk insurance against expropriation by an entity that at the moment has no expropriating capability? Many interesting questions. Despite this, we had made just such a proposal to them about a year ago, although on a somewhat more modest and doable scale.

But no! The UN steps in with its all-knowing approach, aided by the World Bank. "This must be a competitive tender!" decreed the midlevel bureaucrats. And you must demonstrate the ability to mine 20 million tons of coal per year or you cannot even qualify to bid. Note that 20 million tons of anything is a lot, and of coal it is about three-quarters of what a really big utility, like TVA, uses in a year. And it was not being proposed that anyone was building the TVA in Kosovo. We suggested that maybe two million tons was a more reasonable number, much closer to what the new plant would actually need, and maybe the "20" in the draft documents was a typo. But our attempts to point out this anomaly fell on deaf ears, all of them stuck in the sides of the heads of not very bright international civil servants and "we know what's best for 'these people'" do-gooders.

Hence Paul and I found ourselves sitting in a meeting with the aforementioned General Clark, former head of NATO, retired four-star general, Rhodes scholar, and unsuccessful Democratic candidate for president. He was not large, actually about my size, dressed in a well-tailored charcoal-gray suit. Small hands, very gentle handshake. He was accompanied by an associate named Mike, who had worked with the general when he was in Belgium running NATO and, now retired, had thrown in his lot with Wesley K. Clark & Associates. He had, for some reason, a Hotmail address. Maybe he wanted to get all that e-mail on mortgage refinancing and body part enhancement.

Because we aren't total dummies, at least not all the time, we already had an "international helper" on our team, a guy named Bill, who had been ambassador to Serbia during the very same war that Gen. Clarke had run. We had him come to the meeting. It was even funnier than one would have anticipated.

The two of them greeted each other warily, and it was clear, as we expected, that they knew each other. The meeting began, and what followed was a very high-level game of who knew who or what more than the other guy. Clark would mention someone he knew in the Kosovo hierarchy, defined to include the World Bank and the UN, and Bill would respond that he had met with said person last week. Bill would suggest influencing Minister XYZ, and Clark would say that he was the godfather to XYZ's daughter. Clark said things like, "They love me in Kosovo," and Bill would say, "Except for the ones whose houses you bombed." You can see how it went. Paul and I just sat back and watched.

My favorite line was when Bill said, "You know, Wes, I'll never forget the time I called you from Pristina and said how bad things were getting for the Kosovars. Of course, it took a while for the call to go through since

they had to go get you off a golf course in Brussels. You said I should
fly to Belgium and brief you. So I did. You listened carefully, you asked
really good and thoughtful questions, and then you told me to go back
to Serbia and carry on. When I asked what you would do if the situation
deteriorated further, as it was clearly going to do, you said, 'Bill, keep me
informed, but there's not a thing that I can do for you.'"

It was priceless. Finally after all the parading around and leg lifting to
see who could pee on the tallest tree, we did discuss, at least for a couple
of moments, our little 20 million ton problem. Both parties averred that
this should be easily fixed. Clark suggested that he could also help us in
Kazakhstan, although what kind of help was unclear since he had never,
to our knowledge, bombed any of the Stans. The meeting ended with the
general certain of his ability to help, and his staff interested in following
up. On our side we said we needed to think about it. Paul and I each got
nice thank-you notes from the general, which was a classy touch. I would
have expected him only to correspond with the CEO.

Over the next several days we worked out a contingent arrangement
whereby Clark & Associates would go to Kosovo, work their magic, and
get the foolish qualification changed. When they did so, we would pay
them a $10K success fee, and consider them for more business.

It is interesting to note that the general's guys, with whom I was negotiating, said initially that the general would prefer to be paid the $10K up
front and then see what he could do. My response, politely rendered, was
"Well of course he would, honey! We all would! But we want some real
work done here; this is not just showing up and making a speech. If we
wanted that we would have hired Colin Powell." I couldn't help myself.

So what happened? Clark Associates sent the aforementioned Mike
to Kosovo, not the general, and he made the rounds to the predictable
players—the US ambassador, the minister of energy, the UN factotum,
the nasty and arrogant World Bank person, the commissioner of privatization—and sent back a brief report. Mike said, basically, "I met with a
bunch of people, they all said it's too late, this will be really hard to do."

I had several long conversations with the general's staff. I suggested, as
politely and as dispassionately as I could, that we really hadn't thought we

were contracting to get an FSO Grade Seven to represent us, not even a retired ambassador, and that what we expected was that the general should get off his butt and get over to Kosovo and make this happen. I was ensured that this would be discussed with said general. I suppose it was.

But at the end of the day, after the prequalification documents had gone from draft to final, with the 20 million ton requirement still clear as a bell, the general had in fact not gone to Kosovo. He may have been too busy helping the Democrats take back the Senate.

He did finally make a phone call to the US executive director of the World Bank, asking for a delay of the bids. I don't know why, exactly, since this wouldn't do us any good. And we had already decided to link up with a Czech company and bid jointly, since they could meet the mining requirement, but not the financial strength requirement, and our situation was vice versa. It is interesting to note that the Czechs have hired former secretary of state Madeleine Albright as their international helper. I'm just glad we're not paying her. At least she's not a general or an admiral. Or a guy.

Love and kisses,
Bob

Afterword: We never built a huge, new coal-fired power plant in Kosovo, and despite all the "help" of the World Bank, no one else did either. We never paid the general a dollar for his invaluable assistance in finding out that this project was difficult.

You don't always do that well in dealing with famous people. At least we never tried to hire General Petraeus and his girlfriend.

chapter
thirteen

Singapore, It's So Clean You Can Eat off the Streets, Except They'll Throw You in Jail

April 2007

Dear Dad,

Off to Asia, middle of March—I am sitting in the Singapore Airlines executive lounge on a Sunday night in mid-March and NOT watching the Oscars, unlike most of America. I have an eighteen-hour flight ahead of me, on Singapore Airlines, nonstop from Newark to Singapore. I am pretty impressed that you can fly that far on a commercial airliner without running out of fuel. Because of global warming, it turns out that we in Maryland now live at the North Pole. It snowed in Potomac all morning and all afternoon, so I decided to take the train to Newark rather than risk flying out of Dulles, where half the flights were announced as delayed, and the ones listed as "on time" were lies. And when I got to New Jersey, it was cold and snowing here too, as the North Pole seems to be following me.

I may stay in this lounge forever, it's warm and they have a very nice Sauvignon Blanc and mixed olives and cheese sticks! No peanuts for some reason, however. People are strange, I have sagely concluded. In the fancy

airport lounge in Madrid, they had small red-colored aluminum foil envelopes that said on the outside, in clear yellow letters, FRUITS SEC. We all
know from our childhood Spanish that this means dried fruit, so I passed
it up, cursing gently to myself that this must be some sort of Spanish
perversion, and they really like sweet and chewy bits of apricot and pear
and apple with their drinks. Well, no. I finally watched some people open
the red envelopes and eat the contents, and they were PEANUTS! Boy
was I mad. How come they call those dried fruit, I for one would like
to know? Are the Spaniards conspiring against us to keep the peanuts
for themselves? And it wasn't like there was that much more to eat there
except some cookies, which do not go so well with wine no matter what
the Mondavi brothers tell you.

Why Singapore, with its lovely tropical climate, one might ask?
Because it's not the North Pole, one might answer. But really, our story
begins about three weeks ago when the regional president for Asia walked
into the CEO's office for his annual evaluation. This is the obligatory
meeting to review the previous year's performance and discuss compensation earned therefore. Us big executives get salaries, but we also get
bonuses and long-term compensation (stock options and the like) that
are in general supposed to reflect what a good or bad job we have done
during the past year in keeping the shareholders happy by us responsibly
managing their assets. People tend to prepare carefully for such meetings,
as we are talking about real money here.

"So," says the regional president, "I liked AES better in the old days,
now there are lots of people in Arlington telling us what to do, it's hard,
so I quit."

This was not, to say the least, what anyone would have anticipated for
the beginning of the meeting. Nor had anyone been hinting to this person
that we didn't like him and maybe he should go elsewhere.

"So I'll take the severance package, and what about my bonus for last
year?" he adds cheerfully.

There follows something of a stunned silence on Paul's part. I am sure
that what to do in such a situation is part of the Harvard Business School's
curriculum, but maybe Paul was rusty. Finally, after several moments of

conversation in which he endeavors to determine if the RP is serious, Paul says, "Well, there are a couple of problems here. First, if you quit, you don't get any severance. Second, if you're not going to be around, then it's unlikely that I will use any of the bonus pool on you. I think I should instead reward the people who stick around and get their jobs done."

I won't go into the rest of the subsequent odd discussions, but this was considered quite a strange and weird turn of events. Hence we all finally decided that we would remove the executive from his job, since he had already quit and clearly he didn't much want to do it anyway, and we should find someone else to take his place. But in the meantime, we had a region to run. I was asked to go and hold things together until a new person is recruited and arrives, and since I am an accommodating type and they pay me, here I am in Newark. And, in a mere eighteen straight airborne hours from now, Singapore.

Interesting things about Singapore not related to work—it is hot and sweaty and rainy here. And not just little, cute, misty, *Singin' in the Rain*-Gene Kelly dancing around Paris with an umbrella-type rain, but serious buckets of deluge. Umbrellas are plentiful and routinely carried by all. Of course, we are about eleven inches from the equator, so this is probably justified. OK, maybe that's not so interesting.

There are lots and lots and lots of malls and shopping plazas and shopping centers and shops and kiosks, etc., all with shopping in their name and as their avowed purpose, and many of them are interconnected—like in Minneapolis—so that if you're clever you can travel for miles and never go outside. I don't know who buys all the stuff but it's mostly clothing and places to eat. This is a city serious about its food and wearing apparel.

I have a small serviced apartment with an air-conditioner that I cannot figure out how to turn off and a stove that I can't turn on. Also small ants. I don't know if they can work the stove either. So I found a hardware store to get something for the ants. I could not help but notice as I cruised the shelves that while most of the bottles in the "insecticides and poisons" section were modest in height and volume, there was something that looked like a half gallon of milk, labeled SNAKE REPELLENT.

You may recall that when dining at truly authentic Chinese restaurants for dim sum, one of the dishes available on the little metal carts they push by is chicken feet. I have tried these and, really, there is not anything you can actually eat. It's all gristle and bones and toenails. I now note for the record that at many of the local restaurants you can also order "Thai style chicken feet." I honestly do not believe that there is a need in the world for two different chicken feet recipes.

The yogurt section of the small supermarket near the apartment has both aloe vera- and pink grapefruit-flavored yogurt. And here I thought aloe vera was a lotion or maybe a houseplant that never died. Or a character in *The Rocky Horror Picture Show*.

Some of the folks in our office told me that it was easy to walk home to the apartment. So like a goon I tried it. "How hard can it be," I thought, "since the apartment is on the river?" It turns out that we now have data: no one in Singapore actually knows where the Singapore River is. But you can get exceptionally cranky and sweaty trying to find it. I decided to get a compass before I tried this again. By the way, I saw very few persons out walking. They know better.

It's not your grandma's China anymore—we have a good-sized office in China, which was high on my list of places to visit, so I went. I had not been there for any serious length of time in probably ten years. It should not be surprising that even if one starts with a small base, ten years of 10% economic growth makes a big difference, thanks in part to the miracle of compounding. But it is surprising anyway.

Thank God there is somewhat less smoking, especially less smoking in meetings, but at the banquets there are still packs of cigarettes laid down at every place setting.

More cars than ever before, lots more cars, and lots more traffic and more coming, I am sure. All the bicycles and all the motorcycles of the early years have gone away and been replaced by cars. When we first started coming to China in 1991, Beijing had one "ring road," a sort of beltway around the city. There are now six. We can't even build a second one in Washington, although it has been on the planning agenda for thirty years.

At all our meetings, it is clear that the Chinese we meet with are much better dressed. For one thing, they have abandoned the charming habit of prior years, which was leaving the labels on the sleeves of their suit jackets, not the price and size labels, but the ones that say ADOLFO or BRIONI or other fake Italian names. At these same meetings, however, if you ask for green tea you still get a cup of it with all the leaves floating on the top. This poses certain etiquette questions, like, how do you drink this? Do you use your tongue to kind of push the leaves out of the way? What if a leaf gets stuck on your lip; is it polite to remove it with your fingers? Then where do you put it? I asked Paul about this and he said he just eats the leaves. A wise practice.

And still the instant coffee. In our offices in both Singapore and Beijing, when you rummage around in the kitchen, all you can find are hot water and jars of Nescafé instant coffee. If you ask for coffee at a meeting, you get instant coffee. I do not understand this. There are, however, 150 Starbucks in Beijing, and I bet there are that many in Singapore. And thank God for that.

We are seriously considering an investment in a Chinese wind farm. One of the things I was to do in Beijing was to meet the partner who is selling us 49% of his interest in the project. I did not have a chance to go to the site although others have, so I am pretty confident they have windmills (unless they showed us someone else's). At the meeting the potential partner, an investment firm called Guohua, impresses one as a straight shooter, and this is remarkably rare in China. Here's a silly but important example. We walk into meeting, sit down, get tea, exchange business cards, and start. The Guohua folks bring in a slide projector and launch into a PowerPoint presentation on their company—what they do, where they are, what their numbers look like, and then more explicitly with maps of their wind sites, how much capacity they have, how much is in development, etc. OK, you may be saying to yourself, "Is there a point here?" Yes. I must have been to more than a hundred such introductory meetings with a hundred potential partners on a hundred potential business opportunities in China, and this is the FIRST TIME anyone has ever showed me what I would characterize as a Western style, straightforward, PowerPoint presentation. I have never seen one in China before ever.

The St. Regis hotel next to our office has excellent high-speed Internet service, and a truly beautiful and large fitness center. You could be in New York but the Internet service would be not as good. But . . . the Holiday Inn in Hefei, capital of Anhui Province (described as "small, inland, and rural") also has excellent Internet service and a very nice fitness center. Wow.

It's not all sweetness and light. The Anhui provincial authorities are trying to shut down our plant in Hefei, the capital city. So off we go to Hefei to discuss this with them. Fortunately we have a very strong contract that will create significant costs for them if they shut us down. Once we finish litigating, that is, and get the award, and then litigate over collecting the award. Perhaps we can negotiate a more sensible outcome.

During our discussion with the Anhui Electric Power Supply Bureau they launch into a traditional refrain: we are poor country, our people are not wealthy, they cannot pay their electric bills so please don't enforce your contract. I note to myself that we are sitting in the lavish eighteenth-floor conference room of a brand-new and very elegant glass skyscraper that the power bureau has built for itself. And we will be going to dinner at a fancy Chinese restaurant at a local hotel that they also own. I think the "we are so poor" act may be wearing thin.

We go to the obligatory Chinese banquet with members of the power bureau. There is lot of the wretched Chinese brandy called mao-tai (not to be confused with mai tais, a perfectly good Hawaiian drink) but no one insists that I drink it, so I don't. I select the local beer instead, but it is surprisingly weak. There is, as the evening goes on, much toasting and much hilarity. I am the only Westerner and the translating is fitful. It is OK, however, as there are no insects, and no snake on the menu. The local regional specialty is bamboo, not the little slices you get in cans at the Safeway, but whole big chunks of it, pieces of the stalk a couple of inches around and six inches long, like you could harvest from your backyard. You peel off the outer layers and eat the inside. It's OK but a little fibrous. Kind of like eating a young pine tree but not as resinous. And it's better than the sea cucumbers by a long shot.

There are two big pieces of news at the national level while I am in Beijing, since the National Party Congress is having its biennial session. One is the passage of a law allowing private property. I am not quite sure how they have gotten this far without same, but everyone seems to think this is a fine thing, and I agree. There is also a change in the tax laws for tax equalization. What this means is that foreign joint ventures are no longer tax advantaged. So much for courting foreign investment.

In the Beijing airport, I see something I have never seen anywhere before—advertisements painted right on the moving slabs of the luggage carousels. This is pretty darned creative, actually. But the planes are all jammed, every seat taken, and there is really, truly, no leg room, and nasty food. I am working on a theory that something about the physics or chemistry of it all means that it is impossible to have good cooked food in an airplane. By anyone, anywhere. Well, except for Vietnam Air and the dumplings. But they'll learn soon enough.

Also at the St. Regis hotel in Beijing, I try room service, and am delighted to find Wiener schnitzel on the menu. But when I call room service the person responding says, politely, "And how would you like that cooked?" I switch to spaghetti.

And best of all in the capital of Anhui Province, at a normal, big, semi-fancy Chinese restaurant in Hefei, at a big lunch at a round table, with two of our Chinese partners, we were served—crisply fried thin rectangles of pork! It was just like bacon except for the almost square size of the pieces and it wasn't smoked. So either the Chinese invented bacon (along with gunpowder and the Internet) or the evil Hemphill family influence has penetrated this tiny backwater town of 4 million.

Indubitably Dubai

From Beijing I fly to Dubai where we have an office covering the Middle East, which we define as being part of Asia. I don't think we have told the Asians this, however.

Everyone who goes to Dubai remarks on how much construction is going on, including me in a previous letter, and they're right—25% of the world's cranes are here. It is even more than when I was here a year ago, a level of wretched excess that I never thought could be exceeded. But never bet against excess, other than in a monastery in Bhutan.

Unfortunately, 25% of the world's road graders are not here, so when all these buildings are finished, there is going to be a traffic problem the likes of which will never before have been seen. Same roads, twenty-seven times the office space and apartments—could be a problem. One does wonder idly who will buy these apartments and rent this office space? Who will make the electricity to cool and light these buildings? We can handle the second part of this at least. And they'll need a lot of electricity since the traffic will prevent anyone from ever leaving his or her building.

Yes, you can go skiing indoors in the desert. And people do. Snowboarding too, and they rent you the whole package, including the clothing, so all the skiers have the same outfits. And you can watch them. And the indoor skiing facility, a big five story tall but gentle slope, is built into the Mall of the Emirates, the largest shopping mall in Dubai, so you can come off the slopes and go shopping. And every luxury brand name that one has ever heard of is here in the mall. Perhaps this is the world of the future.

Much of the building that is going on is being organized into "cities." Health Care City, Internet City (what's the point here?), Media City, but only Knowledge Village. I don't see why knowledge got shortchanged, but there you have it. And unlike most of the Middle East, there are very few mosques in evidence, and only a scattering of women in full chador in the malls or on the streets. No Religion City. At least not yet.

A Weekend in Indonesia

Because we are a wussy company, we don't make people work over the weekend, which leaves me with time on my hands. I arrange to go to Yogyakarta to see two World Heritage sites I have always wanted to see, the Borobudur and the Prambanan Temples. I don't much like going by myself, but it doesn't seem reasonable to ask someone to fly eighteen hours each way just to spend the weekend climbing around an ancient ruin in the hot sun. Better to save your chips.

When I left Dubai, there was a huge mess at the airport. The day previously, a Bangladesh Airlines flight had slid off the end of the runway rather than taking off. As a pilot you may remember that this is not standard procedure. It caused all sorts of cancelled flights, and things were still being very slowly and ineptly sorted out the next morning. And here I thought Emirates airline knew what it was doing. Jakarta has had, in the month before I went, at least three fatal airline crashes, the most recent one of a Garuda plane that went off the runway at Yogyakarta, the very same airport into which I am flying. Plane broke up and caught fire, and all those in business class were killed. The back of the plane was safe. Nonetheless, I go. I figure that the pilots on Garuda Airlines (named for the sunbird of Hindu mythology, peculiar name to choose in an Islamic country) will now be extra careful flying into this airport.

We land and take off entirely safely. And I notice with some curiosity that I do not see the burned-out shell of an airliner on the end of the runway. Of course, leaving it around would not really be good for the morale of the passengers.

To be a cool traveler, it is important to call this city "Yogya" and not by its full name. I don't know why there are both a Jakarta and a "Jogjakarta" as it is sometimes spelled, and after asking a couple of people and getting blank stares, I decide to adopt a Buddhist view of the matter—being is nothingness or possibly the world is an illusion, or at least these two cities are an illusion. The city and the surroundings are distinctly Asian but not big-city Asian—lots of motorcycles; much immediate greenery (rice) between the buildings; no particular clarity between the city and the suburbs and the countryside; the normal welter of small, open-front Asian shops; and very little English in the signs. And warm and lots of flowers. Very limited number of head scarves in evidence, and I see maybe one full chador in two days.

Borobudur is a ninth-century Buddhist temple, a very large stone structure, in essence a square pyramid of five levels. All around each level are amazing bas-relief panels, each probably three feet by nine feet, a very large amount of stone carving. And set into the walls in many, many niches and arches, usually above the strips of panels, are 504 images of Buddha. I did not count them, but there are a lot. They vary slightly depending on the direction they are facing and the level of the temple. Probably two-thirds are damaged to some extent—missing heads, missing arms, but many are perfect. It is impressive and beautiful. My guide keeps wanting to go on up to the next level but I insist on seeing every one of the carvings. After all, this is why I came. Unfortunately he is not very good at reading them, and I do not have a book to elaborate. But you can see that it is the life of Buddha. And that assembling such an enormous and elaborately detailed structure took a huge amount of manpower and many carvers. Impressive. It has also fallen down a bit in several earthquakes and been carefully reconstructed, initially by the Dutch, which is equally impressive.

Prambanan Temple, where I go the next day, is nice but has been damaged by a recent earthquake, so you cannot get very close to it or walk on or into any of the six large individual structures. This lessens the impact, although it too is elaborately carved, but this time in Hindu style, with the story of the *Ramayana* depicted on all the many bas-relief panels set in the base of each temple. There is an interesting video in a theater on the grounds. Once the narrator finishes lambasting greedy industrialists for spoiling everything—why this is part of the video is never very clear, I don't think greedy industrialists make earthquakes—she sets forth in some detail the story of the *Ramayana*, tying it to the various panels that you could not get close enough to see. I concentrate hard on this, since (a) it is famous, and (b) I paid a dollar to sit in this nice theater in the air-conditioning and watch a DVD. However, although it seems to be a long and convoluted and interesting story, I am no doubt too much of a greedy industrialist as I can't find much of a moral in it or deduce any particular religious instruction. Yet it is widely lauded as a Hindu epic. Hanuman and his army of monkeys are nice.

An added bonus—both sites have immaculate grounds and beautiful tropical plantings, in many cases with the particular plants carefully labeled. Second bonus—I am the only Westerner at Prambanan, one of only three or four at Borobudur. Third bonus—the Hyatt hotel where I stay is beautiful, with elaborate water features, overwhelming tropical plantings, gracious service, and good Internet connections. Gosh, you can surf the web from your balcony as you watch the plumeria blossoms drop into the many pools. Fourth bonus—generally things are inexpensive. A guide and a nice car and a driver for six hours was fifty bucks. But the wine is expensive. A non-bonus—on Saturday evening we have the dreaded native touristic dancers, or NTDs, as Paul and I have taken to calling them. Not to be confused with STDs.

A Visit to Palm Oil Land

As I may have told you, we are getting seriously into the business of creating greenhouse gas offsets and selling them to people who need them, principally the Europeans. There is a whole complicated story here, but in simplest terms:

»   The Kyoto Protocol of 1995, whose longer name is "The United Nations Framework Convention on Climate Change," create, for the industrialized nations who have signed on, overall caps on the amount of CO_2 and the five other greenhouse gasses (GHGs) that can be emitted. The overall absolute amount of GHGs allowed each year is chopped up, first into an amount for each country, and then within the country into an amount for each major emitting facility, such as a power plant. Each year the particular plant has to report on how it met its limit, and if it is over the limit, there is a fine of 40 euros per ton before 2008 and 100 euros per ton of CO_2 thereafter. Since power plants emit a lot, this can be a bunch of money. A 200 Mw coal plant, running 85% of the time, would emit 15 million tons in a year, for example.

»   This is what's called a "cap and trade" system, so the power plant has two choices—either simply reduce its output of power, since there is no good way to take the CO_2 out of the exhaust and stuff it somewhere, at least not as of yet; or purchase the reductions someone else has made if he can make them more cheaply than you can. That is the "trade" part.

»   To further complicate matters, reductions below the regulated cap from regulated plants are OK to sell in the industrialized countries, but there are other sources of CO_2 and other GHG emissions from many types of facilities. For example, decomposing animal wastes (OK, pig poop) generate methane naturally as they degrade. Methane is one of the GHGs, and is twenty-one times as troublesome as CO_2. Hence, if you can capture and dispose of methane you can earn twenty-one times the credits or allowances that you can for eliminating CO_2.

» The final complication is that, while some 180 countries have signed the Kyoto Protocol, only 34 of them are actually subject to the limitations—the EU and certain other industrialized nations, e.g., Japan. And you cannot do the nonregulated source reductions in the 34 countries, but you can do them in the other 146 less-developed locations. If this all works right, this can amount to a massive wealth transfer from the developed countries to the less developed countries. And a real reduction in greenhouse gasses.

It took us a while to understood all the jargon and all the rules, which we needed to do as we have plants in Europe that are subject to them. Then it struck us and some other enterprising companies that there might be a most interesting line of business here—making allowances, called "carbon emission reductions" or "CERs," certified by the UN—in third world countries. So we have set ourselves up in the business and are now aggressively seeking such opportunities. Since the palm oil waste decay process is chemically similar to animal waste decay, only it produces more methane per square mile (and smells better), we are building a business around palm oil.

"Huh?" you say, reasonably, "how does that work?"

Palm oil is made by a crushing/pressing process from the nuts of the oil palm (rather than from chocolate chip cookies or old flip-flops, for example, hence the name), in modest factories or mills. This process uses steam as well as mechanical grinding, crushing, banging, shaking, and whatnot sorts of processes, and there is a lot of stuff left over once you have the oil separated—in fact you get only about 18%–22% oil by weight out of a bunch of palm oil fruits. There is some wastewater and much organic matter produced, and this is treated in a series of open lagoons, rather than just dumping all the muck into a local river. This treatment amounts to letting the waste sit in the lagoon and decompose with the help of some anaerobic bacteria. And yes, you get methane gas from the process, which until we discovered global warming was not considered a problem. To fix this, one just covers the lagoons, collects the gas that arises naturally from there, and flares it. Then take your credits and sell them to the Dutch for 15 euros a ton. Nifty, huh?

When you say to most of us at AES "240 Mw CCGT" (a particular type of power plant) a whole file of information opens up in our heads, since this is the business we have been in for twenty-six years. We know what this kind of plant looks like, we know what it costs, we know where to buy the equipment for it, we know how long it takes to construct, we know how efficient it is or should be, we know the fuels it can burn, and so forth. When you say to us "30 million ton/year palm oil mill," the file that opens has no data in it. It was in an attempt to populate our mental files with this data that we set up a trip to a mill and offset-producing location for Paul. Nothing like seeing a place to better understand it. And smelling it, it turns out.

Malaysia produces more palm oil than any other country in the world. This product is used in cooking, in cosmetics, in lots of stuff. It is relatively inexpensive to produce given the right climate. It has none of the dreaded trans fats, whatever they are. It is also, potentially, a source for biodiesel, a substitute that works fine in place of the diesel derived from refining petroleum. Malaysia is peculiarly well suited to this production. It has close to 50% of its land in cultivation, thanks to only modest mountain ranges (average for a typical country is probably closer to 35%), and of that a full one-third is in palm oil trees.

We flew from Singapore to Kuala Lumpur, Malaysia's capital, known to locals and anyone who wants to be considered a knowledgeable traveler as "KL." I asked about the little cuddly marsupials, but was told that they live in Koala Lumpur. Because agricultural/industrial activity is not generally found in capital cities, we then took a small helicopter up to Ipoh, a town of 600,000, and drove on a well-paved but winding road to the mill we were visiting. I tell you what, you fly at about a thousand feet over the countryside, you can see things pretty clearly, and what you can see is mile after mile after mile of palm tree fields, all laid out in neat rows, all the same height, all the same color of green. Talk about monoculture—it was amazing!

The mill was amazing as well. Run by a group of Chinese brothers, it was very, um, noisy, dirty, hot, smelly, and slippery. The cluster of palm oil nuts, called fresh fruit bunches, come in, looking like about three somewhat furry footballs in size. The nuts surround a central axis, but the whole thing is made of a dirty brown fiber, with thumb-sized nuts poking their little red heads out. Apparently the nuts do not like to depart from their friends in the fiber, because there is all sorts of processing that goes on the get the suckers separated. Also lots of conveyors and big drums rotating and steam going here and there and banging and clanking. Streams of denutted bunches pile up in big heaps, streams of nutshells move here and there. One of the brothers took us on the tour but it was remarkably loud in the plant, and his English was not all that clear to begin with, and the result was that I cannot really tell you exactly what was happening at each specific step. I can tell you that it was very oily underfoot, and when climbing the stairs you really did need to hold on to the railings. Which of course were themselves covered with oily stuff and bits of fiber. Plus there we lots of open or uncovered belts and conveyors and stuff, which is actually quite dangerous. I thought to myself that this place made our worst power plant look like an Intel clean room. Paul remarked that he almost never felt that places he visited were actually unsafe, but this one was.

Our tour ended and then the *pièce de résistance*—the waste ponds. We know how to have fun. Off we go to the outskirts of the facility, where there are three lagoons filled with ugly and bad-smelling black glop. Some of it is bubbling gently in the hot sun. Not big Yellowstone geyser bubbles, but small and distinguishable bubbles—the methane coming to the surface. And it smelled unpleasant, not destructively bad like animal waste or meat rotting, but annoyingly bad. Our team of contractors was there working on the cover for the first lagoon, which really is nothing but a big swimming pool cover equivalent, except once we put it on, we don't take it off. It is said that the material, a dark green plastic, is so thick that you can walk on it, and it did feel pretty tough. But the lagoon was not yet covered so we did not have that dubious pleasure.

If all this sounds simple, it is, and that's the beauty of it. We put in the capital for the covers and the flares, we do all the enormous and rigorous record keeping required by the UN—the agency that validates the CERs—and we pay the mill about 20% of the proceeds as a royalty. The construction of the covers and flares should take only two or three weeks per mill. We are busily signing up as many mills as we can, with a target of having 190 Malaysian mills under contract and either producing or in construction by year's end. And we just really started this activity at the beginning of the year. It is fascinating, if gritty. And fibery. And oily. We were assured as we left that the black glop that we had all managed to get on our khakis would come off in the wash. We shall see.

We pause this fascinating narrative to bring you my collection of favorite commercial names from this trip:

Spring Onion Oil Soda Multi-Fresh (not very good thin crackers in Vietnam)

Beijing 100, for All Your Hair (Singapore hair *crème*)

Clothing for Ladies and Gants (Indonesia)

Ten Minuteman Air Soda (soft drink in Indonesia)

And the grand prize winner, a fairly modern-looking lodging establishment on the road in Vietnam—the Phuc Duc Hotel.

Hanoi and Quang Ninh Province

People with dark skin are said to be from Quang Ninh, because of the coal dust that seems to characterize much of the province. Vietnam mined 25 million tons of coal last year and exported 10 million of this, mostly to southern China. That may not sound like much compared to China's 2.3 billion or the US number of about 1.5 billion. But it all came from Quang Ninh, one of Vietnam's fifty-eight provinces. And we drove past about half of it on Thursday. All right, that's an exaggeration; we only drove past a third of it.

We have a major project here that I have written to you about before. It's a 1,200 Mw power plant, coal-fired (naturally), in Quang Ninh, next to a major coalfield that will provide the fuel. Vietnam is short of electricity (rolling blackouts in the major cities in the summer) as well as having electric demand growing rapidly (7% last year, same expected this year) and electric demand is increasing actually faster than economic growth. That said, I sure wish they would move faster.

Our team pointed out that I was here exactly one year ago for the formal ceremony and party marking the opening of our office. It's all pretty much similar this time except there are if anything more motorbikes on the streets. And we have made progress on a number of fronts, but not as much as we would like on the key front. For example:

» Our environmental impact assessment is finished, the Vietnamese team has visited the site, done their modeling, checked for endangered species, etc., and should issue our permit in about a month. This is a huge deal in the US, and quite important here as well. The fact that we are tearing down a mountain and rerouting a river seems not to have fazed anyone. We are also resettling about thirty-five families, mostly fishermen who live along the rather small and unimpressive Mong Duong River.

» We have written the specs for the plant, solicited bids, and received back four bids, one Japanese, one from Black & Veatch (a US architect and engineer firm linked up with suppliers of Chinese equipment), and two from Korean firms. The latter two appear on first reading to meet both our technical and commercial requirements. This is always a worry until it is nailed down, especially given the significant price increases in steel and other finished commodities that we have recently seen.

» We have reached agreement with the Vietnamese on the general principles that will govern our agreements, and have been "released" to do the technical negotiations on the contracts that are key to this deal— the power purchase agreement and the coal supply agreement. We all acknowledge that getting the prices done will be the last thing to be finished, and is the most crucial, but having all the other stuff filled in is quite important. This is a good sign. We are also in the most recent five-year plan; our plant is cited by name. This may be the one time when I actually like central planning.

» The real estate rights to the site have been released. Remember, this is still a pretty serious Socialist country and the government owns all the land. Getting the rights is thus a big deal. However, as the site will actually hold two large power plants, at least it will after the bulldozers and back hoes get done with it, the site has actually been released to Electricité de Vietnam (EVN), who is building Unit One, while we are building the second. We will share some common facilities on the site, mostly water intake and discharge structures. The EVN guys put in their request for investment approval about fifteen months ago. We all expected that it would be routinely granted, especially given the shortage situation and since they are clearly the home team here. But then, WTO status intervened, and the requirement to change some of the internal laws arose, and . . . they just got their approval in March. This is important because they are in charge of the site preparation for both their plant and ours, and also in charge of the relocation effort. Actually this is a good thing. However, we had thought that it would go a good deal more quickly than it has gone. At least it can now get started. Interestingly, EVN will bear all the costs of this work, we think maybe as much as $50 million, as they need to move about 5.8 million cubic yards of material. We only repay them when and if we get to financial close. In comparison, our plant now in construction in Bulgaria, which is sensibly built on flat ground and has no need to reroute major waterways, had site prep excavation amounts of very much less than a 100,000 cubic yards. And no rivers. The less good news is that all this work will probably take a year, maybe fifteen months.

We have been trying to key getting the PPA negotiated and signed for the June visit of the VN prime minister to the US. Which brings us to why I was here. The contract and the government guarantee and other stuff is all being treated by all three of the following: the Ministry of Finance, the Ministry of Foreign Affairs, and the Ministry of Industry. The latter is probably the most important, as it has the responsibility for the electric sector under it, and this is where EVN is located organizationally. They have formed a committee of the three agencies, EVN and Vinacomin (the coal supplier) and we have secured for them a US TDA grant so this committee can pay for lawyers to sit on their side of the table and assist them during these negotiations.

As I mentioned in an earlier letter, having the US government use US tax dollars to pay for lawyers to negotiate against a US company trying to do business in a foreign country does seem odd. Ah, but it's even more weird than that. We are actually supplying to TDA the bulk of the funds to be used to pay the lawyers for the other side. All this may seem tortuous as well as odd, but it is completely transparent and legal and in fact accepted practice. And the lawyers are being helpful, believe it or not, as they are educating the Vietnamese side as to what the contracts must have in them in order for this project to attract financing from the international lending agencies, Asian Development Bank and OPIC among them. So all this is actually a good thing, strange as it seems. But it took a long time to arrange, and the TDA "grant" of mostly our money was only executed about a month ago. The Vietnamese also took this as a sign of US government "support" for this project. Since they are still largely a government-driven economy, they don't really understand that we aren't, and that such support generally is irrelevant to us.

So where are we? Unfortunately, we can't start building until the site is ready, and that won't be for a while, so we can continue negotiating the PPA for lots more months. We can't really figure out any good way to construct artificial deadlines here to get the other guys to move. Even my suggestion of tying this to the visit of the PM was met with head shaking and perplexed looks. The minister of industry is cordial, but seems harried and also emphasized that this is a big project, their first foreign independent power plant in six years, and he wants to make sure that it's done right. I reply that that's fine, but we have all done these before (the Viets did two in the late nineties, both successful, although both way smaller than ours would be) and we know how to do these, so let's get on with it. But he is unimpressed by my American can-do attitude. The best he will commit to do is to try and move things along. The meeting is actually brief even by US standards, as he has to fly off to the middle of the country where he has power problems.

It's always useful to see the site where you plan to build things. Just to make sure it isn't a swamp, or there aren't big hills on the property or rivers running through it. Hold on, it *is* a swamp with big hills and a river running through it. . . .

To get there is easy, in a manner of speaking, but tedious. Basically you get in a car with a driver whose hand has been surgically attached to the horn, and you drive four hours, mostly north and west from Hanoi. You get to drive past the legendary Ha Long Bay, through the city of Ha Long, which is at about the three hour point of the journey. You get to see lots and lots of beautiful rice fields and people in the traditional conical hats working the fields, and water buffalo doing nothing but eating or sitting around. And on the road lots of motorcycles and for the last hour an enormous number of midsize coal trucks, mostly green but some orange and some yellow and all with a kind of black sheen that you get from coal dust. In fact the dust is everywhere along the road, covering the sidewalks and the plants and, one presumes, the people. It is quite ugly and pervasive. We aren't talking freeways here, but a nicely maintained two-lane concrete road that runs right down the middle of every town, serving as the main street. So all the canopies of the small stores are black with the dust and one wonders about eating the fruit and vegetables for sale along the road. With almost no exceptions the cycle drivers wear scarves or masks covering their noses and mouths, and one can surely see why. And the coal trucks keep rolling by, heading toward the port of Ha Long.

Tourist note: Ha Long Bay is a World Heritage site and pretty famous tourist destination. They probably don't tell you that it is also a serious industrial port and working harbor, complete with coal barges putting around and large boats taking on cargo and so on. Just past the working parts of the harbor, there do appear to be beautiful nubs of dramatic basalt or granite or some such black rock sticking up as if in a Chinese brush painting, but it is pretty hazy and hard to see. I am disappointed, I admit. Maybe it's better in a boat and with better weather. But it's not just a few of these small islands, it's a welter of the things. And they continue almost all the way to the site, as the road, QL 18, essentially runs parallel to the coast. After a bit the road turns up into the hills, some of which are squared off and being excavated.

We turn off QL 18 onto a bumpy, dusty, twisty, dirt road into the site. Finally we get there. We all get out and look at a drawing of the site layout. We determine that we are standing in the middle of the future coal pile. There are in fact large hills on the site, covered with miscellaneous vegetation and some hardy small daisies. There is a nasty little green-ish-brown river winding through the site. There is also a bunch of piles of coal and a small coal loading dock on the river. Boy, there is coal every-where in this place. There is lots of black dust around. There are a few very poor-looking shacks on the banks of the small river. There is not a bathroom. If you needed a site for a big power plant, near the coal, this is as good as any. Except for the hills and the river.

We return from the site, technically near the town of Cam Pha, and stop at Ha Long at a very nice Vietnamese restaurant with a view of the harbor. We have a lovely lunch while we watch the coal barges being pushed back and forth. As we drive back to Hanoi, I marvel at all the statues and posters along the road—you may think that socialist realism as an art style died with the fall of the Berlin Wall, but it is alive and well in Vietnam. We just want it to stop being applied to the power plant sector.

One last note—I left Asia and returned home. The dogs still recog-nized me, and Linda did as well. The dogs required me to feed them several hot dogs to convince them, however. Linda was easier.

We went to Houston for Easter, where one of the things in my Easter basket was a "giant popper," a cardboard tube about the size of your arm and as long as an umbrella. When you twisted the bottom portion, it exploded inside and shot streamers and confetti out the top. Naturally it was made in China and naturally there were directions, precisely reproduced below:

In the wind weather outside. Please choose the right direction.

Don't against to the bare electric line.

Don't attack people. The products discharged by pressure of air. No pollution. No fire. No flavor. Assure safety.

I found this to be good general guidance for many things.

Love and kisses,
Bob

Afterword: I mentioned earlier that we eventually financed and built the large power plant in Vietnam. The palm oil venture was a different matter.

I hate biology. Chemistry and physics and electrical engineering are about all you have to know to be in the power plant business. And as a species, we have a pretty good grasp of those disciplines. But we do not know nearly enough about biology to really describe it as a science, whose basic definition is predictability. Biological processes are never as simple as burning gas in the presence of oxygen to get energy as heat, plus water and CO_2 as by-products. Biological processes are always five or ten or twenty intermediate steps with alternate and redundant pathways to finally get from A to B.

We approached the "offset creation" business as if it were chemistry. The organic material decays, methane is produced, we flare it, and viola—we have created an offset that we can sell in Europe. But the first four words of that sentence are where the complexity lies. How to begin? The "organic material" is not consistent; some decays fast, some slow, some not at all. Some decays into methane, but there are other decay products as well. Temperature matters, pH (acidity of the water in the ponds) matters, circulation matters, dilution or concentration matters. It's little bacteria doing the work and they are more finicky than you would think. Simple, first-order math calculations completely gloss over how much methane comes out of your uncontrolled wastewater ponds.

The guys running the palm oil plants don't care, they only want to end up with treated water that meets the standards and they can dump into the river in compliance with their permits. Whether there is more or less methane than forecast matters not at all to them, in fact they never paid attention to it until we offered them money for a product they may not have realized they were making. In short, our forecasts of methane production from the plants with whom we contracted proved to be off by two-thirds. And we did not understand the decay process well enough to know how to or if we could fix this. Couple this with a glut of offsets for sale in Europe, and you have a recipe for a failed business. Two-thirds less product for the same capital investment meets half the expected price equals one-sixth the anticipated revenue for the same capital and operating cost.

This only occurred to us over time as we watched the numbers continually come in way below estimates and tried to figure out why. We never really did, at least not precisely, and eventually even optimists like us came to the conclusion that this was a bad business and we should get out. So we did.

chapter fourteen

Carthago Delenda Est and Maybe Israel too If You're an Arab Not from Jordan

November 2007

Dear Dad,

I think I have said this before, but taking the Channel Tunnel train from London to Paris is overrated, especially if you leave from St. Pancras Station at five thirty-five in the evening in the month of November. I had forgotten how quickly it gets dark in England in the winter. By the time the train leaves you cannot see anything out the windows. It took me twenty minutes to determine that I was seated facing backwards, a position that I dislike and that I have convinced myself makes me nauseous. But it appears that there is no inner ear process going on here, and once the modest acceleration stops and you're just rolling along, you cannot really tell if you are going forwards or backwards. I would suggest an analogy to US policy in Iraq but this is not a political letter.

Here are three things I note about this hotsy-totsy, high-speed Eurostar train:

1. It is more than a bit shabby, with soiled carpet, worn leather on

the armrests, etc.

2. It is screwed up with regard to its very modest technology. My ticket said "car 11 seat 44," which seems reasonably clear, except that when I tried to get on the train car unmistakably labeled number 11, I was told that I should get on car 8. Was everything off by three? Car 8 was three cars to the right (which turned out to be to the forward direction) of the car that actually had "11' in its little digital display box. And the rest of the cars were arranged in an orderly numerical progression so that 8 came right after 9. There are no obvious answers, so I would of course like to blame the French for this, but I cannot figure out how to do so credibly. Maybe it's an antiterrorism bit of sleight of hand? Now that Sarkozy is president and likes the US and has had his fashion model babe of a wife divorce him because he won the election, I do feel a certain warmth for the fine French people. Lafayette, we are here, or at least we might be here if you keep being nice to us.

3. They have wretched English food on the train, the two choices of entrées being salmon pie or braised whitefish with brown sauce. Errg. The French gift for technology, the English gift for food—could this be backwards? So I just had the salad, which was served with no dressing. Fortunately it was diminutive and they had bread. When you're going backwards into the dark at 120 mph, the small things matter.

This somewhat weird dinner break provides time for one to ask the following questions: Who was St. Pancras anyway? Is he related to St. Gall Bladder? Do they all come from the Isles of Langerhans? Why is St. Pancras the only one who gets a London tube stop? Perhaps Google, which knows all and tells all, can answer these questions for me. But not while I am on the train. There's no Internet connection.

Travel notes: don't go to Paris when some group of French people is striking. Of course, since this is most of the time, this could limit one's visits to Paris. I got off the train at the Gare du Nord and then needed to go to the airport. But the metro was not running and the trains were not running, so the taxi lines were very long, as in, one hour to wait in line in the cold for a taxi. I do not recommend this even in Paris, romantic city of lights. But I finally got to the hotel at the airport, got a nice glass of wine, got the good news that Linda had made it onto her plane and thus will in fact meet me in Tunisia as planned. Which leaves me free to further contemplate the approaching wonder of our "weekend break" in exotic Tunisia.

Day Two—I arrive in Tunisia, ready for the beginning of my tropical vacation with Arab overtones. Whoa, it's raining. It's raining and windy. It's raining and windy and cold. What the hey is going on here? Is this the delightful tropical monsoon, misplaced from Asia, no doubt by global warming? Global warming being the most recently anointed Proximate Cause of Everything Bad.

No, this seems to be actual cold Mediterranean rain. And wind. Since they shot *Star Wars* here, I just assumed it was warm and tropical and sunny like Luke Skywalker on Tatooine. Hah! Bad assumption. And it is embarrassing to note that they made the Internet just so you can go on www.internationalweather.com or something and see what the weather really is wherever you're going. But did we do that? No-o-o, and this is an unpleasant surprise. I huddle in our room and wait for my dear wife to catch up with me here in frigid Tunisia. Too bad I only brought short sleeve shirts and shorts and sandals. This packing strategy is beginning to look flawed. I do have a lot of suntan lotion, though.

My wife arrives, miraculously making connections through Paris (she didn't need a taxi at least) and we have a very mediocre dinner at this fancy hotel which was glowingly recommended by *Departures* magazine, the high-end travel and rich bauble mag only sent to folks who are crazy enough to pay Amex $300 per year to have a platinum card, which actually doesn't get you that much except a travel service that specializes in over-charging you. And a magazine with bad information. But we persevere, as this is our first "vacation," even a short one, in a long time. One of the things we find is that there is no heat in the room, despite the thermostat, a trap for the unwary it turns out. You can turn the sucker up to thirty degrees (centigrade one imagines, but maybe it is actually Fahrenheit, that would explain the meat-locker temperature of the room) and nothing happens except the fan runs with a nice chirping sound. Finally we ask at the desk about fixing the heat and extra blankets and if they know anyone willing to trade us some Polartec for some sunblock. They bring us the blankets and, believe it or not, a portable space heater. We consider this weird at a five star hotel but we don't give it back. Perhaps central heating has not been invented here yet.

Day Three—We finally drag ourselves out of bed at 11:00, but we have reserved, in a fit of touristic excess, a taxi for all day starting at 10:00, which was at one point even going to be nine o'clock. Hmmm. I then find, when showering, that the drain on the shower floor does not work, which means that the water rises above the rather minor lintel in the shower and floods the entire bathroom floor. As I am graciously taking the first shower, I thus see the whole disaster occurring but am powerless to stop it, other than by turning off the shower in the middle of washing off the soap. It's one of those things that happens gradually, the frog in the boiling water, and every minute or so I expect the drain to start working, but it refuses. "Be careful when you go in the bathroom," I helpfully tell my wife when it is her turn, "there's a little water on the floor." A little? We could have Moses in the bulrushes in there by the time I am finished. I wonder idly if I have misread the nice little bronze plaque at the entryway, maybe it didn't say Leading Hotels of the World, maybe it said Leaking Hotels of the World.

Our extremely patient taxi driver is waiting for us, possibly patient as he knows we will pay him for the whole day cause that's the deal anyway. Or because he's a nice guy and he doesn't mind hanging around because driving is actually a pain. He does not enlighten us on his motives. Off we go to visit Sidi Bou Said, which is supposed to be a very quaint hillside town. But as it is listed in all the guidebooks as "quaint hillside town well worth visiting," and has been so listed, one assumes, for some time, how quaint can it now be, five million visitors later? Answer: not so quaint. It is the predictable whitewashed buildings with blue doors, and about a hundred shops in a five-block area, all taking from the same wholesale supplier, and all offering the same carved camels, items made of very thin leather, "colorful" ceramics that probably leach lead, belly dancer outfits with beaded brassieres, key chains, coffee mugs, postcards—you get the picture. Perhaps this stuff is all made by "local craftsmen," but if so they all went to the same School for Local Craftsmen, and they all learned to make exactly the same stuff. I suspect Chinese influence.

We stop at a small rooftop café and try to have some coffee, having had none because we started late and there is no coffeemaker in the hotel room. The expensive and very cold hotel room. However, despite the lovely view of the Bay of Tunis or the Mediterranean or possibly the Rock of Gibraltar, the menus keep blowing up in our faces. I am freezing and, yes, I'll say it, increasingly cranky. We leave, find the cab driver, and ask him if there are any restaurants or cafés in Tunisia where one sits inside. Linda is inspired and asks, in very nice French, if we can go to one at a hotel. "Sure," he says agreeably, "there is a café in a hotel next to the Carthage Museum." We are still game so off we go to Carthage. I am too cold to resist.

We end up at the Villa Didon, a very modern hotel on a steep hill next to the Carthage Museum. Great views of the harbor or bayou or whatever it is. We hang out at the bar, having cappuccino, and being hungry. The waiter brings us the short menu and we place orders for the tarte du jour and a croque monsieur. The latter, as you know, is a classic French ham and cheese sandwich, toasted. In theory. Ordering a ham sandwich in a Muslim country is an adventurous move, but there is so little else available that I conclude it is the only viable option. We have had no food all day and that makes the best traveler peckish. But that is not the initial problem. The problem is the fact that it takes forever to arrive. I would argue that making a toasted ham and cheese sandwich should not take forty-five minutes, but I am an impatient American. We are at least seated in a very cool and modern bar with lots of cool young Tunisians. Not a set of running shoes in the crowd, which is how you tell that they are not Americans. Unfortunately, to be young and modern and Tunisian is also to smoke furiously, so that is not as good. The "food" comes after many, many long minutes, and the sandwich is awful. The "ham" is some sort of bright pink-colored exploded bologna (not ham-colored but hot pink fashion-colored—think bubble gum but brighter) and the cheese is white goop. We pick off the toast and eat it. The tarte is a cookie covered with really gelatinous vanilla pudding and the odd slice of banana. We must have picked a bad day to have the "tarte of the day," maybe Monday would have been better.

We go to the Carthage Museum since we are there already. Lots of bits of marble ruins—pediments, capitals, columns, miscellaneous heads and faces, some unclear stone structures and so forth, nothing very well explained, at least not in English. It is worth perhaps noting that Carthage was destroyed by the Romans, who apparently were really fried about the Hannibal and the elephants thing. They burned everything down and, as one representation shows, "left not one stone standing on another." This could explain why there is not so much left. It is therefore a small museum, mostly the museum of fragments. As Cicero was fond of saying in his oratory, according to Miss Kiracofe, my tenth-grade Latin teacher, "Carthago delenda est." Translation: Carthage must be destroyed. And it was. Given the weather and the food, I am beginning to think that this was a good thing.

Day Four—We give up and change our travel arrangements so we can go to Israel a day early. The very expensive Tunisia hotel has been unimpressive at best, the weather is cold, windy, and rainy, the food is lousy, and there is little of interest to see. So much for this tropical paradise. On top of all that, Tunisia turns out to be hard place to leave, especially to go to Israel. Shades of "Hotel California." There are no direct flights to Israel, and the flights to and from other places do not operate every day. The only flights we can find to let us leave early for Israel take us through Amman, Jordan. We wonder idly what Israeli security is going to think of our change in plans and our flight path from Tunisia, through Amman, to Tel Aviv. We make it to Amman smoothly, and I have an onward connection to Tel Aviv right away. Unfortunately I have to leave Linda in Amman, as she has a telephonic board meeting that interferes with the flight to Tel Aviv and that she cannot miss. She, lucky girl, gets to therefore wait for a flight out of Amman at 5:30 the next morning. I get to Tel Aviv about nine in the evening, and it is dark and suspiciously damp, but at least it's a lot warmer.

Day Five—Well, here's a surprise, it's raining and windy in Israel, too. I begin to suspect that late November may not be the ideal time for a Mediterranean vacation. Linda, after enduring the "airport hotel" in Amman, arrives, takes one look at the weather, and decides that she has important work to do indoors, including taking a nap. For some reason I decide to walk along the ocean to the Tel Aviv neighborhood of Jaffa, which we can see from the window of our fancy beach hotel. It's on a point on the coast and looks sort of old and made out of stone. The guidebook says—I abridge—that it is full of galleries and restaurants and miscellaneous old stuff. So off I go, in a momentary break in the rain. And, sure enough, once I am approximately halfway there, the rain comes back in typhoon strength. Thank goodness for my serious Orvis rain jacket, but my pants and shoes are soaking. I duck into a small building on the beach with a piece of military hardware in front of it, which turns out to be a nice little museum dedicated to the Irgun, the underground Israeli resistance fighters during the period up to independence. One might call them terrorists today, and in fact they were. They are called patriots in Israel, not surprisingly, even though their history includes blowing up hotels and embassies (the UK one in Rome). As one of my old HEW bureaucrats once said, "It depends on where you sit, how you stand." I am the only person visiting the museum, so the staff is glad to see me. I wander all through it, and then they play the well-made twenty-minute movie in English for me. From this one can conclude: the British were bad guys, the Arabs were bad guys, and the Jews were internally quite quarrelsome, and had a very hard time getting themselves to all work together and not degenerate into a Jewish civil war. This part of the history is not well known, thinks I.

I continue the hike up to Jaffa but precious little is open when I get there so I walk around in the rain and look at the wet stone buildings and the windows of the galleries. This is a lot of fun, I muse. Maybe I'll go back to the warm room and do e-mail.

Day Six—The trip to Israel originated because Linda has developed relationships with several leading medical institutions there as part of the work of our investment company. Israel has been at the forefront of developing novel treatments for cancer, especially blood cancers, using immune system therapies. She is bringing a whole flock of folks over to meet with the Israeli medical centers the following week, and needed to spend some time with them getting everything set, so we decided to blow off Thanksgiving (sort of a dumb holiday anyway, in my opinion) and spend the week doing partly work and partly vacation. Today is the partly work day, so off we go (ah, yes, in the rain, it turns out) for our meeting with one of the good doctors for a fascinating tutorial in the power of what cutting-edge immunotherapies can do for cancer patients—without the toxicity of conventional "modern" treatments. It is tremendously impressive and suggests to me that if any family members get serious cancers, the US is not necessarily the gold standard of treatment anymore.

That evening we go to a very good restaurant with several of the Israeli scientists. One of them selects a terrific wine, which turns out to be what he calls and the label confirms is a "dry Riesling." And here we all thought Riesling came only in gallon jugs and tasted suspiciously like generic pancake syrup laced with rubbing alcohol. Best food I have had on the trip, finally, thank goodness.

Day Seven—It's time to be tourists. We book a car and a guide to go to Masada and the Dead Sea and two nature preserves and a winery. And I arrange so that we don't have to leave until nine, a schedule more befitting a "vacation." It is a two-hour drive to Masada, and if you were to begin the drive in the foothills of Jerusalem (which is on the way but which we skip as requiring too much of a commitment, besides it's raining so maybe the desert will be better) you would see nothing but rocks and stones and scrub brush going up into Jerusalem, and then from Jerusalem to the Dead Sea, and south along it to Masada at its southern tip you would see rocky, stony, tan desert with almost nothing growing. This is a desert person's desert, cut up by wadis with maybe the occasional small tree, but in essence objec-tifying the concept of "barren." And you would ask yourself why exactly anyone would want to spend so much blood and treasure fighting over this place.

Jerusalem is set on the top of a series of pretty high hills. You drive up a long steep road through narrow canyons to get to it from the coast. Along the way you see a series of rusted-out military vehicles, personnel carriers, and armored trucks mostly. They are all painted the sienna-brown color of rust-inhibiting primer. Our guide, Michael, is a pretty aggressive Israeli.

"The Palestinians never had Jerusalem as their capital, it was Caesarea, they are just making that up about claiming Jerusalem." And "How would the United States like it if some Mexicans were shooting rockets into El Paso and Brownsville?" He explains that these are the vehicles that got knocked out during the Israeli assault in 1948 to capture Jerusalem from the Arab Legion. They have been left as they fell as a memorial to the Israeli soldiers killed in the battle. Every year on Remembrance Day citizens go out and repaint the vehicles. This is pretty sobering, and maybe a better memorial and a better reminder of what took place when the country was established than any large white marble memorial would be.

Masada, when one finally gets there, is impressive as a fortress location—located on a flat bluff, separate and standing out from the series of bluffs that define the edges of the Dead Sea. It's probably two thousand feet above the level of the sea and the surrounding shore; you can barely make out the fortifications at the top of it looking from the ground. It is, our guide tells us as we pay the admission fee, the most expensive site in the Israeli national park system, the most visited, and the one that economically carries all the others. There are a lot of people, but it's not bad really. There is a nifty big Swiss made cable car that runs from the base of the adjacent mesa all the way to the top of the fortress, boarded after you watch an eight-minute movie about the place. It's impressive and looks like ruins on the top, which is reassuring. The story is simple. Herod built it in around 35 BC as a retreat and maybe winter palace, although perhaps he thought he could hole up here if his adoring populace revolted from his not-so-benevolent rule as King of the Jews, but appointed by the Romans. Kingship as an appointive office. Bear in mind that from Jerusalem to the Dead Sea, heading due east, is thirty minutes of total barrenness by fast car, though all down hill. Then you head south for another ninety minutes of more Dead Sea on one side, gullies and barrenness on the other. There are a couple of green spots, kibbutz where they have taken advantage of modern water purification technologies and the existence of some springs and are raising dates, etc., but this is not a nice, welcoming bit of terrain to traverse, even for a winter vacation, and even if you are the king. But if you're the king, I presume you have slaves or taxes, and you can more or less do what you want. So Herod had all this built, the impressive stonework and clever water system, on the top of this very tall mesa.

Zoom ahead to approximately one hundred years after Herod, and there is a major Jewish insurrection going on. The Romans are running around putting it down. Four hundred Jewish zealots come to Masada, Herod having been long gone and apparently failing to have locked the door. The Romans decide this is not good so they muster 10,000 legionnaires, and 15,000 Jewish slaves, and surround the mesa with walls and an encampment. Then the slaves build a wide ramp, all made of dirt and rocks, leading to the top of the mesa, the Romans roll a siege engine up the ramp, and beat down the wall. Most archaeologists think that building the ramp probably took ten months. All this time the Roman commander had to arrange for food and, more importantly water, for the 25,000 folks under his command. Note that it is next to the Dead Sea, and since that is water with about a 25% salt content, it's not so drinkable. What a logistic pain. Anyway, having beaten down the wall at last, the Romans call it a day, noting to the rebels in the now pretty battered fortress that they'll be back in the morning to kill and enslave everyone. That night all the surviving zealots choose death over slavery and kill each other, and when the Romans arrive after breakfast everyone is dead. Frankly, I gotta say I don't think much of this story. The Jewish religion, as with all major religions, does not condone suicide, so this makes a sort of uncomfortable story to cast as heroism. And wouldn't it have been nicer to go down fighting and take a few Romans with you? Of course, I was not there. I bite my tongue and refrain from referring to this as the Jonestown of Israel. On the way back we make the obligatory stop at one of the beach establishments and watch people, sure enough, floating in the Dead Sea. They look cold.

Day Eight—Time to go visit the Golan Heights. About six months ago, one of our AES power plant developers (they are an irrepressible bunch of fun-loving guys and gals) told us, in a sort of offhand, by-the-way fashion, that he was working on a 400–500 Mw wind project that would be located in Israel in the Golan Heights. He also remarked that the political risk might be a problem and that the US government folks who insure such things, the Overseas Private Investment Corp., had already taken a pass on this one for "political" reasons. A bit funny since their whole purpose in life is to evaluate and take political risk, but never mind. The World Bank arm that does the same thing had said the same thing. But we soldier on. Perhaps a bad choice of words under the circumstances.

When our august chairman of the board read about this, he fired off one of his intensely literate and intensely direct messages that I shall not reproduce here, but rather summarize, conveying the rough meaning of, "The Golan Heights?? What's the matter, was Iraq busy?" Thus I made a note to myself to visit said location when the time was convenient and see what was what. As in, would I have to wear a flak jacket and a helmet and visit the site in an armored vehicle.

The local developer, a friendly, stocky Israeli named Ayel, pulled up at precisely seven at our hotel in an SUV, not an APC. Good start. John, our guy and project sponsor, was there also, so we hopped in our own car and away we all went. Always good to have two cars in case of an ambush or the need to evacuate casualties. We headed out of Tel Aviv, north, since that, it turns out, is where the fun is—Lebanon, Syria, all those happy neighbors.

Why is this a good idea? Well . . . first, some electrical background (no, it turns out that I cannot restrain myself, but thanks for asking anyway)—Israel has installed capacity of 11,500 Mw for its 7+ million people. This is not a good ratio, and more to the point, most of the capacity is coal fired, using imported coal. The rest of the plants are gas fired using imported gas. And all of it is expensive, as the gas suppliers do not, being Arabs, seem especially interested in cutting the Israeli's a break. It should be noted that they don't cut each other a break either; our project in Jordan burns gas from Egypt and it costs just as much as the gas the Egyptians sell to the Israelis. No hydro plants as this country is pretty dry with no real dependable rivers. No nuclear plants. The most important fact is that last summer their "reserve margin" was down to 4%. In a well-run electric grid we try to keep this number above 15%, because if you get down to less than zero, which can easily happen if a large unit, say one providing 5% of the service, trips off, then you have rolling blackouts. Customers, it turns out, do not like this. They prefer to have their air-conditioning and their lights on rather than off on the hottest day of the summer. And we agree with them, they should have that. So the Israeli system is in some trouble—dependent on outside sources for fuel supply, dependent on high-priced fossil fuels, and with low and decreasing reserve margins. Oh, yeah, and no one wants a power plant in their neighborhood. And since this is a pretty small country, where you can drive end to end in probably six hours, there are not a lot of non-inhabited neighborhoods to put power plants in. These attitudes and this problem is classic the world over, by the way.

But say, how about . . . windmills! Or rather wind machines or wind turbines, as we say. Current state of the technology: they work, they make power in good wind sites at a cost of $0.08–$0.09/kWh (coal is probably $0.06–$0.07), they have no emissions, and if maintained properly the machines are highly reliable—when the wind blows. It appears that Israel actually has a decent amount of wind and sites where modern wind machines would make sense. It also has a grand total of—wait for it—10 wind machines installed in the whole country. Germany probably has 37,000 (the world leader), the US has 18,000, etc. We ourselves have 2,000, just little old AES. As perhaps you can tell, ten is not a big number. I have now seen all ten. They're nice. They are also small (600 kW, current machines are pushing 2,500 kW) and fifteen years old. We visit them this morning, in company with Ayel, whose family owns them. He and his dad put up these machines fifteen years ago, which was the dinosaur age in wind, and they have kept them working at 95% availability, a very respectable number, ever since. And this despite the fact that the original manufacturer, a defunct Austrian company called Villas Technology who I have never heard of, is no longer of this world. This makes procuring spare parts harder, at the least. But the Israelis, at least the older generation, are a pretty tough bunch. They have, for the last two years, been working on a much bigger installation in the Golan, on the order of 400–500 Mw. This is a very big number in the wind biz. We have three big wind farms in Texas, and none is larger than 300 Mw, and they don't have Syrians for neighbors. But these guys have been carefully going to all the local orchards, of which there are many, and carefully signing up individual turbine locations, and they now have more than 150 such small pieces of land under contract.

They plan to put the machines in the corners of the orchards, and the farmer loses a couple of trees but more than makes up for it in the income from the land lease. And they will soon have an agreement from the Israel Electric Corporation for the interconnection, and then an agreement to purchase the power at around $0.10/kWh. This is pretty impressive if they can pull it off, and here is where they need our help with the not small capital required for this. We can also help them in scaling up their operations; the total operating staff is currently two, both nice guys, and a dog. I was not sure of the technical qualifications of the dog. Oh yes, they also need support convincing the turbine suppliers that they are real and that they deserve to be allowed to purchase wind machines. It is the worst kind of seller's market on wind turbines right now. The kind that makes the suppliers picky and arrogant and high priced and demanding: "Gee, we're just about sold out for 2010, did you want to place an order?" "2010," we think to ourselves, "we have a lot of stuff in the pipeline, but nothing that is permitted yet and nothing that has a power purchase agreement, and we don't know yet if the tax credit legislation will be extended in the US, and you want us to irrevocably commit to purchase two hundred machines at $3 mil per machine, with no rights to redirect them to Europe and no rights to resell them in case all our projects fall through or the tax credit doesn't get extended, and you want an answer and board approval and a $100 million deposit in two weeks?" I think you get the picture.

So, $0.10 a kWh, probably paid in Israeli shekels. Lots of sites, pretty good wind resource that will give you 35+% capacity factor, which is excellent. Technical interjection: wind sites are rated by how often one can expect the stupid machine to be turning and thus actually making electricity. Since this particular part of the business is essentially all capital and very minor operating costs, i.e., no fuel, then more is clearly better. Capacity factors of 100% would be fine. Wind don't blow that way, however. The best sites anyone has monitored in the world get you to the high 40s. The number of hours in the day the wind blows is important, but so is the speed, as there is some output relation that rises with the cube of the wind speed. This attention to capacity factors is not peculiar to wind. Most dams without storage, which is the vast majority of all dams in the world, and almost all small ones, are what is called "run of the river." If the water flows you make power, if not, then you know the answer. If I actually knew Yiddish I would say bubkes. The run of the river dams tend to have 35% to 45% capacity factors. Solar panels have the same problem, with really good numbers being 20% to 22%. The problem with solar is that there is more cloud cover than you think and the sun is not always directly overhead, which is where you get the best results. I suspect you can confirm this by going outside. Especially at night. Nothing seems to be simple or easy, even in the wonderful world of renewable energy. But we digress.

So, 400–500 Mw, $0.10/kWh, good interconnection, a utility that really needs and wants the power, all permits completed, a good local developer really looking for our help and participation, what's not to like?

After two hours and half of driving from Tel Aviv, we get to the control center, really a small building with a computer, a kitchen, and a bathroom, sitting at the base of the small hill where at the top one finds all the wind machines. Nice but modest. Four extra wind turbine blades are lying in storage in the front yard, bought at the bankruptcy sale of the original manufacturer. We chat, we look at pictures, we look at maps, we look at the one computer in the place, we listen to the stories of the original installation, we put on our coats as it's pretty damn windy. We drive up to the top of the hill. It appears from the bottom to be fortified. Leftover from the war, I think. No. It *is* fortified, in the infantry sense of trenches and pillboxes and multiple rows of concertina. It's a well-designed, platoon-sized position on the top of the hill, in quite good shape. Not manned, just ready. Sandbags all in good repair, fields of fire cleared, overhead cover more than adequate. And along the ridgeline on whose highest point the fortification sits run the line of ten wind turbines. OK, no one seems particularly freaked as they jump over the trenches to get to the machines. And the dirt roads wind among the wire and the gun emplacements. In the distance is a derelict tank left from the first conflict, I suspect as a reminder. More conversation ensues, we inspect the wind measuring mast. Actually once you get to a wind turbine there's not really much to see. We ask about bird kill, they say no problems, there has been a study. Maybe birds don't like barbed wire. I then note around the edges of the site more barbed wire, with nice rectangular yellow signs hung on it saying, in Hebrew, Arabic, and English, Danger, Mines. It is also posted with the red upside down triangle that is the universal signal for minefield. I will say that this is the first wind farm I have seen interspersed with a minefield. A real minefield, not an allegorical minefield, as in "permitting here is really a minefield." Strangely, there were also small deer running about. One presumes either: (a) they have learned to read the yellow signs and stay out of those areas; or (b) the mines are set to detonate at too high a pressure threshold for the deer to trigger, i.e., these are mines for tanks. Of course, the deer that I saw were really small, so maybe that supports explanation (b).

We have also a nice view of the UN establishment/encampment that monitors the cease-fire. This is pointed out to us, as is Syria, which is both visible and pretty doggone close. But it is also all extremely pastoral and calm and bucolic. Lots of orchard and vineyards—you could be in parts of California heading into the Sierras, or many locations in Spain. And lots of Druze villages around; the Druze are a local ethnic group that are not exactly Arabs and not really Jews and are sort of Christians, but generally hard to categorize. We drive though several and they have McDonald's. There are also Druze villages on the other side of the Syrian border, and at the end of the long valley is Mount Hermon, the highest mountain in Israel, which is half Syrian, and where there is a ski resort on the Israeli half. There is already some snow on the mountain. It is all very interesting and very slightly odd, but no one but us seems to think so. I will say, if the Syrians decide to attack, you will see them from a long ways away, and they certainly do not hold the commanding heights. So far they have shown no such inclination, and have kept the area far quieter and in better order than the Lebanese. For whatever comfort that would give one.

Our trip ends with an opportunistic visit to Nimrod Castle, an impressive Crusader-era castle overlooking one of the valleys, built on top of a serious hill. Battlements, vaulted spaces, places to shoot arrows down on attackers, lots of big blocks of marble, and wonderful views out over the valleys. Mark Twain visited it and called it the most beautiful ruin he had ever seen, but then he hadn't been to Cambodia and Angkor Wat. It was built by a Muslim sultan in the 1200s, as the large and quite well-preserved inscriptions clearly explain. Despite this inconvenient bit of big marble, for a time it was thought to have been built by the crusaders, so thought, one presumes, by early Anglo archaeologists, but now it's pretty clear. It is also the largest castle in Israel. The translation of the inscription extolling the wonderfulness of its builder includes the title, "Slayer of Willful Deviationists," which I find a great descriptor. I presume I would have been included had I been around then.

Day Nine—It's the Shabbat, which technically started at sundown the day before and ends at sundown today. Nothing is open, not even any of the stores in the international hotel. And even stranger, there are no domestic airplane flights, which is inconvenient as we need to go to Eilat to see some solar project developers and their project site. Eilat is at the very southern tip of Israel, on the Red Sea, and has been uncharitably described as a lot of five star hotels at a three star resort. Even the guide-books, which are loath to say ill of anything much, suggest that for better diving and snorkeling you should go on to the Egyptian parts of the Red Sea. But we have to go to a kibbutz there, so Eilat it is. You can drive for four hours to get there, through more desert (I think it's the Negev again but I get confused) but we decide to save time by flying, at least as soon as the planes are allowed to take off.

Except the hotel sends us to the wrong airport, the international one. This is annoying. We are next directed in a cab where we are let out at a different but not nearby terminal, which, sure enough, has signs for Israir, the carrier we are looking for, and Eilat. After about twenty minutes of detailed security questioning—"Where do you live?" "Why are you trav-eling together?" "Why didn't you do the research to know that Tunis would be unattractive in the winter?" "What are the names of your dogs and why did you choose those names?"—we are informed we are at the wrong airport, again. At least this second airport does have a lot of flights leaving for Eilat—just not ours. Our third try works, although of course we have now missed the plane that we had specially picked to get us to Eilat in time to see something of the area before the sun went down. We are revived when the developers and the business head of the kibbutz meet us for dinner and take us to a very good Japanese restaurant in the hotel. Since this is probably one of my favorite cuisines in the world, and since for reasons of bad planning and closed facilities we haven't had anything to eat all day, this works.

Day Ten—We are picked up at the hotel by one of the senior kibbutz members and off we go, north, away from the little sliver of sea coast and big hotels and into the very real desert. It surely is dramatic, as landscape goes. And no pesky trees or vegetation to obscure the views. Although parts of the Golan were suitable only for pasture, as least there was stuff actually growing there. Not so here.

The area of Eilat includes the resort and port area on the Red Sea, which really isn't very big, sort of like Cancun, and then another kajillion square miles of desert, before you get up to Beersheba and the Mediterranean coast and things get somewhat less sandy and rocky. There are ten kibbutzim in this region. I am not sure the whole idea had been invented when you were doing UN peacekeeping here in 1948. Basically these are elective communities of families who form a communal economic and living group. They have always been placed out on the edges of things, on the frontiers, and they have inevitably started with an agricultural base. Think farmer's co-ops in very inhospitable "arable" land, but way more inclusive and intrusive. They have never been more than 3%–4% of the population, but have contributed a very significant portion of prime ministers, fighter pilots, members of the legislature, etc. I think it is likely they have had a disproportionate share of influence on the culture of the country, and certainly have gotten a lot of press. In the Eilat area, all ten together add up to about two thousand souls, with the largest being probably eight hundred and the smallest fewer than fifty.

The one we are dealing with is called Ketura, and it is about an hour north of Eilat. We start with a very cordial meeting with the mayor of the region who has a visionary plan for making the area the renewable energy focus of Israel. After the tour of their date palm plantation, we are asked if we know much about kibbutzim and if we would like a tour. Yes, indeed. A member of the kibbutz named Bill is on hand, and happens to be a licensed tour guide. He also happens to be from Bethesda, MD, although he is now a naturalized citizen of Israel, but his parents still live in Rockville, next-door town to where we live in Potomac. Darn small world.

Economically this kibbutz is engaged in date growing, dairy cattle, fish farming, and production of nutraceuticals using algae. They are very entrepreneurial and very businesslike. But inside, it is classic communalism. As far as I can tell, there is almost no private property. All meals are served in the dining hall. All medical care, all pensions, all education including college is provided for or paid for by the commune. There are seventy families, and the commune owns ten cars. If you need to use one you do. They even have their own auto mechanic. And all laundry is communal. The "members" are all adults, and if they work outside the kibbutz then their salaries are paid to the central kibbutz treasury. I suppose they own their own clothes, but they don't use money on the kibbutz for anything. Membership is voluntary, and also elective. If you want to join, two-thirds of the members have to vote you in. You can leave anytime you want, but very few people do. They have not been around long enough to have a feeling for second-generation members yet, but many of the kids seem interested in returning and becoming members. But none of this is conveyed in a messianic or peculiar way, it's much more matter-of-fact, with frequent acknowledgement that this is not for everyone. I find it fascinating. I do not, however, think I will sign up, although I note that it is warm and not raining.

The business deal, briefly, involves using some of the kibbutz land that is not really suitable for anything else for a large solar installation. This means lots of ground-mounted collectors, hooked into the grid of the IEC, and receiving the $0.24 per kWh that is the Israel determined subsidy price. Actually it is probably not enough for this project to be immediately profitable, and there are higher rates available in Europe. But the sun in the Eilat region is amazing. NASA has compiled very good maps of "insolation," not to be confused with "insulation." This is a fancy word for how much the sun shines. The numbers for the general Eilat area and this kibbutz are about 20% better than Italy or Spain, so this whole thing is worth considering. The guys who have put this together are members of the kibbutz and have done a lot with very little money, but now they need someone with some experience and some real money to get this over the finish line. And they have big ideas about doing this in Jordan as well, which is just across the border about a mile away. Every other country here is very close, reconfirming that this is a small dang place. But the border is very modestly fortified and there is regular and easy crossing—Jordan, with a fit of common sense regrettably rare in the Arab world—long ago made peace with Israel.

The deal that the kibbutz wants is still a bit vague, and if they want too much for what they have done and what they bring, then this won't work, but it is lots of fun to talk with them and they are smart and well connected and nicely grounded. We agree to think about the terms and send them some draft language. Maybe it's because it's not raining, or maybe it's because I get lunch for only the second time on the trip, or maybe it is because I don't see any minefields around, but I am optimistic that we can do something here.

Shalom,
Bob

Afterword: We never went back to Tunisia. And I don't plan ever to go there again unless and until the Middle East becomes friendlier than Disneyland. History says that this will take some time.

We never built a wind farm in northern Israel. That, too, is a fine outcome, and the "friendlier than Disneyland" applies to that fine country as well. Overcoming bad zip codes is slow work.

chapter
fifteen

We Continue to Persevere in Happy Foreign Climes

November 2007

Dear Dad,
More notes from the road, this time the international road, during 2007. Yes I was a busy boy.

Nonhazardous Waste at Ras Laffan
I am at the meeting on the operations, business development progress and opportunities, and strategy for our Asia region, being held at a fancy hotel in Dubai. We have recently realigned our organization, and now Kazakhstan is no longer in Asia, it is in Europe and Africa, and the Middle East is no longer in Europe, it is in Asia. No sense getting too set in your ways as to geography. The safety and environment guy is giving his presentation. He puts up the slide on a recent environmental audit of our Ras Laffan gas-fired power plant in Qatar. There are four categories of findings: serious, high, medium, and low. The English professor in me refrains from asking why this typology doesn't seem to make much sense or at least

doesn't follow, and why serious is worse than high. Couldn't we just have used "really high" for serious? But never mind that.

The slide indicates that there were no serious findings, four high, and I forget the rest. Starved for actual content, I ask, "What was the substantive nature of the four serious findings, and have they been fixed?"

The safety guy responds that one of the findings was "failure to have a documented procedure for the disposal of nonhazardous waste." Something about this nags me. He attempts to go on but I can't hold myself back.

"What is 'nonhazardous waste'?"

"It is all the waste that is not classified as hazardous, and since this is a gas plant, there's no ash to dispose of, which is usually the bulk of the waste in this category," he graciously answers, wondering what kind of an idiot he's dealing with.

"So it's like, paper towels and coffee grounds and requests from head-quarters and bent paper clips and the remains of your lunch from Burger King and stuff like that?" I ask.

"Yes," he replies politely.

Suddenly I flash back to when I first moved from Washington to Chattanooga, Tennessee, which was a cultural shift of probably greater intensity than from Washington to Dubai would be. When I was first there I noticed that you had to put out your trash cans every Tuesday for the pickup. But I also noticed that about 50% of the time when I put mine out, it wasn't emptied. I finally asked my next-door neighbor what was going on. She was a very gracious Chattanooga native. She explained in her beautiful accent, "Well, you have to put out trash on Tuesday and garbage on Wednesday. You cain't mix the two or they won't pick up none of it."

"Damn, I am a Yankee even though I'm from Nebraska," I thought. "Well, what's trash and what's garbage?" I asked.

This stumped her. "Well, you know . . ." she explained.

I never did get an answer that made sense. Trash seemed to be dry and garbage wet, but baby diapers were trash not garbage. Ashes from the fireplace were garbage not trash. There was no garbage/trash dictionary or Rosetta stone. I ended up going to the dump a lot. They didn't seem to care whether it was trash or garbage. But I felt so inadequate.

"So we need a written procedure for this? What would such a proce-dure say—'Empty the trash can every so often—do not eat'?"

There is no answer for this question so I decide to shut up and let the meeting proceed. We have become a big company and sometimes it ain't pretty.

The Perils of English Food

It is sometimes said that English food is "much better" than it used to be (it used to be like eating dirt, or in the better cases, fried dirt), and a few idiots have even gone so far as to characterize it as "world class." On this short junket to the land of our forefathers (why couldn't they have been French or Laotian?), I am staying at an aggressively midlevel hotel in Berkshire, approximately forty-five minutes west of Heathrow. Its name is Coppid Beech Hotel. I have contemplated this, and speculated that either a coppid beech is some species that no one has heard of except Rosemary Verey or Graham Thomas or some other English garden freak, or it is something that you do to beeches to make them more, I don't know, English or some-thing. If you were English you'd understand.

I know it is midlevel, as there is a roundabout and a gas station across the street. But, sadly, no McDonald's. This is a conference of the BP alter-nate energy folks and as an invited speaker I am either the entertainment or a voice of sanity in the midst of excess. BP is the biggest and richest oil company in the world. But they don't have conferences at the Four Seasons. Maybe there's a connection.

As I arrived late and am not good company for anyone, and don't know anybody here anyway—I am speaking tomorrow but my host is off in Amsterdam—I am not having a swell dinner with anyone. Which is OK with me as I have been on an airplane for eleven hours from LA and am feeling uncompanionable and somewhat grungy.

After I run at the fitness center I come back to the room to find that there is no minibar key, as in, they didn't give me one when I checked in. I go back downstairs and the nice desk people say, "We don't have enough for each minibar, so you need to go back to your room and call room service and they will bring you a key to the minibar." I am not making this up.

Great moments in Euro hotel management: let us pause for a moment and consider the economics of minibars. Generally speaking, they put in stuff that costs $1.00, and then charge you $4.00 for it. In the land of high finance we call this "gross margin," and it is the ratio of net revenues ($3.00—you pay $4.00 but the stuff costs $1.00) to revenues ($4.00). At AES, for example, it is in the thirties—we get a dollar for every three dollars of revenues. And we are both delighted and the envy of the neighborhood. Here it is 75%. Wowee, kids, it's like the lemonade stand where the ingredients were free because your mom gave them to you, and the labor was free because it was you, so every glass sold was pure profit. Technically the ratio was therefore infinite, but that's hard to do in the real world. Every human being in the hotel biz knows that minibars are gold. Except those in Berkshire, it seems.

I get annoyed and say, "Never mind, I'll just order something from room service." How bad can it be? Note: this is a phrase that, in almost every human situation in which I have experience, foreshadows, um, disaster. The menu seems decent, has cheeseburgers and veg stuff and chicken satay and goat cheese salad. So I order the two latter. It comes quickly—too quickly perhaps—along with a half bottle of some Portuguese red, since, although it is on the menu, there is no Pinot Grigio.

The satay is not cooked, so nice yellow fat globs are still in residence in various locations on the chicken pieces, and the satay chunks have that bright pink inside color that we all love in chicken. The "peanut sauce" is a really odd shade of yellow gray not found in nature, and almost gelatinous. You could probably float a poorly cooked chicken chunk on the surface of the sauce. The side dish of chopped cucumbers is almost edible but is just that. The Thai immigrant wave has not overwhelmed this part of Sussex. Or if did, it took one look, turned around, and hightailed it back to downtown London.

The goat cheese with friseé is a goat cheese hockey puck sitting on two of the famous oat breakfast biscuits—why, why, we ask again and again—and seven very small bits of friseé, I counted. Oh, price—ten dollars per dish.

The Portuguese plonk, however, is actually quite good. I eat two chicken bites, all seven friseé leaves, and half the goat cheese hockey puck in honor of the NHL finals that may be going on, or may have ended six months ago. I am not much of a hockey fan. Ever since the Dodgers moved from Brooklyn to LA.

I find that, what with e-mails and being sweaty from running and all, I have moved expeditiously through the wine, Marques de Caceres to be precise, and so am forced by circumstance and survival instincts to order up another half bottle. Inspiration strikes! "Say," I ask conspiratorially to the chipper room service lady, "do you have any nuts?"

"We do," she says, "would you like some?"

"Very much," I say smoothly.

And, HOORAY, they bring me another half bottle of decent cheap wine and the first edible item of the evening, peanuts and sembei! It's not so tough to eat well in these third-world culinary countries; you just have to know what to order.

In Turkey, *Koc* Is Pronounced "Coach" but They Don't Make Fine Leather Goods

As the most available member of the AES executive team, I was sent to the biannual meeting of the US-Turkish Advisory Council, held on the grounds of the Koc Holdings compound in Istanbul. I am the official AES representative, and Koc is a big deal.

Since I had never been to Istanbul or Turkey before, I was careful to have the address for the meeting written down. I gave it to the driver of the taxi at the hotel, he looked at it, consulted with the dispatcher, nodded wisely, smiled, and took off. We crossed the suspension bridge over the Bosporus—my hotel was on the "Euro" side of Istanbul, the Koc offices on the "Asian" side—and then started negotiating the traffic-laden area.

Soon we were driving up and down narrow, steep, and winding streets, bordered by big and not very attractive residential apartment buildings on each side, cars parked on the sidewalk, laundry hanging out to dry from many of the windows. "Hmm," I thought, "Koc Holdings, third biggest conglomerate/business unit in Turkey, has its headquarters in this kind of neighborhood . . . maybe . . ."

The driver stopped several times and yelled out the window at passersby for directions; the first two times he received advice to continue driving past buildings with laundry. Finally we emerged and stopped in front of a vast expanse of immaculate green lawn, with a walled compound at its end, a guardhouse with uniformed guards, and beautiful office buildings visible beyond the walls. "Aha," I thought, "this might be it." This insight was assisted by the fact that across the wall nearest the guardhouse, in really big gold letters, were the words Koc Holdings.

The conference ran from nine to three in lovely facilities on top of a ridge, with a view of the Bosporus, guys in white coats pouring coffee, and so forth. All the proceedings were in English, which was a nice concession. Of the forty people there, it probably split twenty-five Turkish, fifteen American. Mustafa Koc, chairman of the place, and Frank Carlucci, former secretary of defense, were the two cochairs of the conference. The Turkish delegation had three former foreign ministers, a TV personality, a former Turkish ambassador to the EU, a number of well-regarded academics, and the like. No other Turkish businesspeople, probably for obvious reasons—why invite your competitors.

The US delegation was less impressive—a midlevel State Department guy, two or three RAND people, a couple of Carlyle partners, a head of a foreign affairs foundation in NY named Rita Houser (I think she is supposed to be famous but I never heard of her), no academics or bankers or lawyers, and no other industrial folks but me. Oh, yes, and Dr. Henry Kissinger. He is old. And short. He may have always been short. I think he might have been paid to come, since he didn't stay for lunch. He said in that deep, slow, gravelly voice of his that despite forty years in the US has never lost its German accent—the better to underline his authority, no doubt—things like, "The Middle East is a problem," and "Israel did not do well in Lebanon." OK then.

Mostly the program consisted of the Turkish side making presentations and then there was a brief period for two questions, and then the next presentation. I learned more about the Cyprus problem than I had ever planned I would. But not much about the business climate. Also a lot about the secular vs. Islamist question in Turkey, with the answer being, in general, with regard to the future, "We don't know but we think we're OK, unless of course things change and we're not." The more incisive folks suggested that economic development did much to reduce the interest in Islamic politics.

There was also much about the EU and its slowness in considering Turkey's application, and Turkey's related annoyance, which seemed in fact rather patient and forbearing on the part of Turkey. But no one predicted a train wreck. There was a too brief but very good discussion of the economy, which is doing remarkably well, largely the result of the Islamist party doing what the IMF told them to do.

Iraq came up, of course (another "problem," according to the good Dr. K.) but no one, American or Turkish, had a clue as to what to do. It was also agreed that it would be nice if the Kurds stopped blowing things up. Then we had lunch.

At lunch the conference managers had flown over Al Eisele, the editor of the *Hill* magazine, "the most knowledgeable publication about Congress." He gave a somewhat partisan talk and said it was hard to predict the election, but Iraq was an issue in some races and that the election could be important, depending on the outcome. Gasps of astonishment all around.

The food was pretty good, the people were smart, and it was nice to sit outside in the sunshine and look down at the Bosporus. I did get a chance to speak briefly with Mustafa Koc, conveying our interest and the best regards of John MacArthur, a longtime friend of the family and AES board member. He was warm and open, but was clear that they were not bidding in this round of privatizations of Turkish utility companies. We are and we had really hoped we could entice them into partnering with us. They have had trouble with the government in concluding the sale of the privatized oil refining business that they won last year. And since it was $4.5 billion deal, perhaps a bit of problem arranging all the money has arisen.

But the gracious Mr. Koc also said he would be happy to have further discussions on the next round of sales, but I did not have enough time with him to really discuss what that meant. It could have just been pleasantries.

The next meeting of the group will be in Washington in six months. I don't know exactly how these are organized, but I didn't get any assignments. I hope that isn't a bad sign.

Because of meetings in Kazakhstan on Tuesday and Wednesday of the following week, I was forced to stay over the weekend in Istanbul. It was really nice, even if Henry didn't come by for a drink.

Visit Beautiful Kazakhstan, Where the Unpredictable is Predictable—What?
Tuesday morning in September, after a long flight, a long passport line, a long baggage wait, and a short night, I walk out the door of the hotel wearing my finest lightweight summer suit and ready to go meet the energy minister only to find . . .

Winter comes early to the cruel and lifeless steppes, home to some of the finest C minus architecture in the world, combining the skills of second-rate Western architects with the sensibilities of the ruling Kazakh strong men, the guys who think sheep's eyeballs are a delicacy, to bring you really garish and remarkable stuff, strewn haphazardly around a perpetually windy and swampy site located far from anything of value or interest. Yes! It's Astana, the NEW capital of Kazakhstan, decreed by first pres (and pres for life, at least so far) Nazarbayev in 1997, and modeled on the wildly successful Brasilia, where no one likes to live either, although it's not so cold.

Fortunately there is, despite the relative newness of the town, substantial traffic to make one feel at home. And, in another modernistic departure, the local drivers have adopted a complete disregard for traffic lanes, a tactic last seen in Manila. Globalization at its very best!

Our offices in Astana are housed in a twenty-story new, modern office building that is covered with tiles colored a remarkable French's mustard yellow. I don't believe I have ever been in an office building before that was yellow, or worn a tie this color. It is said that the local Astanoviks call this building "the banana" but all that means is that these tropic-starved folk have never actually seen a banana, which is at least a nice shade of yellow until you put it by mistake into the refrigerator, trying to be tidy and helpful, and it turns immediately black and shriveled up, and your wife comes across it by mistake, digs it out, looks at you, and dangling this nasty thing by its stem says, "Don't you know you are not supposed to put bananas into the refrigerator?" This seems at best a rhetorical question because if you did know probably you wouldn't have unless you wanted to create something looking like it came from a low quality archaeological dig.

While the building color is not fetching, at least our office has a high-speed data line, although the pricey intercontinental hotel ("best in town") has only dial-up (!!!). I had almost forgotten that such a backward technology existed. And for good reason . . .

Late in the very cold day, we cannot get the fully booked early flight from Astana to Almaty, where we were bound for the next day's meetings, and thus we took the ten o'clock flight in the evening, which puts one in yet another not very good intercontinental hotel about 1230 in the very early morning. Again.

Here they have a different approach to in-room hospitality; they supply you with all the appliances needed for a minibar, and a couple of wine glasses, and a very well-printed list of the prices for all the things in the minibar, only they make the minibar empty as a clever trick! But I am an experienced world traveler and I immediately called the desk and said, 'Hey, where's my minibar?" or something to that effect.

The desk clerk, probably determining that I was delusional—who can't find his minibar, I ask you—or else having seen the original *Clerks* movie, said he would take care of it right away. Thirty minutes later, I called room service and ordered two beers, having given up on the Emergency Minibar Restocking Team.

Twenty minutes later I called room service again and asked where the legendary two beers were—with or without Goldilocks—who was not Kazakh or she would have skinned and eaten all three bears rather than just lying down for a nap.

"How much time does it take to deliver two beers?" I asked testily. "When will they be here?"

"What?" replied the room service person.

"When?" I said again. "The two beers, I would like to know when the two beers will be here, when?"

"One?" she asked. They eventually arrived, but without an opener. Fortunately I used my Swiss army knife to open the luke-cool bottles and celebrate a small victory in the never-ending battle against mediocrity, aging, and world hunger. Or world thirst.

Almaty, it turns out, is nicer than Astana and looks like the inside of a windowless conference room, with people showing you slides with about a jillion numbers on them and speaking at you in translated Russian or translated English, sometimes both at once. No, wait, it's a budget meeting and I am being held hostage without coffee until the "coffee break." It's sad when conference organizers take these break things literally. No wonder I couldn't tell where I was.

My conclusions from meetings and meetings are:

» We got a lot of stuff in K'stan, and it's getting more valuable by the day. What we really are is American oligarchs (dude, where's my jet?), who picked up assets on the cheap ten years ago, and didn't even have to shoot anyone or push them out of helicopters. Of course, since the roof of the boiler building had fallen in, and the 4,000 Mw plant was only capable of producing 250 Mw, and we could only sell 50 Mw of this, it wasn't obvious at the time that this was a diamond mine.

» We have managed to develop a lot of good people here running these assets, and they are all pretty pleased to have survived and to see that these things are now becoming useful. And I think many of them are relieved to actually work for an honest company. Except the crooks, of course. But we try to fire them.

» It's still pretty corrupt. Your $4 million tax bill can disappear, the governor of the province assured us, if you'll just have a one-day study done by this company he recommends, for $100,000. You'll even get a copy of the study. At least it's nice that this helpful offer comes directly from the governor.

» — Rather than do business in Russia, which is not only corrupt but also dangerous and geopolitically weird, we are luring companies from Russia down to Kazakhstan with promises of . . . no, not lush young women or men or caviar or vodka or fancy cars or alligator briefcases full of euros, but CHEAP ELECTRICITY! Strangely, it is starting to work, first with a metal smelting company, then with SUAL, a giant aluminum company.

» We have enough smart and dedicated people here to continue to make this work. We just have to hope that the government runs the country in a sensible enough way that incomes rise, at least some small fraction of the remarkable oil and mineral wealth trickles down, and global warming comes quickly enough to make the winters tolerable.

Cameroon by Night Is Not a Delight—Yes, Another Food Story and More

You know, this international travel to exotic locations actually isn't all that jazzy. I am sitting here in Yaounde doing e-mail, looking out my window at not very many lights in a dark town that you really don't want to walk around in at night, although it is the major commercial center of the country and thus has six tall buildings, but only one decent (and we use the term advisedly) hotel, the Meridien, graded B minus and trending down, where I have just had via room service half a bowl of not very good pasta with tomato sauce and three (3) olives. "Spare no expense! Give the American guy a third olive!" says the kitchen staff, "Even though he'll sure be surprised when he finds out that we left the pits in them, ho ho!"

I also had two rather small bottles of what was supposed to be the local Cameroonian beer, ordered with as much clarity and patience as I could muster, twice, and delivered once as nothing, as the young woman came to my room and asked about the beer, delivered a second time as mugs of beer not bottles, but now present for duty as Beaufort, a fine, light Irish beer with a golden English lion but not Simba lord of the jungle on the label.

My quest for local color, limited this evening to the beer, is not successful, and not for lack of trying. I even said it in French: *"Le bière de Cameroon, en bouteilles, s'il vous plaît."* I obviously need to master the vernacular.

And this is my reward after sitting in a grade C conference room, on a not really comfortable at all hard wooden chair, watching PowerPoint slides, for ten straight hours of briefings and discussion of a whole series of initiatives being undertaken by the Sonel people. Who really are trying hard, but gracious me. One hour would pass, the issue of setting up a transmission systems operator would be thoroughly discussed and presented, then that gang of Sonelians would get up, troop out, and another group of six or seven would come in, fresh and eager, all ready to be introduced and, except for the expats, all with names like Mary Ntanang and Joseph Yoekobo and Charlemagne Nana and Vladimir Foubegou. Who could make this up? Was there some rule here that you had to give your kid an American or European person's name? Or are these transliterations of African names? Or are these adapted out of courtesy to us ex-colons, since we would be hard-pressed to remember or pronounce the name of Yufonui Sinajie—another real-life example.

They are dying to discuss with me the initiative of separating the accounting system into three sub-units, each with its own balance sheet and income statement, organized into generation, transmission, and distribution. We still own the whole thing, no matter how many pieces we divide the accounting into, and then report on—to ourselves, of course. Not clear this is progress.

No break for lunch, although there was cold pizza left over from yesterday. I tell you what, these gentle and attractive Cameroonians do NOT know how to make pizza, which is hardly strange given their African/French colonial/British colonial heritage. The pizza is not nearly so good the next day, although it was pretty awful on Sunday when warm. Well, sort of warm. One piece of olive per slice. Maybe they know the chef here at the Meridien. All this is washed down with a cup of instant coffee, which the wily support staff has disguised by putting it into a large carafe, thus making one think that it might even be brewed. No such luck. I note for the record that coffee is in fact grown in Cameroon, said to be quite good coffee, it just doesn't seem to be brewed here. Africa, land of mystery.

Love and kisses,
Bob

Afterword: As mentioned earlier, we eventually sold our major asset in Kazakhstan for quite a lot of money, and got out of Cameroon financially intact.

Turkey is another matter. One could not have asked for a better partner in a 50/50 joint venture than the Koc family. We were delighted when they finally decided to join with us. They are highly successful businesspeople, they are widely respected, they have the kind of money that it takes to play in the infrastructure game, and they have clear understandings of the requirements of international business. But "partners" are hard, and a venture when each decision requires both parties to agree is potentially a flawed structure. Language interferes, cultures interfere, values interfere. One party wants to go faster than the other, one party uses a different discount rate than the other, one partner provides less capable people to the venture than the other. The list is endless, and all these matters of potential conflict cannot be negotiated before the venture is set up, because the list is endless. It is more amazing to find a joint venture that works, by at least an order or magnitude, than it is to find one that has failed.

The venture worked for a while. But AES finally decided to get out of Turkey, as it was not seen as a sufficiently big market that would support the level of resources necessary to do business there, even with, or perhaps especially because of, an ambitious partner. Given the current situation along Turkey's borders, this was a great idea when evaluated by looking back, but it was not one for which the company takes any credit. Sometimes luck happens.

chapter sixteen

Geese Are Harder to Shoot Than You Would Think

December 2007

Dear Dad,

So what do you do when Paul, your CEO, asks you if you'd like to go goose hunting with him tomorrow? And it's the end of the day Friday and he has just engineered it so the board has approved a $240 million take or pay purchase of solar panels for projects where we don't quite have permits. Or in some cases, land rights. Since it's hard to answer this question without the requisite background, here is the background.

Paul and his wife, Rodanthe, moved to Easton five years ago from McLean. As you may remember, Easton is across the Chesapeake Bay from everything, and you have to go over a long bridge to get there. The "there" is generally called the Eastern Shore, which makes no sense as Maryland is not what you would call an island or even a peninsula like Florida, nor is it one of those geographical oddities that, like Costa Rica, exists where the continent necks down, so there isn't really a "western shore," it's the only shore there is, given that "shore" usually means "ocean shore." We might also note, pedantically, that this strip of land continues on south and turns into part of Virginia, at which point it is mysteriously called the Northern Neck. Except that it is either the southern neck if the whole thing is a neck, or it's the eastern neck if we are now referring only to Virginia. But never mind that. The point of this small lesson in local oceanics is that it's a honking long way from our offices in Arlington to where the CEO lives. We did finally break down and get him a car and a very capable guy to drive it, so that Paul doesn't fall asleep and crash into the guardrails when he is driving in at four-thirty in the morning, which you have to do to get to work at a reasonable time. Seemed a small thing to do, and much cheaper than having to have a real executive succession plan.

It is unmistakably nice in Easton, which is on the western side of this small peninsula (or neck) that makes up the Eastern Shore, while all the beach towns—Ocean City, Dewey Beach and Bethany Beach, for example—are on the eastern shore of the Eastern Shore. There are many rivers and suchlike that drain into the Chesapeake, and thus lots of river-front properties, and lots of boats. In olden times, which is defined as when Reagan was president, it was entirely farms and an annoying bit of boring flatness to drive through fast on your way to Rehoboth. And the waterfront part of it was used by real working people who harvested fish and crabs from the Chesapeake. Then someone discovered how cheap it was and how nice it was to have your own dock and boat, especially if you didn't have to get up before dawn everyday no matter what the weather and go out and fish for oysters. Rich people have moved in and bought large pieces of property with river frontage, and the place is in the middle of something of a boom. Vice President Cheney has a house in the area, for example. This conversion into a weekend retreat for Washington big dogs may be timely as the shellfish and the fish are in something of a decline. But the rural culture that was high on huntin' and fishin' still thrives.

Paul likes it so much that he has now, in addition to his lovely house and eighteen acres on the water, purchased a five hundred-acre farm, also on the water. It is an interesting but odd bit of property. For probably twenty-five years now the farm has been owned by an absentee landlord, an elderly party who lives in Key West, and managed by a contract farmer who also doesn't live there. Hence the outbuildings are all falling down, except for the concrete barn that is used for farming purposes and besides won't fall down for another several hundred years. Who ever heard of a concrete barn, but there you are. Another interesting part is that whenever a vehicle or piece of farm equipment realizes that it is at the end of its useful life, it has crept off into the wood line and thickets and quietly died. When you hike around the parts that are not farmed, you continually stumble upon old Camaros and Pacers and tractors (six by last count) and even the odd large truck, which in this case actually has a tree growing though its bed.

There is much wildlife. Lots of deer in the thickets, and tons of ducks and geese lured by the abundant water and the farming that still leaves lots of uncollected corn and soybeans in the fields in the winter. Also lured, I suspect, by the change in the population from classic poor rural to higher-end residents, which, despite this story, means fewer people with guns blasting the birds and animals. Or perhaps the same number of people with guns, but less economic need and goodness knows less accuracy as drivers of hunting efficiency.

In addition to the substantial detritus of an internal combustion graveyard, Paul has discovered that his new property has six—count them six—goose blinds dotted about it.

We now pause for further explanation. As you will no doubt recall, when I was growing up you never took me hunting or fishing, nor did you go hunting or fishing yourself without me. You did teach me how to play a lot of great card games, which I consider a more than fair trade, although you shorted me on poker. When I actually got a BB gun you were apoplectic that the air base MPs would come by and confiscate it since it was not legal to shoot it anywhere. This does raise the question of why I even had one in the first place, maybe Santa brought it. This whole area of guy-ness has been missing in my upbringing and subsequent adulthood. Obviously I did not miss it terribly, since when in the army they gave me a gun and told me to shoot at stuff, not only was I happy to oblige, but I turned out to be a pretty good shot. Somewhat to my surprise. But I have done none of that on a recreational basis, ever. I do not have a shotgun, nor a camouflage parka, nor hat, nor duck boots, nor a prize-winning retriever or any of that stuff. I have no strong political position on this, and don't think it is necessarily a bad thing to shoot stuff, although I suppose we should eliminate other human beings from the list, particularly well-behaved children and loving spouses.

Geese do strike me as a reasonable target, so to speak. They are bold and unattractive, they have multiplied unmercifully in the past decades as hunting restrictions have been put in place, and they now foul (as it were) numerous properties that have water at hand—something the clever landscape architects never quite thought of when designing the attractive "water features." You can buy expensive systems to keep geese off your property and thus prevent the loud honking at night and the really remarkable amount of goose manure that is deposited everywhere. I would prefer to shoot deer, which are really destructive vermin, but absent that Geese Will Do.

But wait, nothing in modern American culture is that simple. Shooting geese is, it turns out, at least in Maryland—where we have never seen a regulation we don't like, and where the political establishment constantly talks to people in Massachusetts and California to make sure that we haven't overlooked some new regulatory approach—highly regulated. Well, there's a surprise. You don't just get a gun and a license and go out and blast away. First, there's a season. For geese it is middle of December to the end of January. Why? There is no answer to such an existential question. On the pro side: because geese are down here for the winter. They are, after all, Canadian geese, and it is cold in Canada in the winter, so who wouldn't want to fly south. Why they stop in Maryland rather than going on to a condo in Fort Lauderdale is not clear.

The whole thing is further confused by a different season for snow geese, which are, it is said, even more criminal than Canadian geese, in that they pull plants up by the roots and demolish crops, etc. Of course, this view of snow geese explained to us by the hunting guide of our party, who just may have a particular point of view on these matters. In simple terms, it probably doesn't make a lot of sense to allow hunting of stuff that is not around. On the con side, it is cold and damp in MD in this particular time period. Also it gets dark early. And light late. And since the additional restriction is that you can only shoot them in the daylight, this further limits the window of availability.

There are more rules.

Restriction #1: you cannot shoot them with a rifle. Well, a shotgun is better anyway as it fires shot—could that be why it has that name?—and thus has a broad distribution of the little pellets. The standard is for all the pellets to fall within a thirty-inch diameter circle at forty yards. Of course a rifle is one bullet, so that's different. The downside of the big circle is that each pellet has correspondingly less of the energy of the gunpowder discharge so they don't go very far. Forty yards seems more than enough to me, since we are not talking about killing water buffalo that have gotten irritated and are charging you with evil intent. Just geese.

Restriction #2: your shotgun may only have two shells in it, even if its magazine or internal architecture would allow for more. No, we have no idea why this is the rule, it's just a rule. Maybe it's so that you won't follow the flight of the geese as they fly away from you and inadvertently turn into your hunting partner and blast him with your third round. We don't know.

Restriction #3: you have to shoot them in the air; you cannot wait until they land in front of you as you sit disguised in the middle of the cornfield, and the now-earthbound geese start pecking at all the fallen corncobs that the John Deere harvester somehow neglected to harvest and thus are waiting there on the ground to become goose food. I do wonder if there is a setting on the John Deere for "maximum missed corncobs." You can't go out and sprinkle food on the field to attract the geese, but if you just have an inefficient harvester, what are you to do? The "on the wing" thing makes no sense to me. They are a lot harder to hit in the air as this implies that they are in fact flying and this further implies velocity and erratic movement, and thus you need to lead the suckers and anticipate where they are going and shoot there and so forth. If they're on the ground gorging on corn you can do a much better job of hitting them, which I thought was the point of all this. And, not to come across as unnecessarily argumentative, but how exactly does one tell, once you got a dead goose filled with buckshot on your hands, that it was shot in the air as opposed to on the ground? Does it have telltale corn fragments embedded in its underside? If flying, is it clear that all the shot hit its belly? I mean, hey, those birds can do some acrobatics, who knows where you're gonna hit it. This seems to me to be an unenforceable rule, unless the game warden is sitting right there with you in the goose blind, or lurking at the edge of the field in the tree line, in which case he better watch out that we don't shoot at him in our enthusiasm.

Restriction #4: each licensed hunter may only shoot one goose per day. I sense that this rule is applied retroactively and in aggregate, as hunting (now that I have been once, I am of course an expert) for geese is something of a team sport, perhaps similar to the game we played occasionally at Yale with the really large six-foot inflated ball—bladder ball I think it was called—where your side tried to push this mother over the goal line of the other guys and vice versa. There was no way to distinguish in that muddy mess—for some reason it was always played after a rain—who had done what. Or think about tug-of-war—truly a team effort. Goose hunting is same. Hence if three hunters and three dead geese leave the field of conflict, I guess the rule is obeyed, even if two of them are blind paraplegics and thus unlikely to have done in said geese.

Restriction #5: you have to have a special license, both state and federal. What, you may ask, does it take to get such a license? Are there tests like in drivers ed? Do you have to go through a simulator, like to get a license to become a nuclear plant operator? Is there a waiting period, like that required to get a gun license in Virginia, so that you have five days to contemplate the protection of your home from goose invasions or the enormity of possibly taking the life of another sentient being? Right, a goose . . . well maybe not that sentient. Oh no, the requirement is that you have a credit card, or if not that, the requisite amount of US currency. I guess you also have to be able to tell them that you have a name since they have to write something on the piece of paper, but that's it. And the license-selling stores are conveniently usually also gun- and equipment-selling stores, a very handy one-stop concept. I bought mine at Chesapeake Bay Outfitters on the way to Easton from Potomac. And it was even open at five in the morning! No, that's not a typo. Burger King isn't open then, 7-Eleven damn sure isn't, but on Route 50 heading from Annapolis over the bridge to the Eastern Shore, you can get yourself a license to kill. I felt strangely like James Bond at least with respect to waterfowl. What the waterfowl felt was not recorded.

Back to our main story. So, your CEO asks you to go goose hunting with him on the same day that you are supposed to fly to Boston and spend time with a bunch of relatives of your wife. Fortunately I like Paul a lot and he has been very supportive of me, so I am NOT reminded of TVA. I had been there in my new job a week, having been recruited by Dave Freeman, who was at that point chairman of the board. He gaily thrust me into the middle of the TVA power bureaucracy to run the newly established conservation division, carved out of the turf of some other people who were longtime Tennesseans and not all that happy to see me. It should also be said in my nondefense that I did not see a thing wrong with this, and was supremely confident, in the arrogance of youth, that I could do anything asked of me and was probably smarter than these slow-talking people anyway. In some cases this was true, in others not. One of the most interesting "nots" was in picking up cultural cues and adapting quickly. The principal greeting in Chattanooga when a resident meets someone from outside is to say, "Hello, glad to meet you, have you found a church yet?" I will admit that this confounded me. It was not a greeting I was expecting or used to. I would have understood *"Ikaga desu ka?"* or *"Como esta usted"* way better. My initial reaction was to say, "Have I found a church yet? There's one on every dang corner, how hard could they be to find?" But that would have been wrong.

So when I was first introduced to my immediate boss, the manager of power, a nice and as it turned out ineffective man whose named I forget, maybe Nate something, he greeted me pleasantly and a little bit diffidently. I later figured out that they were all a little afraid of Dave Freeman who had, truth to tell, been running around breaking a lot of china in an organization where even the tiniest chip on the smallest and least expensive cup was regarded with something akin to horror—they did not settle differences by arguing them out. Nate Something gave me the customary, "Glad to meet you, have you found a church yet?" Not "Are you getting settled in? How do you like it here? Is this your first time in Tennessee?" etc. I was slow so I said, "No, no, I haven't." And then he said, "Well, then, I would like to ask you to join me this weekend at my church." Eeek! How bad was this? Somehow I finally recovered my senses enough to lie that I had already been invited to *another* church, but thank you for the kind invitation. Whew, close call. Fortunately he did not ask again, and I learned enough to reply yes I had, the Episcopal Church on Signal Mountain, and then everyone left me alone.

But this was not like that. I asked Paul what "hunting geese" entailed. It turns out that it entailed getting up at four in the morning and driving from Potomac and my warm cozy bed to stand around in a goose blind as the sun rose. Note: goose blinds are not heated, so the weather was what you got and it was December. "Well," I temporized, "I don't have a gun." "No problem, I have an extra one you can use." "Uh, do I need a license or anything?" "No problem, you can stop at Chesapeake Outfitters, they're open early, and it's on the way." I was out of excuses since I figured saying that I had to go to church, having just found one, would not be convincing for a Saturday morning. "Sure," I said, "that would be fun."

Paul's driver, Robert, gave me the directions to the farm and indicated that he would be coming with us and that I would really enjoy it. But the kid was a Marine, almost anything after that would seem enjoyable by comparison.

I show up at the appointed time, license in hand and wearing long underwear and other layers of warm clothing. Fortunately it is in the high thirties and not raining or snowing, so it does not seem that bad. At least not inside the car.

The guide, Paul, and Robert all have full camo gear on. By sheer good luck I have on an olive drab coat and gray jeans. The red baseball cap seems to have been a mistake but the coat has a hood so I can look mostly green. At least the others have not painted their faces.

The first thing one does in this ritual is put out the decoys. The guide, a nice, talkative local guy who is also the National Guard recruiter and a volunteer fireman has brought the decoys. There are a lot of them. About 120. And most are two-dimensional, full-size replicas of geese mounted on sticks that you stick in the ground. There are also some full- size ones and some that have goose heads and then a sort of brown wind sock thing attached to the stick the head is on. All of these move slightly in the wind, which it turns out is useful as geese expect motion from their comrades. I cannot tell if we are distributing them in a pattern but we put them all around the blind, then the guide drives the truck off somewhere.

The blind is in the middle of a cornfield. It is much more elaborate than I had envisioned. Think about a bunker to use in case of an air attack and you'll be closer. It is a rectangle, about half the size of a Conex container, and sits entirely below the level of the ground. There is a nice wooden bench across one side, the walls are wood with support posts, and actually the entire thing is made of wood, including the floor. It is serious construction, nicely engineered, not just some hole in the ground. Two-thirds of the top is permanently covered, but one-third has a long rectangular sliding top made of small angle iron, with wheels attached that are mounted on rails. It is sort of like a garage door, except it moves horizontally back and forth to cover and uncover the blind. This metal frame is covered with wire fencing to which have been tied lots of corn stalks. Thus when it is closed the area looks like a goose blind with a cover of dead corn stalks on it. But geese aren't so smart, so it's apparently fine.

The process is also interesting. First you load your gun with two shells, making sure you know how to put it on "safe" and then how to take it off safe so you can actually shoot it. The shotguns don't have sights on them, really, just a bead on the end. One sights down the barrel and puts the bead at the end "on the head of the goose" and then fires. This is said to be enough of a lead for as close as the geese will be to us.

You start with all four of us, the guide and us three shooters, standing up in a nice sort of row and looking around the sky for, yes, geese. This is interesting for seven or eight minutes. Eventually some fly by, but "by" is a relative term. Mostly they look like little dots in the sky, as they are prudent enough or lucky enough to avoid us by a very wide margin. What we want them to do is come over to the cornfield and begin to land next to the decoys so we can then shoot them. What they want to do is fly merrily round here and there, mostly to and from the water that is nearby. Or maybe to the local Howard Johnson's for some flapjacks, who knows. The leftover corn does not seem to attract.

The next part of the ritual is even better. When some group of geese look like they might actually see the decoys and the corn and comes a bit closer, we close the top of the blind and sit down on the benches. All except the guide, who sticks his head through the corn stalks and starts using his goose caller: *honk, honk, honk*. Those of us sitting inside have no idea if the geese are coming or not, how close, what side they might be on, etc. I finally understand why this is called a goose blind. If by some miracle a goose does get close enough to shoot, then the guide quickly slides back the top, says something like, "Go shoot them," and we pop up looking for geese. Looking in which direction is not so clear, maybe I missed that part. But you have to be quick because if the idiot geese actually land then you can't shoot them. I guess maybe you could shoot over their heads and that would encourage them to fly. And if you don't hit anything, then the ritual starts all over again. Look at the sky, discuss whether it is getting cloudy (for some reason clouds encourage geese to land in cornfields), note disparagingly that it was a full moon the night before so probably the geese were out feeding by moonlight and are now full and content to float around on the water, discuss other hunting trips you have been on, explain the difference between geese and swans, etc., and every so often listen to the sudden chorus of *boom, boom, boom, boom* as some other folks in some other blinds find geese foolish enough to come by for a visit. There were lots of others sitting around like us, which is somewhat remarkable. Paul did accommodate us by stopping at Dunkin' Donuts on the way to the blind, so we were each able to kill and eat several donuts and drink a lot of coffee. This may actually be the purpose of goose hunting.

The alleged geese were only close enough to us for us to fire our guns two times. The first time a flock flew over us low and were wildly bombarded by us crack marksmen, they flew away successfully, pooping on us as they went. Of course, were I a goose with someone unexpectedly shooting at me from below, I might well react in the same fashion. The second and final time a single (and obviously mentally retarded) goose decided to land and chat up our decoys. Maybe he'd been introduced by eHarmony. All three of us rose up firing rapidly, and one of us—probably Robert the former Marine—nailed him in the air. On balance: geese three, hunters one.

Eventually we tired of the fun and the geese stopped flying around anywhere, so we climbed out of the blind, pulled up and packed up all the decoys, and walked back to our trucks. Then occurred the final ritual, the Distribution of the Goose. You take it, no really I couldn't, you take it, no I'd love to but I have to go to Boston, well you could take it with you to Boston, we can pack it in ice, good I am sure my relatives would like a dead bloody feathery goose for Christmas, I appreciate it but wouldn't your kids like to perfect their biology skills by cleaning it?

I quickly left before the reverse tug-of-war between Paul and Robert was resolved. The following is an e-mail from Paul that gives you the ultimate goose outcome.

Merry Christmas.

It's unfortunate that you couldn't take this tasty goose with you to Boston. We actually cooked and ate the darn thing tonight. The kids cleaned the goose and I cooked it. Rodanthe and her mom just wished we had ordered Chinese instead. Fortunately, I had some deer "appetizers" in advance, so all had plenty to eat. Next time, we'll go out goose hunting on a day when the geese are actually hungry. Then you can bring a couple of them home for dinner—I'll share my recipe.

Love and kisses,
Bob the Mighty Hunter

chapter
seventeen

Chiusa Does Not Mean "Hello" in Italian

August 2008

Dear Dad,

It all began, I suppose, at the movies.

Linda loved Diane Lane in *Under the Tuscan Sun*. I preferred Liv Tyler in Bertolucci's *Stealing Beauty*, perhaps the most sensuous movie of the "rent a villa in Tuscany for the summer and invite all your beautiful and artistic friends over and have great intellectual conversations while drinking excellent wine, eating fabulous food, and surveying the olive trees and the vineyards from your hilltop estate" type movie ever made. Jeremy Irons was in his "I still look like a human being" phase, which probably ended with *Die Hard: With a Vengeance*. Naturally what happens when you really sit down to think about this is you realize that you don't have any artists and poets and sculptors as friends, all you know are lawyers and investment bankers. Egad. But anyway, about a third of the way into the summer, we had the usual vacation conversation:

Conversant #1: Are we taking a vacation this year?

Conversant #2: Well, of course we are. Let's rent a villa in Italy.

#1: Um, it's late June, and people plan this stuff a year in advance. Plus we don't have any money and villas ain't exactly cheap.

#2: No, there's bound to be something available. [Note absence of reference to money.]

#1: Maybe. When do you want to go?

#2: August. Nothing else is happening then. But the house <u>has</u> to have a high-speed Internet connection, and the cell phone has to work, or else I'm not going.

#1: But if nothing else is happening in August, why do we need e-mail? And our cell phones don't work here in Potomac.

And so forth.

But in the spirit of "Hey, why not," one of us duly searched the Internet, found a "villa," which as you might imagine is what everything is called, including the one-room chicken coops. I made as sure as one can that it actually had Internet service and that cell phones worked, determined that it was available the second week of August, sent forth a modest amount of dollars—unfortunately tied to the euro—got our tickets with airline miles, and there we were.

It should also be noted in the spirit of fairness that I got pretty excited, and so bought a bunch of guidebooks and maps about Umbria, since (a) the house was near Padua, wherever that is, and (b) as do all well-educated Americans, I believe that Italy is divided into four basic regions: Rome, Sicily (which Naples is part of somehow and where both pizza and the Mafia were invented), Tuscany, and Umbria.

Amazon sent the maps and the guidebooks and I sat at our breezeway table eagerly exploring them. "Where the hell is Padua?" I finally exclaimed after much fruitless searching. "They left it off this damn Umbria map."

Well, yes, they did, but only because Padua and Venice (another referent for the villa) are not in Umbria. Nor in Sicily or Rome. Italy has gone and created several additional regions! Must be part of the worldwide trend toward ethnic fragmentation, like the Kurds or the South Ossetians in Georgia. And are there North Ossetians, by the way, and if so are they the same as or different from the southern ones?

The villa turned out to be in the Veneto, the flat plain lying to the west of Venice and south of the Dolomites and extending down to somewhere, maybe Umbria, maybe Emilia Romagna, whoever he was or she was. New maps and guidebooks were ordered. Very confusing.

There were some early signs of trouble . . . not including my lack of geographical knowledge of Italy, which is hard to blame on someone else, maybe my fifth-grade teacher. For one thing, when I went back and read the fine print carefully instead of just looking at the majestic pictures, what we were actually renting became somewhat more clear. It was not a gigantic, historic, three-story limestone villa with two wings surrounding a majestic if somewhat formal garden with parterres and statues and fountains and urns with flowers and serious big iron gates. It was a small apartment with an even smaller kitchen in one of the wings of the villa. The left wing to be exact. The villa itself is home to its owners, a countess and possibly an accompanying count, although this never became clear. The apartment had two bedrooms, two bathrooms, a kitchen, and a combination dining room and living room. It was said to accommodate ten should you come across an accommodating group of midgets. It was a flat, as the Brits would say, in a villa, not a villa. You did get to walk around in the grounds, however, unless there was a wedding going on. Yes, the villa—the real villa, that is, not the flat for the Americans to pretend they lived at a villa—was also rented out for weddings and, I suppose, receptions. We found this out after we had made the nonrefundable deposit, and only by reading the evaluation form of one of the previous renters who had also found himself surprised to be in the middle of a wedding, not his own, during his vacation. But when we checked there were no weddings scheduled for August, although the agents did acknowledge that the villa was a popular wedding venue. This should have been a sign, but it was too subtle for us; we were just relieved that there were no weddings planned.

The next not so good sign was that when we were sent directions to the villa by the agent, the directions were for someone coming from Milan. Which is way to the west, whereas we were coming from Venice, which is much closer and to the southeast of said location. When we inquired, the agents apologized—they had also gotten the check-in time wrong, failing to even read the information on their own website—and sent a different set of directions.

So we packed up and with our new directions, our second set of guidebooks and maps, and our strict instructions to bring 1,000 euros in cash for the breakage deposit for the owner, we took off. The directions to the house had a certain number of shortcomings. Like "After exiting at Treviso south, immediately turn left before the traffic circle," which was impossible as there was no road between the exit and the traffic circle. And the omission of several key T intersections where one had to turn in some direction not noted. Mostly by luck and by having spent an hour on Google maps, I had a more or less idea of where to go. But only more or less.

When not cursing the lousy directions as I drove the twenty-five miles to the villa, about two-thirds on narrow back roads, I did take time to notice several things:

» The place was very flat. The Veneto must be a plain, I concluded. I am nothing if not an observant traveler.

» Corn, corn, and more corn, all quite tall. Just about every piece of agricultural land with a crop on it had corn. Got corn? You bet—big fields, small fields, the little triangles at the autostrada exits, the next-door neighbors' twenty-by-twenty plot—everywhere. I estimate that of all the land in cultivation, fully 85% was growing corn. I knew the directions were bad, but I did not expect that they would have taken me to Nebraska.

We now offer several thoughts on the subject of "Why corn?"

1. It is a staple of Italian cooking, as in cornbread, cornmeal muffins, corn fritters, corn soup, tortillas, etc.? Well, no. Italy is about pasta and rice and not so much corn. I took a cooking course from Marcella Hazan in Venice a while back, and corn was not featured at all in any of the recipes for the entire seven days. OK, there is polenta but not so much, and not according to Marcella.

2. Italians love corn on the cob? Probably not, as there was no fresh corn available in the markets that were right in the middle of the

cornfields. None. Nor at any roadside stands, of which there were none.

3. They were growing it to feed to cattle? Maybe, but I don't think I saw a single cow or pig the whole time we were there, and we drove around a lot.

4. They are making ethanol with it? Could be, but there was no evidence of this in the gas stations. Hence it must remain a mystery, which is the answer of the Catholic Church to many things, and since this is a Catholic country, the answer works. It was a lot of corn.

» Hot, hot, hot. Well, it was August. Hot and sunny to be precise. Better than cold and rainy, which is what it was when me and Marcella were hanging out at the Hotel Cipriani, mastering non-corn Italian recipes. On that fabulous occasion I decided that checking on the weather in November in Rome was a good enough proxy for Venice, and thus brought only short sleeve shirts and stuff with me. Another trick of Italian geography! Tricky Venice is not close to Rome — I almost froze there. *Death in Venice* without Thomas Mann, the heat, the beautiful Tadzio, and all that other stuff you can find in Wikipedia if you cannot be bothered to actually read the novella. I do not think it is at the top of Amazon's list of best sellers.

With some good luck and more good guesses, none of which should be necessary if one has what are called "directions" (but the providing of same is apparently not a skill mastered by the rental agents of villas), I did end up at the place. The countess greeted me and seemed surprised to see a hot, annoyed, single American when all the information that had been sent to her implied eight persons. Perhaps she thought the rest of the party had gotten lost in the cornfields.

The villa was large and historic and so forth. It was also a bit down at the heels, paint on the shutters way past its shelf life and cracking off, the limestone stained from the rain, the garden only intermittently maintained, the central fountain not working and full of green goo. It did have a sign on it that I translated as DO NOT DRINK THIS WATER—IT IS NOT

CLEAN, although one would have thought that all you had to do was look at it and figure this out for yourself. But never mind.

The countess showed me through the apartment, and it did have the number of rooms specified. And was at the top of two flights of broad marble stairs. The bedrooms had air-conditioning, although not the kitchen, dining room, or living room. The place was clean and decorated in the dark and kitschy style your grandmother might have used if she frequented garage sales and only bought cheap cut glass and large pictures of dead fish. There was a stereo we could never get to work, and a TV set that had no channels that I could ever find that showed the Olympics, even in Italian. The kitchen had been hived off the dining room so it was essentially long and thin. It was equipped with a stove top where three of the four burners actually worked, an incomprehensible microwave that told time correctly and did nothing else I could deduce, a dishwasher and a refrigerator with a glacial back wall of ice. Fortunately the previous renters had left two beers in the fridge. I immediately had one, and went back downstairs to see if I could get the Wi-Fi system to work. After much negotiation with the countess, including a call to her son and a discussion on the cell phone with him, it did. So, I did not have to decide whether or not to abort.

After the second beer I decided that I would take stock of the kitchen and get some supplies. For a place with room for ten people, it was pretty surprising. No blender and no Cuisinart and no mixer, and only tiny wooden cutting boards, but that was predictable. However, no whisk, only one decent knife, no corkscrew, no wine glasses, no cheese grater. I checked again to make sure that I was actually in Italy, not Albania by mistake. As do all good Hemphill family members when confronting such challenges, I decided that the correct remedy for all this was to make a list.

The countess recommended the market in the village of Levada, about a three quarters of a mile away. To get there one passes by the central monument of the place, a larger-than-life-size bronze replica of a soldier standing erect on a tall plinth of rocks held together with mortar. He is in full military gear including helmet and pack, but has his arms raised over his head, holding his rifle by the end of the barrel, with the clear intent of tossing it away. The iconography seemed less than heroic, but perhaps appropriate given the history of the Italian military in the twentieth century. The "store" in the town was open, but turned out to be a bar, not a store. Everything else was closed, but it was a small town and it was late Saturday afternoon.

Fortunately, there was an alternative, an *ipermarketi* named Emisfero, about three miles in the opposite direction. It was open, the parking lot was full, and it was interesting, especially if you're a sucker for markets and if you're hungry and out of beer. What was inside was a little unpredictable. There were, for example, no fresh mushrooms but twenty-one kinds of prosciutto (counting speck, a northern Italian kind of smoked, dry-cured ham that is different from prosciutto in a way not understandable to non-Italians) and seventeen kinds of salami. And a whole entire aisle of nothing but pasta! And really good red and white local wines for 2.50–3.00 euros. There was a nod to environmental sensibilities—the sturdy plastic bags for carrying things home cost eight euro cents each—but no one I saw was bringing them back to refill and thus recycle them. But MasterCard worked.

On Sunday I went back to the *ipermarketi*. Oops, closed as well. I suppose I should have known this although nothing in all the material that was sent to us said anything about this. Fortunately we had enough supplies that I could make pasta with pesto and other goodies. And the cheap wine was excellent.

One of the few benefits of the "villa" was that the countess had a small and friendly dog you could pet, and a big vegetable garden. Several times she brought us baskets of tomatoes, basil, eggplant, and the inevitable large number of zucchini squash. I figured out what to do with all the tomatoes and basil and eggplant. Zucchini, it turns out, do not add value to a *pomodoro* sauce.

On Monday we verified that the cell phones worked and that the Internet worked on all three of the computers that we had brought along. I went back to the market but since Linda was busy working I took the opportunity to drive around a bit more. Finally, slow learner that I am, I began to figure out what at least a couple of people had mentioned to me generally—that Italy closes down in August. You think when you hear this that it is hyperbole. After all, this is a modern country, connected to the global economy, third largest GDP in the EU, 58 million people, and so forth. But, actually, the two most important words in Italy in August are *chiuso* (closed) and *aperto* (open). And mostly everything is *chiuso*. The stores and the shops are all *chiuso*. The restaurants and *trattorias* and *albergos* (inns or hotels) are *chiuso*. About half the self-service gas stations are *chiuso*—why, one asks, when they have no employees in the first place? There are no cars on the road. You can drive for miles and not see another car. There are no cars in the parking lots in front of the stores that are closed. You can park anywhere you like, even at the tourist destinations. The houses all have metal shutters on the doors and windows, and all the shutters are down. There is no one walking on the street. I did see the occasional older person riding his bicycle along the very narrow roads, which would have been suicidal had there been any traffic other than me, but there was not. Even the churches are closed, and even on Sunday. So much for viewing the glorious ecclesiastical architecture or fabulous stained-glass windows. It is actually sort of creepy. We asked ourselves where all the people who had left had gone to—they had to go somewhere. Maybe the beach. It was like being in a zombie movie where the zombies have eaten everyone, but then gone on vacation themselves.

We took advantage of this lack of people and traffic to drive around and see the sights of the Veneto. There are many small towns that still have their medieval walls—Castelfranco, Castellata, Asolo, Marostica. Sure enough, there were medieval walls. In one location the guidebook said that the brickwork of the walls alone was worth the visit. It wasn't. And once you were there, while the parking was easy, there wasn't much else. It was even hard to get something to eat or drink as most of the eating and drinking places were closed. We sat in the middle of the piazza in the center of the wonderfully preserved town of Castellata, at the small *gelateria*, in cute little chairs in the shade, with an excellent view of the *duomo* and the surrounding medieval architecture. Probably thirty tables, a sea of blue-and-white chairs, us, and another couple. No street life, no pedestrians, no cars, nothing *aperto* except the *gelateria*. Strange.

We drove to Bassano del Grappa. It was recommended as the home of grappa, the very bad Italian attempt at brandy, and besides it had a wooden bridge by Palladio over the small river in the town. Yes it did, we made sure by walking across it. But it was just a nice wooden bridge over a small river.

Asolo and Marostica were actually the most interesting of the small, not very interesting, mostly *chiuso* towns we visited. Each of these is sort of on a hill with a fortress or *rocca* on the very summit, although these are such small hills that "summit" overstates this. We climbed all the way up to the top of the *rocca* at Asolo, which meant many steps and much uphill trudging—well, twenty minutes—in the hot sun. And, sure enough, at the top, *chiuso*. You could look through the barred gate to the inside of the fortress but even if it had been open, what you got was a small lawn surrounded by big walls that you could not climb up on. A Danish couple made the climb at the same time. They suggested this was a lot like going to Copenhagen and seeing *The Little Mermaid*, to wit, once you saw it, sure enough, it was a small bronze statue sitting at the water's edge. They were too polite to say "and so what," but it came across in the universal language of shrugs and body language that said, "OK, check this off, and now let's walk back down to the shaded piazza and see if we can get a glass of wine."

This strategy worked fine at Asolo but not at Marostica, where we sat for twenty-five minutes waiting for a not very busy waiter to discover us. Marostica's claim to fame is that in September there is a chess game played in the square, using live humans. This is for some reason a big deal, and we did go and stand on the board laid out in the piazza. The squares are big. Well, that's interesting. The waiter seemed to be auditioning for the role of one of the kings in the chess game—the piece that almost never moves.

Because we did not plan this as well as perhaps we might have, we did not think to bring along any DVDs. However, in Castelfranco there was a Blockbuster. And it was open. Since this was such a rarity, I decided we should stop and get some movies. On the first night we watched *Che Pasticcio, Bridget Jones,* where Renee Zellweger reprises her very successful role in the first Bridget Jones movie, and the rest of the actors reprise their roles (Hugh Grant looking mildly embarrassed this time, which he well should have), and the plot reprises itself. The difference in the sequel is that

Zellweger is even fatter than before, and the Italian title means, "Bridget Jones has a little too much pasta," which was surely the case. The next night we watched *Indiana Jones e l'Ultima Crociata*. We did the math and found that this was made nineteen years ago, which would explain why it now comes across as so incredibly cheesy and the special effects so unbelievable. The Italian translation is "Indiana Jones and the Ultimate Crock," which is close to accurate.

On one of the later days in the week, having exhausted all the recommended visits in the plain, we took the train into Venice. It is said that visiting Venice in August is foolish as it is hot and crowded with tourists. And it is said correctly. We decided to go over to the island of Murano instead and look at the famous Murano glass. They do have lots of shops there which sell the famous Murano glass, a lot of which is now made in the famous Czech Republic. We could tell that no one among the throngs was really Italian as they were all dressed in shorts and running shoes and T-shirts. So this did not solve the mystery of where all the Italians had gone. Some of the glass was actually nicely done, although most was touristy and souvenir-like, and of a certain sameness after the ninth or tenth shop. As soon as we left the train station, I decided I needed to buy a hat because the sun was so intense, so I spent the day walking around wearing a Venetian boatman's style straw hat with a generously sized blue ribbon on it as a hat band. Printed upon the ribbon was the word VENEZIA, which of course is Italian for—no, we won't tell you, you have to guess. I suppose it was useful; if you temporarily forgot where you were, and the canals and stuff weren't a clue, you could always read your hatband. Fortunately, there are no pictures, since we had agreed not to take my picture as part of the deal for me to buy the hat. I left the hat behind as a gift to the countess.

Suitably glassed out, we took a water taxi for the obligatory stop at the Piazza San Marco and saw more tourists and the lovely, even breathtaking, architecture of the plaza. None of the pigeons landed on us, so we decided not to press our luck and went home to have more pasta. And to try one last time to figure out something useful to do with the zucchini.

Amore and kisses,
Bob

Afterword: Don't go to Italy in August. Really. Go to Greece, they need the money.

Acknowledgements

I had help from several people in the chapter on the collapse of AES. Roger Sant, Paul Hanrahan, Barry Sharp and John McArthur all spoke to me extensively about this tough period of our history, and their input made this a much better chapter.

I would never have attempted a second book, without the encouragement that I received from writing and publishing the first book.

A number of noble and generous people supported Dust Tea, Dingoes and Dragons. There must be some quaint saying I could quote along the lines of "you never know who your friends are until you ask them to write a review of your book." But many people did more than that.

I am especially grateful to Andres Gluski of AES, who sponsored a book signing and then bought copies for all the AES employees who showed up, which turned out to be more than 200 people. Chris Johnston and Tom Firth sponsored a similar gathering, inviting all their Bank of America colleagues and customers. Keith Martin at Chadbourne and Parke held an event at their Washington office, with all their many legal customers in the energy field attending. Kristen Larson convinced the International Club of Santa Barbara to invite me to speak and thereby plug the book. Lisa Shaffer and Diane Wewerka each asked me to speak at their book clubs. And Harris Miller and Deborah Kahn opened their house to me and invited their extensive array of friends so that I could shamelessly market to these very tolerant people.

Many friends and relatives bought numerous copies of the book to give to their friends as presents. Sam Adams, Rita Trehan, Victoria Harker and my neighbor Holly Cana were real champs in this regard.

I am grateful to all the people who went to Amazon and did write reviews of Dust Tea—and favorable reviews at that. Thank you all.

Gary Ackerman (in his own wonderful energy publication, The Burrito), Mark Boyadjian, Ballet Teacher, Kumar Barve, Stephanie Chandler, Buggirl, Lyle D. Woodard, E. Sharp "Book-a-holic," Alexander Lee, Sweet Diva Reader, JENNIFER, Deborah Kahn, Andrew Levine, Steve Wells, John Huetter, C. G. Scammell, Robert A. F. Reisner, Libby O'Connell, Tony Kranz, Michael Ware, Corinne Onetto, Kristiane Lambert, Andrea Glass, Steve Flaim, Shelley Chung, Tobin Crenshaw, Rich Confalone, Jean Solari, Gil Porter, Lex Sant, John Hemphill, Lindsay McAuliffe, Victoria Vinton, Dawn Bissonette, Vicki Siegel, Ziyad Awad, Holly K. Hemphill, David Kipper, Todd Swanson, Roger Sant, Richard Kingsland, Tristan Grimbert, Laure Grimbert, Don Liddell, John Blake, Jason Birn, Cheryl Kessler, Alice Lemon, James Jenkins, nFlyandShoot, Susan Jenkins, Jody Allione, Bob Jenkins (in verse no less!), Mary D. Jenkins, John Motta, Luis Herrera, Robert G. Yokoyama, Matt Burkhart, Roccio Monico, Brad Mantz, Matt O'Connell, Tim Wollaeger, Woodward Boynton, Jennifer Hemphill, Adah Almutairi, Avid Reader, Dee Long, Leah Bissonette and Jonathan Brown.

Many others sent me encouragement and commented favorably on how much they liked the book, some with surprise, but we'll take whatever we get. I am not sure I have everyone, but the list included:

Jonathan Aberman, George Abraham, Jason Anderson, Ed Arulanandam, Dennis Bakke, Italo Ballestrelli, David Barrick, Paul Barry, Matt Bartley, Steve Bartram, Santino Basile, Leanne Bell, Massimo

Bernardi, Don Beyer, Catherine Bierman, Stephanie Birn, Dixie Blake, Guy Blanchard, Maura Blaul, Julie Blunden, Brian Bolster, Terry Boston, John Bottomley, Tom and Judith Boyd, Jamie Burke, Ellen Burkhart, Kara Callahan, Jaspar Camacho, John Carrington, Carmen Catanzariti, Felipe Ceron, Uri Chang, Sharon Cohen, Nancy Conley, Nick Coons, David Corcia, Genevieve Cullen, Greg Curhan, Tom Calder, Tony Colman, David Davis, Glen Davis, Scott DeGhetto, Frank DeRosa, Phil Deutch, Jennifer Didlo, Rauf Diwan, Barbar Drizin, Werner Dumanski, George Durazzo, Ellen Dux, Claire Dwoskin, Lounette Dyer, Jeff Eckle, Mark Ein, Valeska Ellis, Dora Elmore, Don Facciano, Roger Feldman, Mark Fitzpatrick, Eric Fornell, John Fouts, Kerri Fox, Brian Frank, Scott Gardener, David Gee, Brent Glass, John Goins, Fernando Gonzalez, Liz Goodgold, Rob Gray, Bill Green, Einar Gulstad, Bonnie Guo, Beatriz Gutierrez-Larraya, Joan Halbert, Ned and Annie Hall, Tammy Halligan, Mary Ann Hankin, Paul Hanrahan, Sam and Vivian Hardage, Susie Hart, David Hemphill, Berit Henriksen, Michael Herson, Sharon Hillman, Chip Hoagland, Aldyn Hoekstra, Tim Howell, David Jacoby, Alan James, Bengt Jarlsjo, Chloe Jenkins, Aina Jumabaeva, Jolanta Juszkiewicz, Tim Kaine, Richard Katz, Veronica Kayne, Doug Kimmelman, Bill Kingsley, Terry Kipper, Etta Kolombatovich, Diana Kutlow, Peter Labbat, Joseph Laia, Jim Lambright, Tom Lane, Mark Leslie, Garry Levesley, Toby Levine, Ina Liddell, Peter Lithgow, Constantine Logothetis, Federica Lombardi, Maggi Luca, Bob Lukefahr, Ron Lumbra, Dave Magill, Fred Malek, Laura Manz, Frank Marino, Olivier Marquette, Fred Martin, Jeff Martin, Hilary Maxson, Marina McCarthy, Nancy McCaleb, Nancy McConnel, Maureen McDermut, James McKeever, Rick McQuain, Emily Mei, Steve Meyer, Connie Milligan, Tania Morabito, Francisco Morandi, Rob Morgan, Martha Morris, Marsha Morrow, Glenn Mosier, Pat Murphy, Stuart Murray, Rog Naill, Venu Nambiar, Prabu Natarajan, Julian Nebreda, Nancy Nenow, Tom Newton, Rob Nicholson, SuLin Ong, Aygul Ozen, Andrew Perlman, Robin Phillips, Bryan Poffenberger, Ilene Price, Sandra Rennie, Deborah Reyes, Alan and Julie Richardson, Laura Rittenhouse, Brian and Judy Robertson, Chuck Robb, Martin Roscheisen, Marjorie Rosenberg, Judy Rowland, Alan Salisbury, Ken and Brenda

Sanders, Mike Scholey, Nina Shapiro, C.P. Shankar, Jonathan Silver, Cal Simmons, Linda Sullivan, Keichi Suzuki, Mariusz Szkudlinski, Maria Taft, Helen Tarnoy, Scott Taylor, Steve and Ruth Taylor, Christi Tezak, Tom Unterberg, Sharma Upadhyayula, Trae Vassallo, Julia Velichkovia, Jai Verma, Chaim Wachsberger, Biddy Walker, Jeff Walsh, Mark Warner, Olivia Wasennaar, Julie Way, Bruce Weintraub, Daniel Wolf, Raymond Wood, Jay Worenklein, Catherine York, Nick Yost, April Young, Niclas Ytterdahl, Gary Zahakos, Nan Zhang, and Flora Zhao.

About Robert F. Hemphill

Mr. Hemphill for much of his career was employed at AES, a global electric power generating and distribution company, where he served as Executive Vice President and Chief of Staff to the CEO. Hemphill was one of the three executives who began the company in 1981, growing it from a million dollar six person start up. AES owns and operates 38,000 MW of power plants in 21 countries around the globe, is publicly listed on the NYSE, and had approximately $18 billion of revenues in 2013.

Recently, Hemphill was the founder and CEO of AES Solar Power Ltd from its inception until his retirement in December 2013. The company, formed in March 2008, is a joint venture of the AES Corporation and Riverstone LLC, an energy focused private equity fund. AES Solar is a leading developer, owner and operator of utility-scale photovoltaic solar plants connected to the electric power grid. These installations, ranging in size from less than 2 MW to more than 250 MW, consist of large arrays of land-based solar photovoltaic panels that directly convert sunlight to electricity. Under his leadership, the company designed, permitted and constructed fifty-one solar plants (526 MW) in seven countries: Spain, France, Italy, Bulgaria, Greece, India and the US.

He has also been a senior policy official at the Department of Energy and Deputy Manager of Power at the Tennessee Valley Authority.

Mr. Hemphill graduated Magna Cum Laude from Yale University and earned an MA from UCLA and an MBA from George Washington University. He served as an airborne infantry officer in the US Army in Vietnam, and in the Special Forces.

His first book, *Dust Tea, Dingoes and Dragons*, was published in 2014 and won the National Indie Excellence Award for Humor, three Gold Awards from the Nonfiction Authors Association (Humor, International Business, and Travel), and was a San Diego Book Awards finalist in the "memoir" category.

His interests include geraniums, unsuccessful participation in Final Four pools, sporadic exercise, competitive duck cooking and tribal art.